RUNIC RECORDS
OF THE NORSEMEN IN AMERICA

Runic Records
of the
Norsemen in America

By O. G. LANDSVERK

Erik J. Friis, Publisher

The research for this volume was sponsored by the
Landsverk Foundation, Rushford, Minn.

Copyright © 1974, by O. G. Landsverk

Library of Congress catalogue card number 73-8072

ISBN 0-8057-5457-1

MANUFACTURED IN THE UNITED STATES OF AMERICA

Contents

Note to the Reader

The January 26, 1974 issue of the *New York Times* carried a report which indicated that the ink with which the Vinland Map was written may be no more than fifty years old. This is certainly in error and cannot go unchallenged. Since this book was with the printer when the *Times* article appeared, these comments must be restricted to a few lines.

As a professional scientist and research writer during some thirty years, the author would caution against uncritical acceptance of the estimated age of the ink from any ancient document. Only two of several reasons can be discussed. Whether microchemistry or some other method was used, the sample of ink which could be secured for measurement was necessarily *extremely* small. This reduces the accuracy which is possible and often makes the measurement meaningless. Add to this the fact that no "clean" sample of the original ink could possibly be obtained. One reason is that all air carries pollutants, such as various dissolved chemicals, some of which may be corrosive, and dust, much of which consists of small particles of rock. It is well known that such air pollutants vary widely from place to place and from time to time. Therefore, the effect on a sample of ink from five centuries of exposure cannot be known or predicted. To this extent the measurement may not only be in error but cannot be interpreted. No reliable estimate of the age of the ink is probable. (In Los Angeles a piece of aluminum window screening is often completely corroded and disintegrated within five years by the chemical action of the air.)

The medieval character of the Vinland Map is clearly and completely demonstrated in Chapter 8 of this volume. The massive evidence speaks for itself and needs no elaboration here. It has not been and cannot be overthrown.

Foreword

Originally it was the intention in this volume to deal with the entire subject of the presence of Norsemen in America after 1000 A.D. as indicated by their runic inscriptions. This would have required a large book. Research has expanded rapidly in this field during the past few years and it has attained a degree of success which could not have been anticipated. It involves large and widely scattered areas in what is now the United States east of the Rocky Mountains and it extends over a period of three and a half centuries.

The tool without which this progress would not have been possible has become known as Norse dated cryptography. It consists of dates from the perpetual, medieval church calendar, often accompanied by Norse-type ciphers. These were concealed, largely if not exclusively, by Norse priests in runic inscriptions and in at least two Latin texts.

The existence of this cryptography had been unknown over more than five hundred years when cryptanalyst Alf Mongé discovered it in 1963. Since that time he has solved about six dozen runic puzzles of which approximately one half have been discovered in Norwegian runic carvings. A few are from Sweden and the remainder are scattered to the westward over thousands of miles to the Orkney Islands, Greenland, and in New England, Illinois, Minnesota, and Oklahoma in the United States.

Fortunately for the preservation of the history of the Norsemen on the North American continent, at least three of these puzzle-happy priests had apparently been assigned to accompany expeditions to the Vinland of which the sagas speak and had reached areas which lie far beyond it. Fortunately, also, they had chosen to continue to exercise their unusual art in the wilds of a strange land. This implies the presence of other Norsemen and relatively stable and promising conditions.

1

Up to this time, eighteen dated runic inscriptions have been discovered, and solved, in what is now the continental United States east of the Rocky Mountains. Because the dates fall into three closely spaced groups, and because the cryptography within each group is similar, they are apparently the work of only three puzzlemasters. One group covers the years from 1009 to 1024 A.D. in Massachusetts and Oklahoma; another, from 1114 to 1123 A.D. in New England, from Maine to Rhode Island; the third, which consists of two inscriptions, includes a beautifully decorated horn from the vicinity of Winnetka, Illinois, north of Chicago, whose date is 1317 A.D., and the Kensington inscription from western Minnesota, which was carved in 1362 A.D.

These inscriptions all harbor secret dates from the medieval perpetual church calendar. Those that are from the early twelfth and early and mid-fourteenth centuries, also contain Norse-type ciphers which deliver brief messages. Both dates and ciphers are, by definition, cryptograms. They are *embedded* in runic inscriptions but this no more makes them runic than a fish is the same as the water in which it swims. Such dates, and ciphers, often required misspellings of words and other distortions when they were fitted into the runic inscription. Such anomalies clearly do not have their origin in runology or the medieval Norse language. They can only be explained in terms of the cryptography which created them.

That this is so is emphasized by the fact that many Norse puzzles, including the eight early eleventh-century American inscriptions, have no translations whatever. The runes are used exclusively to represent numbers from the perpetual calendar. Because the sound values of the runes are not used, no words can be formed and the inscriptions can have nothing to do with the medieval Norse language. The runes, and their arrangement, are dependent solely on the cryptography which is present.

The need to limit the scope of this volume was given added impetus, in June of 1971, by a remarkable new discovery of a group of three runic inscriptions along the banks of a narrow salt-water estuary in the Phippsburg district of Maine, about fifty miles south of Augusta. The hidden dates and ciphers in their inscriptions helped to expand and consolidate what was already known about the Icelander Eirik Gnupsson. He had assumed the name Henricus when, about 1112 A.D., he was made special legate of Pope Paschal II and bishop of Greenland and Vinland. As a result, the content of this volume is concentrated, to a considerable degree, on the surprising amount of time and energy which Henricus apparently lavished on Vinland.

With the publication of these chapters, roughly one-half of the Norse cryptography which Mongé has solved has been made known. Most of the remainder is on file with The Landsverk Foundation which is dedicated to research on the Norsemen in America. The solutions will be published when suitable opportunities present themselves.

In general, the less complex runic puzzles appear on these pages because they lend themselves better to illustrative purposes. One very outstanding example, whose cryptography is too extensive to be included here, has been called *Hettusvein* from a person who is mentioned in the inscription. It is one of the nearly six hundred runic inscriptions which were excavated from the ancient wharves at Bergen during the late nineteen-fifties and early sixties. Its most significant feature is that it contains virtually every form of cryptography which is found in four of the most important Norse puzzles from the western hemisphere. They are the Vinland Map by Henricus (1122 A.D.); Spirit Pond Number 3, from the Phippsburg area of Maine and also by Henricus (1123 A.D.); the Kingigtorssuaq inscription from northern Greenland (1244 A.D.); and the Kensington inscription from western Minnesota (1362 A.D.). *Hettusvein* was itself dated 1328 A.D., only about a generation before the carving at Kensington. This implies good intercommunication among the puzzlemasters.

Since 1963 the discovery and decipherment of Norse dated

cryptograms have established a number of important historical facts in addition to those which have been mentioned above:

1. Many concurring factors make it virtually certain that it was a segment of the Norse clergy who were the puzzlemasters.

2. Presently known Norse dated puzzles in the United States cover a span of three and a half centuries. Interest could only have been sustained this long because the puzzlemasters were intelligent, original, and innovative. Yet they never departed from the basic rules of the game.

3. Virtually all dated puzzles from the early eleventh century used the decimal system, but in place of the Arabic digits they substituted the numerical values of runes and a special system of numbers which was called pentathic.

4. As late as the early twelfth century (Henricus), some Norse puzzlemasters mixed so-called ancient runic symbols with their own medieval runic alphabet. The ancient runes had been abandoned for normal runic writing several centuries earlier.

5. No one had known of the existence of Norse dated puzzles for well over 500 years when Mongé discovered them in 1963. As a result, a claim that such constructions are modern hoaxes cannot be sustained. The chapters which follow contain many examples of runic inscriptions which have been misinterpreted in the past because the presence of Norse cryptography was not known.

The subject of Norse dated cryptography was introduced to the public in 1967 in *Norse Medieval Cryptography in Runic Carvings* which was coauthored by Alf Mongé and O. G. Landsverk. Two years later, a second book by Landsverk was issued with the title *Ancient Norse Messages on American Stones*. In the years after 1967, many articles on the subject have appeared in various magazines and newspapers. In addition, many new solutions have been distributed as they have become available to the considerable mailing list of The Landsverk Foundation. It is an indication of the rapidity with which the subject is making progress that all but a few of the solutions which are discussed in this book are being made known for the first time.

The contents are divided into several sections. Chapters 1 and 2 describe the history of the discovery of runic inscriptions in this country decades before anyone suspected that some were dated. They also attempt to analyze the reason that this definite, and quite extensive, type of evidence of the presence of Norsemen was, to a large extent, denied and ignored.

In Chapters 3 and 4 the runic alphabets and the Norse perpetual church calendar are discussed. The basic tools which were used by the Norse puzzlemasters are also discussed and their function in Norse cryptography assessed: runes, the perpetual calendar, pentathic numbers, and the decimal system.

Chapters 5, 6, and 7 demonstrate the procedures which were used to construct Norse-type dated puzzles and ciphers. They also show, by the complete analysis of many examples, that the dating and cipher art of the Norse puzzlemasters is in no sense runic. It merely uses runes, and the medieval Norse language, as vehicles in which the cryptography is embedded. It is important to understand this fact clearly.

The five chapters from 8 through 12 constitute, in effect, an outline of the activities of Henricus, bishop and papal legate to Greenland and Vinland from 1112 to 1123 A.D. The outline is based on a total of seven dated inscriptions in New England in which his name is concealed. He was also the author of the two legends which are adjacent to Greenland and Vinland in the Vinland Map. In addition to a hidden date, they contain a three-part ciphered message. This cryptography is actually the reason for the existence of Henricus's part of the Vinland Map. The most important parts of the message are his own name and the date from the calendar.

The last three chapters deal with important special subjects. The source of the many features which the Spirit Pond Number 3 and the Kensington inscriptions have in common is discussed in Chapter 13. Two theories are proposed which singly, or working together, may explain how the Kensington runemaster could have had the opportunity to study, and to adopt, some of the procedures of Henricus more than two centuries later. Chapter 14 contains an analysis of the Narssaq dated puzzle from early fourteenth-century Greenland. This Norse cryptogram, and many others from Western Norway, provide a significant backdrop for the appearance of the Kensington inscription about forty years later.

Runic cryptograms presuppose the existence of other more conventional inscriptions in the same and in neighboring regions in the United States. There are a considerable number of rock carvings which have been discovered over large areas east of the Rockies. Many are certainly runic but they bear no dates or ciphers. Chapter 15 is an introduction to this important field of research which will unquestionably merit, and receive, much attention in future years.

Finally, a few definitions will be helpful. The terms Norse and Norsemen are used frequently in these pages. As they are used here they do not refer to the inhabitants of modern Norway. They identify a person or a group of people from late medieval times whose ancestors originally came largely from Norway. They include, in addition to the people of medieval Norway, dwellers along coastlines and islands across the North Sea and the North Atlantic whose inhabitants came mainly from Norway in the centuries after about 850 A.D. First among them, in so far as this discussion is concerned, are the inhabitants of Iceland and the Norse colonies in Greenland including those who went to North America.

Among the Norsemen who sailed the North Atlantic were also some of Celtic and Anglo-Saxon origin and not a few from Denmark and Sweden who, for one reason or another, became involved in the movement to the west. No attempt will be made here to assess the relative importance of these various elements. The use of the terms Norse and Norsemen is a matter of convenience because it avoids making distinctions between medieval Norwegians, Icelanders, Greenlanders, and those who reached the American mainland. Because of the nature of the evidence which is presented here, such distinctions seldom have any relevance to the issues at hand.

At no time will the term "Viking" be used to designate the people of Iceland, Greenland, and Vinland after 1000 A.D. It is a misnomer. It is true that the Viking period was not yet entirely at an end in northern Europe. However, the Norsemen in these western territories were, at least officially, Christian. Their sailings to the west and south of Greenland had nothing to do with Viking raids. Their basic motive, aside from an active love of adventure, was certainly to find tillable land and other natural resources and a climate which was more tolerable than that in Greenland. From these considerations it is clear that the term "Viking" is inappropriate.

The word cryptography is used here in its broadest meaning, that is, the transmittal of secret intelligence by any means whatsoever. It is never restricted to messages that are scrambled and unscrambled according to a prearranged code between two parties.

The plain spelling of Leif Erikson's name is used here in place of the medieval Icelandic Leifr Eiríkssonr. Because this may disturb some, an explanation is in order. To begin with, the name has already been altered when the nominative R is dropped so that it becomes Leif Eiríksson. Before the author became historian for the Leif Erikson Society of Los Angeles, this question was carefully considered by the society. Its main concern was to influence the American people, and especially the school children, to take an interest in the discovery by Leif and the exploits of the Norsemen. The conclusion was that the more simple the spelling, the better. Later, this was also the spelling which was adopted by the Congress of the United States when, by resolution, it directed the President to proclaim October 9 of each year as Leif Erikson Day. It should be noted, incidentally, that the Norse alphabet had no letter, or rune, C. The letter C in spellings such as Ericson and Erickson are a later Latin intrusion.

Runic Records
of the
Norsemen in America

CHAPTER 1

Brave Men Whom the World Forgot

This chapter will trace an outline of present knowledge of the penetration of Norsemen, after 1000 A.D., into what is now the United States as it is revealed by the runic inscriptions which they left behind them. Emphasis will be placed on that ill-defined region which they called Vinland. Most of the proof on which present conclusions are based will be deferred to later chapters.

The title of this chapter would make a suitable epitaph for the Norsemen who discovered, explored, and settled areas which are remote from the Atlantic seaboard. This is a dramatic but totally forgotten episode of American history. It took place over a long period of years after Leif Erikson had set foot in what he named Vinland abut 1003 A.D.

There are undeniable evidences of the presence of Norsemen in New England, Oklahoma, and Minnesota. They also apparently reached neighboring areas such as the upper Ohio River basin and the Dakotas along the Missouri River.

Those who are familiar with the subject will be aware of the many efforts which have been made to locate the various sites that are mentioned in the so-called Vinland Sagas. It has been very difficult to identify them with any part of the eastern shores of the continent. This is not strange when one considers the fact that the contents of the sagas were passed on from mouth to mouth over a period of up to three centuries before they were recorded. To match the sailing directions and geographical descriptions with the complex contours of the eastern shorelines of North America has proved to be a formidable task.[1]

Over the past century several dozen investigators have tried to pinpoint Leif Erikson's Vinland. About one half decided that he had landed somewhere in New England. Other opinions have varied all the way from Laborador to Florida.[2] While the extremes may reasonably be discounted, no consensus on the site of the original Vinland, or other locations which are described in the sagas, has come about.[3]

The evidence which is presented in these pages infers, but does not prove, that Leif Erikson's Vinland was located south of the Gulf of Saint Lawrence and, presumably, somewhere in New England. But it indicates that the site of the southernmost of Thorfinn Karlsefni's two major camps, which he named Hóp, may have been situated on the banks of a narrow estuary not far from the Atlantic coast in southern Maine. Of the several leaders of expeditions which are mentioned in the sagas it was Karlsefni who made the most ambitious attempt to colonize Vinland.

A native Icelander, Eirik Gnupsson, visited the same area a century later, in 1123 A.D., and apparently recognized it as the Hóp of the saga accounts. He had adopted the name Henricus by the time he began to serve in Greenland and Vinland as a special legate of Pope Paschal II and as bishop. The appointment was made in 1112 A.D. or shortly thereafter. His subsequent actions make it clear that "the neighboring regions," as the pope so ambiguously referred to areas outside Greenland, must have referred primarily, if not exclusively, to Vinland.

Later chapters provide an outline of the comings and goings of Bishop Henricus to and from Vinland and along its shores. He seems, in fact, to have paid more attention to Vinland than he did to Greenland, which was his official headquarters. This implies that Norse colonies were established in Vinland in the early twelfth century and that Henricus was optimistic about their prospects. The assumption is supported by the fact that Henricus troubled to plan, and to carve into stone, seven secretly dated and autographed runic puzzles along a three-hundred-mile-long shoreline from southern Maine to Rhode Island. Even one such intricate puzzle would have required much mental and physical labor. If the sites had been a wilderness, frequented only by Indians, it is highly improbable that he would have made the effort.

It was certainly not one of Henricus's assignments to be a missionary to the American Indians or to the Eskimos. Nothing that is known of the attitudes and actions of the Catholic church authorities in regard to Greenland and Vinland suggests that the natives of North America played any part in their plans. The same can be said of Henricus himself. His puzzles in runic inscriptions in New England are strictly Norse in conception and there is no trace of Indian influence. The two Latin legends, which are adjacent to Vinland and Greenland in the Vinland Map, and which were also his, are also entirely devoid of any reference to the natives of America.

Henricus was almost certainly a skilled and experienced puzzlemaster before he took office in Greenland and before he made his first sailing to Vinland a year or two thereafter. But it would seem that only a combination of three conditions, which he must have felt were fulfilled in Vinland, could have induced him to continue his cryptographic efforts there: 1. Norse colonies were spread along the shores where he carved his inscriptions. 2. He was optimistic about the survival and potential growth of these colonies. 3. He felt confident that colleagues, who also belonged to the cryptographic fraternity, would be interested in solving his dates and ciphers. It should be noted that Norse cryptography continued to be practiced over three and a half centuries in spite of the fact that it extended over one quarter of the circumference of the globe from Sweden to Oklahoma. This could not have happened had not a segment of the clergy maintained a lively interest in it.

There is another factor to consider. As a legate of the pope and a bishop, Henricus had been sent to Greenland, not to gather individual communicants into congregations, but to organize existing congregations into a bishopric. This he accomplished in Greenland even though the see was not established until 1125 A.D., two years after Henricus was last heard from through the Spirit Pond inscriptions in Vinland. Taken together, his official status and his activities in Vinland suggest that he was trying to organize the Church there.

No matter how this situation is viewed, a considerable presence of Norsemen in Vinland in the early twelfth century is implied. If the area was occupied only by Indians, why should Henricus have made what seems to have been three sailings to Vinland and was certainly no less than two? Why, also, should he have spent what appears to have been at least one-half of the eleven years which he served as bishop, in Vinland? Yet, this is what his activities, as they are revealed in later chapters, seem to indicate.

The discovery of runic inscriptions along the eastern shores of North America makes a long and checkered story. As early as 1837 the Danish scholar Carl Christian Rafn insisted that there were runic inscriptions along the east coast but he was discredited by his colleagues.[4] Similar fates were in store for others who agreed with Rafn. It might well also have become the lot of the late historian Hjalmar Rued Holand who from 1907 to 1963 energetically championed the authenticity of the Kensington inscription from western Minnesota.[5]

This famous carved stone was discovered in western Minnesota in 1898 A.D. Its nine lines of runes on one side and three lines on an edge contain 222 runic symbols, and it therefore ranks as one of the longest inscriptions that is known. In 1966, Mr. Mongé demonstrated that the Kensington inscription was unquestionably medieval and authentic because it contains the many-times confirmed date, Sunday, April 24, 1362, which was taken, as usual, from the Norse church calendar. There are also two ciphers which reveal that the name of the puzzlemaster was HARREK and the runecarver was TOLLIK. Both are acceptable medieval Norse names.[6]

New discoveries of runic inscriptions were being made in the nineteen-thirties. A small group of men in New England combined their energies and talents in order to discover, identify, transcribe, and translate inscriptions in New England and in neighboring areas. The only survivor from this group is

Malcolm Pearson, a photographer and technician who resides at Sutton, Massachusetts. In a recent interview, Pearson stated that he was not interested in runes, and knew nothing about them, but that he had a strong interest in preserving an accurate record of all man-made cuts on stone surfaces in the area. As a result, he has assembled a large collection of photographs of such carvings.

Olaf Strandwold, at that time a retired West Coast superintendent of schools, had spent a number of years in the study of runes and runic writing when, in the early nineteen-thirties, he became interested in the New England carvings. After a few years, he had collected twenty-four inscriptions which he was certain were runic. In attempting translations Strandwold did not fare very well because he was not aware that many of these inscriptions were not normal runic inscriptions but Norse-type puzzles. This difficulty he shared with some runologists who attempted to translate runic inscriptions, especially those from Norway and Greenland.[7] A significant part of each are Norse cryptograms.

The value of Strandwold's work lay elsewhere. He wrote two brochures, one in 1939 and a second in 1948. Each contained transcriptions and photographs of about two dozen runic inscriptions. The photography and transcriptions were, for the most part, the work of Pearson.

The first brochure was sponsored by William Goodwin, a wealthy Connecticut enthusiast for the archeology of the New England area.[8] Beginning about 1940, an electrical engineer and manufacturer, Magnus Bjorndal, spearheaded search for runic inscriptions. It was he who published the second brochure. At the time of his death in early 1971, he was preparing a manuscript on the settlements of the Norsemen in Vinland, the result of many years of investigation. Bjorndal was also an active supporter of research into the history of Norwegian migration to the United States in modern times and, in 1970, he was made president of the Norwegian-American Historical Association.

It was almost twenty years after the second brochure was published that Mongé, using the original negative plates, solved four dated and autographed puzzles by Bishop Henricus. If mistakes had been made in transcribing the runes and auxiliary marks, the solutions might well have become impossible. Because the existence of Norse dated puzzles was unknown when Pearson and Strandwold photographed and copied them, nothing could have been added by the two men, or left out, which would have made the solutions possible except by an improbable accident.

There is a third area in which runic inscriptions, which turned out to be Norse puzzles, have been discovered. Mrs. Gloria Farley has led a search for runic inscriptions in eastern Oklahoma over at least thirty years. As a young girl she became aware of the eight large runic symbols which are cut into a massive block of stone in a deep ravine not far from Heavener. The carving is now known as Heavener No. 1.

In 1966, Mongé showed that the Heavener inscription was a gem of cryptographic finesse and efficiency. It is dated November 11, 1012 A.D., and is one of a group of five closely related cryptopuzzles that have been discovered, and solved, in eastern Oklahoma. The solutions of Heavener No. 1, and Byfield No. 1, which appear to have been constructed by the same puzzlemaster in Massachusetts three years earlier, are analyzed in Chapter 7.

The presence of Norsemen in Oklahoma in the early eleventh century is not nearly as surprising as might be supposed at first glance. There is a very logical explanation. After the Norsemen reached Vinland, they believed, apparently over a period of at least a century, that they were settled on the eastern shores of an island. There are two written records, which may be considered reliable, which affirm that this was so.[9]

It may be taken for granted that one of the first enterprises which attracted these daring sailors was to try to sail around their island. By the time they were passing the southern tip of Florida, into the Gulf of Mexico, they knew that this was a continent. The tremendous outflow of fresh water into the gulf, where the Mississippi drains into it, may have tempted them to try to discover a passage through, or around this large area of land. It is likely that they already knew that the Isthmus of Panama could not be crossed by water.

There are also carvings on stone and bone surfaces in other areas which can apparently only be interpreted as runic but which do not contain dates or ciphers. It would, indeed, be very strange if this were not so in the United States as it is in Scandinavia. A number of such inscriptions are illustrated and discussed in Chapter 15. They have been discovered over the past seventy years in the upper Ohio River basin and in the Dakotas along the Missouri River. These carvings were reported by a well-known anthropologist, Warren G. Moorhead, or were discovered by archeologists from prestigious museums such as Peabody at Harvard University and the Smithsonian Institution. As a result, the circumstances of their discovery can scarcely be questioned. The forms of their carved symbols also resemble standard runes so closely that the inscriptions must be presumed to be runic.

The occurrence of dated runic puzzles in the United States can best be understood in terms of their historical and cryptographic background in Scandinavia, and in that staging area for Norse contacts with the North American continent, Greenland. Chapters 5, 6, and 7 describe the more salient features of this background. Of approximately six dozen Norse cryptopuzzles which Mr. Mongé has solved to date, more than one half are from Norway. The remainder, which number about thirty, are found in Sweden, the Orkney Islands, Greenland and the United States. A little more than one half of these are from New England, Oklahoma, Illinois, and Minnesota.

Unfortunately, the loss of runic inscriptions over the centuries, especially in Norway, appears to have been dramatic. There, most runic cryptograms were carved on the interior walls of churches, especially the picturesque but flammable wooden stave churches. Since the late Middle Ages their number has been reduced from more than six hundred to only twenty-five. There is no reason to doubt that the number of runic inscriptions, and dated puzzles, which these church buildings once harbored, have been reduced in about the same proportion.

In spite of this heavy attrition, which may well have been equally severe in some other countries including Greenland and the United States, Mongé estimates that the total number of Norse puzzles in runic inscriptions which may eventually be solved will reach two hundred.

This estimate may well be conservative in view of the rapid increase in solutions during the past few years. A further substantial increase in potential solutions would be certain if the remainder of the ancient wharves at Bergen were to be excavated. A number of important solutions have already resulted from only a partial examination of the approximately six hundred inscriptions which have been recovered to date. Asbjørn Herteig, who has been in charge of the excavations, estimated a few years ago that the site may contain a total of 4,000 to 5,000 inscriptions. Discoveries of runic inscriptions in Greenland have also steadily increased over the past decades as excavations of the site of the cathedral at Gardar, of many churches and of several hundred farms have proceeded. The number of known runic inscriptions from Greenland now number about a hundred. Among them are two very important dated cryptograms, the Kingigtorssuaq inscription from northern Greenland (1244 A.D.) and the recently discovered and solved Narssaq carving (1316) which was excavated near the mouth of Eiriksfjord, at the inner end of which Eirik the Red built his estate, Brattahlid.

The reason for concentrating in this volume on runic inscriptions on the North American continent is not lack of other types of evidence of the presence of Norsemen. However, as evidence which can not easily be refuted, runic inscriptions enjoy unsurpassed advantages. This is, above all, true of those that contain hidden dates and ciphers. It would be more than foolish to fail to make use of this very positive proof. Let us list some of these advantages:

1. Even though this has never been proved even in a single instance, let us assume, for the moment, that runic inscriptions may have been carved within the borders of the United States after the first English colonists arrived. The fact is that a runic puzzle, while it is *embedded* in a runic inscription, is not itself in any way runic. Furthermore, it uses the medieval Norse language as a vehicle but does not depend on it. It is the other way around. It often alters the language to suit its own purposes. As a result, neither the medieval Norse language, or runology, can be used to assess, criticize, or deny the existence of runic puzzles. The runologist Aslak Liestøl, curator of the National Museum at Oslo, confirmed this, without necessarily intending to do so, when, in 1967, he denied that there was such a thing as Norse dated puzzles. The effect of this was to confirm, what the record also clearly shows, that no one, including the runologists, had had any knowledge of Norse dated puzzles over more than five hundred years.

2. Most of the American inscriptions are carved on solid rock or on boulders which are so heavy that they could not have been moved. They are still located where they were carved. Even the three small Spirit Pond inscriptions must have been carved near the place where they were found because one of them has carved on it an outline map of the same area.

3. The dates at which the inscriptions were carved are stated and confirmed from the perpetual church calendar. It is one of the greatest drawbacks with other types of Norse artifacts that it is not possible to date them accurately. As a result *not one* alleged Norse artifact in the United States has yet been *generally acknowledged* to be authentic. In this context the importance of calendrically dated puzzles is clear.

4. The evidence is overwhelming that, in the United States as in Scandinavia, it was members of the Norse clergy who made a game of constructing dated puzzles. Only they possessed at the same time the necessary tools, the required knowledge, and the incentive to carry on this very unusual art.

Norse dated puzzles also possess important historical implications which no other type of artifact has to the same degree:

1. The presence of a dated puzzle also implies the presence at that site of a group of Norsemen, almost certainly accompanied by a priest, who were there on more than a temporary basis. It required much time and effort, both physical and mental, to construct and to carve such a puzzle. It would have made no sense to have left it in the wilderness where it could have been seen only by the natives. As was mentioned above, there is no evidence that the Church, or any of its representatives, took any interest in the Indians.

2. The presence of dated puzzles implies optimism on the part of the puzzlemaster about the future prospects of the colony. It also implies his confidence that a knowledgeable colleague would, some day, arrive who would try to solve his puzzle.

3. In particular, Henricus, who expended so much of his time and energy in Vinland, must have believed in the future of whatever colonies were scattered from Maine to Rhode Island during the early twelfth century.

It is too early to attempt to make an inventory of all runic inscriptions, dated and undated, which are found in the United States. However, the eighteen widely scattered dated inscriptions east of the Rocky Mountains have demonstrated some basic facts. Most important of all is that medieval runic inscriptions do exist with all that this implies. These dated carvings are supported by others which are not dated. Together with many other supplementary facts, this can only be explained in terms of the long-term and widely distributed presence of Norsemen over large areas in the eastern half of the United States.

CHAPTER 2

The Anatomy of Forgetting

World opinion has almost totally ignored the saga of the Norse-men who *maintained a long-term presence* on the North American continent. On the other hand, events of such high dramatic quality were not deliberately, and without reason, shut out from men's minds. An attempt will be made here to analyze the causes for this neglect.

The fact is that a large quantity of high-grade scholarship has been put into the effort to reconstruct the lost history of the Norsemen in America. However, it has had to contend with a serious lack of documentary evidence. Since history must be based on the record as it exists, the omissions have not only made the historical judgment incomplete but misleading.

Documents which describe the extent of Norse activities on the North American continent are limited to the two Vinland Sagas and to a few brief references which add very little. The fault does not lie with the sagas themselves but arises from the fact that they comprise nearly all of the documentary evidence which has survived. As a result it has not been possible to put the sagas in their proper historical perspective.

Historians have estimated that the exploits of the Norse Greenlanders, as they are related in the Vinland Sagas, ended somewhere between 1012 and 1020 A.D. This would be nine to seventeen years after Leif Erikson is believed to have discovered Vinland. Henricus made his visits to Vinland about a century later and there is no hint in what he did or wrote to suggest that the Norse presence in Vinland in the early twelfth century was coming to an end. Quite the contrary.[1]

Did sailings from Greenland to Vinland end temporarily after the unsuccessful attempt at colonization by Thorfinn Karlsefni

21

which is related in the sagas? This failure was well advertised in Greenland, Iceland, and Norway. But it did not necessarily, or even probably, discourage other Greenlanders who had less to lose from making the attempt. Even if such unheralded settlers could not expect that their descendants would commemorate their exploits by writing sagas about them, this would scarcely matter. As colonists, they presumably never returned to Greenland and communication may have been bad or nonexistent from the beginning. This would have discouraged the formation of tales about them in Greenland which might eventually have been recorded. The process of forgetting them may have been very easy.

It is scarcely possible that groups of Norsemen could have settled in Vinland without many sailings between Greenland and Vinland. It is likely that settlers often remained in Vinland whereas the ship, manned by a skeleton crew, returned to Greenland. Those who settled in Vinland were, for the most part, if not relatives, then neighbors and acquaintances of those who remained in Greenland. Such events would be remembered and recalled through many generations. It would be an obvious distortion to assume that the Greenlanders found only the efforts of the sons of Erik the Red and Thorfinn Karlsefni worth remembering. But reports about the fate that befell them in Vinland may have been almost nonexistent. It was not from material such as this that sagas were fashioned.

Yet the Greenlanders did not forget Vinland. How mindful they were of it could scarcely be better illustrated than by the actions of Henricus. Later chapters will demonstrate that he paid a great deal of attention to Vinland. Yet, when he took office he was a native Icelander and presumably a stranger to both Greenland and Vinland.

Another important factor should be kept in mind. After the saga exploits of the early eleventh century the outstanding attractions of Vinland over Greenland, both in climate and in resources, were well known in Greenland and throughout the north. We know this because the saga accounts were in popular circulation until they were recorded two to three centuries later.

The contrast between Greenland and Vinland became greater as the climate in Greenland gradually worsened and as the small amount of tillable land was taken over by large landholders and by the Church. This contrast must have been a powerful incentive to attempts at founding settlements on the continent.[2]

Henricus was a representative of an element in Greenland society which continued to increase in power and influence. This was the Catholic Church whose first representatives reached Greenland from Norway with Leif Erikson in 1000 A.D.

It was the policy of the Catholic Church to assign priests to accompany dangerous ventures such as those to Vinland. It would be out of character for the church to neglect to record which of its communicants departed for Vinland and elsewhere. Especially would this be true when one of its priests was among them.

To assume that members of the clergy in Greenland were incapable of such duties is unrealistic. There is a consensus of opinion among historians that the early priests of Scandinavia were generally well educated. They were often selected from among promising young men of good family. It was considered an honor to become a priest or a monk.

Henricus was himself a member of the respected Valthjoflingar family of Southern Iceland. He was a man of intelligence and great enterprise and he showed a remarkable ability in Norse cryptography. The first two bishops at the famous monastery at Skálholt, which was also located in the southern quarter of Iceland, were Isleif (1056-1080) and Gissur (1082-1118). They were the son and grandson of Gissur the White who played a prominent part in persuading the Icelandic parliament to accept Christianity in 1000 A.D. Both were learned and competent men.

The church establishment in Greenland grew to considerable size. It continued to function over a period of several centuries. There were at least seventeen churches, two monasteries and, at Gardar in the Eastern Settlement, a cathedral. It was constructed of large blocks of stone and lacked only a few feet of being as long as the cathedral of the archbishop at Nidaros in Norway. Around it was a complex of good-sized auxiliary buildings. Thirteen bishops actually served in Greenland during a period of about three centuries from 1112 A.D. The Danish scholar Poul Nørlund describes the churches in these terms in *De Gamle Nordbobygder ved Verdens Ende* (The Old Norse Settlements at the End of the World):

"The churches are usually much larger [than in Iceland] and the walls are constructed of stone by well-developed techniques with alternate thick and thin layers. The massive stone blocks which were used in both the churches, and in some of the auxiliary buildings, are impressive, weighing as they do 4 to 5 and even as much as 10 tons."

It should be noted that the volcanic rock in Iceland is not suited for such construction. The churches in Greenland, and some of their decorative features, are usually ascribed to English influence.

Such a church organization must have possessed both the energy and capability for considerable literary effort. Its period of greatest vigor approximately paralleled the greatest flowering of the saga literature in Iceland. According to Nørlund the Greenland bishops were capable men who had the respect of their colleagues:

"We get the impression that, especially in the beginning, competent men were selected for this distant position and when they stopped in Iceland they were spoken of with great veneration. It was thought of as a position that gave prestige in spite of the fact that this bishopric was not only the most distant but also the smallest in the number of communicants in the Christian world at that time."[3]

But, it might be objected, even if the Greenlanders possessed the ability to write records and produce literature, they could have had nothing to write with. This was probably no more true in Greenland than it was in Iceland whose economy was quite similar. In his well-known volume, *Conquest by Man*, Paul Herrmann devotes more than a hundred pages to the Viking Age, Greenland, and Vinland. He observes that the Greenlanders should have had no more scarcity of materials for making parchment than the Icelanders, since they raised considerable numbers of cattle and sheep.[4]

Whatever the volume of the literary output in Greenland, and whatever its quality, it was totally destroyed when the Greenland colonies disappeared about 1500 A.D. after five centuries of existence. Apparently, only three significant items of literature were saved. One was the Saga of Einar Sokkason. Among other things it relates the process of securing a new bishop for Greenland from 1123 to 1126 A.D., presumably to succeed Henricus. Bishop Arnald became bishop of Greenland in 1126 A.D. The manuscript had apparently been saved because it had been brought to Iceland. A second manuscript which survived in the form of a copy was the contribution of Henricus to the Vinland Map. Its saving required two near-miracles in succession. Henricus's map and legends, or a copy of them, had been incorporated into the Vinland Map at Basle, Switzerland, in 1440 A.D., more than three centuries after Henricus wrote and drew them. How they reached the Church Council at Basle is not known. Another five hundred years were to pass before a single copy of the Vinland Map was discovered among a collection of ancient manuscripts somewhere in Europe during the nineteen-fifties.

If the legends by Henricus in the Vinland Map are not written in the most fluent Latin, and contain a variety of misspellings, it should be considered that he was not trying to display his literary skill. He was constructing a difficult and extensive cryptopuzzle. The Kensington inscription has likewise been unfairly criticized because of misspellings and choices of words which have been questioned. In both cases the anomalies were caused by the needs of the cryptography.

The third direct historical record from Greenland which has survived may actually have been written, in whole or in part, in

Norway. It was a report which was delivered in 1364 A.D. to the Norwegian King Haakon by a Norse Greenlander, Ivar Baardsson, about conditions in Greenland and his twenty-three years of stewardship of the properties of the church there. Father Baardsson was sent to Greenland in 1341 A.D. by Bishop Haakon of Bergen. An important but somewhat ambiguous and now controversial part of the report stated that, in 1342, the inhabitants of the Western Settlement had abandoned their farms, leaving their cattle behind them, and had departed to the continent. After waiting for many years for passage, Baardsson was able to return to Norway aboard a small ship whose crew numbered only eight men. The original report has been lost but its contents are recorded in several references.[5]

These three are literary works of considerable quality, each in its own way. It suggests that the loss of literary treasure in Greenland may have been considerable.

Next to Greenland, Iceland was the natural repository for information about Vinland. The golden age of literature in Iceland continued through the twelfth, thirteenth and fourteenth centuries. In later centuries a great many of these precious manuscripts, handwritten on large pages of vellum, were lost or destroyed by fire, etc.

Because of the type of construction that was used, houses were very flammable in Iceland. While the largest collections of manuscripts were in monastery libraries, these also were not fireproof. Actually, a large proportion of manuscripts in Iceland was in private hands.

That the eventual loss of these literary productions was immense, was recently confirmed by an authority on Icelandic manuscripts, Sigurður A. Magnússon, Icelandic essayist, novelist, and short-story writer. In an excellent article in the Winter Number, 1971-72, of *The American-Scandinavian Review,* he stated that, during the difficult fifteenth, sixteenth and seventeenth centuries in Iceland, the vellum pages of these volumes were used to make clothing and shoes. It is not now possible, Magnússon says, to calculate how much of the old literary treasures perished *"but the quantity was certainly enormous."* (Italics added.)

The losses continued. During the early years of the eighteenth century a fine Icelandic scholar, Arni Magnússon, the "savior" of old Icelandic literature, assisted also by others, collected much of what was left. Because the University of Copenhagen was also the University of Iceland, a large quantity of documents were shipped there. However, says Mr. Magnússon, records exist of large collections that sank into the North Sea along with the ships that carried them.

As if this were not enough, two thirds of the collection that had arrived in Copenhagen was lost in the disastrous fire of 1728. Two years later, all the manuscripts that were kept at the famous monastery at Skálholt in Southern Iceland suffered the same fate. In his *Explorations in America before Columbus,* the historian Hjalmar Rued Holand[6] has this to say about the tragic event:

"This episcopal see in the Middle Ages was the principal repository for Icelandic records. In 1630 it was destroyed by fire and all its records lost. Because Bishop Gisle [Oddsson] had the best opportunity for becoming acquainted with these manuscripts, he later (1637) made a synopsis in Latin of some of the more important documents that he could recall."

The above paragraphs suggest that much more information of various kinds about continued Norse contacts with Vinland must once have existed in Iceland. Except for the Vinland Sagas it was all but totally lost. This points up the extraordinary importance of the dated runic puzzles in various parts of the United States. They have provided guidelines for the presence of Norsemen in America which may otherwise have been lost forever. They prove that, to the degree that the Vinland Sagas have been put forward as substantially the complete history of the Norsemen on the North American continent, this interpretation has been very misleading.

The preceding pages have shown that there has been an almost total lack of written documents by which the Vinland

Sagas could be put into the proper context. There can be little doubt that it is this which is at the root of the very negative attitude which some Scandinavian scholars have had towards all physical evidences of the presence of Norsemen on this continent. While this may in part explain the skepticism, it certainly does not excuse its bias and excesses.

* * * *

The remainder of this chapter will be devoted to some sidelights which the reader may find to be of interest. There has been a tendency to assume that the condition of the Christian Church in the Greenland colonies was generally deplorable and that it was inferior to that in the Scandinavian countries. The record does not seem to support this view.

Again, to quote Nørlund in his comments on life in the Greenland colonies, many of its inhabitants were exceptionally well traveled.[7] As a result, the Greenlanders had, over a long period of years, been acquainted with the Christian religion:

"In Greenland the people were better prepared to accept Christianity than in the homeland. [He is here referring to Norway.] Many of the Greenland colonists were widely traveled and had become acquainted with the Christian Church. It is also true that Iceland had been visited by Christian people much more than Norway."

Meanwhile the situation was far from static in Norway during the same years but it was the leaders who promoted Christianity while large segments of the population were still in strong opposition. This is well illustrated by a passage from the *Saga of Olaf Trygvason* which is a part of *Heimskringla* (the sagas of the Norwegian kings by Snorri Sturluson):

"He [Leif Erikson] was baptized with all of his shipmates.... That same summer King Olaf sent Gissur and Hjalti to Iceland to preach Christianity there. Now he also sent Leif Erikson to Greenland to preach Christianity [1000 A.D.]. The king provided him with a priest and various other holy men to baptize folk there and to instruct them in the true faith."

Gissur and Hjalti were native Icelanders who, according to the saga accounts, had been converted to Christianity by a man named Thangbrand. He was in the service of the king and had spent one or two years in Iceland before returning in 998. As mentioned above, it was Gissur (Teitsson) who, in the year 1000, pleaded successfully before the Icelandic Althing (parliament) for the adoption of Christianity over all of Iceland. His grandson, who also was named Gissur, became the second bishop at Skálholt in Southern Iceland. He was a contemporary of Henricus.

Thus Christianity was officially brought to Greenland by Leif Erikson. The request of King Olaf was probably tantamount to a command and with such powerful backing there seem to have been no serious obstacles to acceptance. Eirik the Red, Leif's father, is said to have continued to rely on Odin and Thor but his wife, Tjodhild, promptly built a small church not far from the dwellings at Eirik's estate, Brattahlid.

The Icelanders made Christianity the official religion by decision of the Althing in 1000 A.D. While strong opposition was expressed during the debate, the edict was accepted by the people without violence. The record shows that both King Olaf Trygvason, and later his nephew King Olaf Haraldsson (Saint Olaf) felt it necessary to use much more drastic means of persuasion in some parts of Norway.[8]

The prompt and generally willing acceptance of Christianity in Iceland and Greenland has been stressed here for two reasons. It provided the most reliable and continuous contact with the culture of Scandinavia and Europe and *it was also the organization within which Norse cryptography was nurtured and by which it was transmitted over the most farflung portions of the Norse realm*. On this subject Nørlund makes these observations: "Greenland can scarcely be said to have had a heathen period. The church connection was exceptionally valuable and prized by the Greenlanders," and again, "The acceptance of Christianity had a meaning for the Greenlanders which it would be difficult to overestimate. The church organ-

ization was one of the bonds which tied the distant colonies most
closely to the civilized world."

This is a view which the tendency to violence and to the
bizarre which is portrayed in surviving sagas about Greenland
and Vinland has tended to obscure. However, it seems to correspond much better with the actual course of events. Perhaps,
like modern motion pictures and television serials, it was the
extraordinary and the violent which eventually survived as
folklore and was recorded. The human characteristics which
determine what is newsworthy have not, perhaps, changed very
much.

Developments which followed a little more than a century
later in Iceland and Greenland raise some interesting questions.
The first bishop of Skálholt in Southern Iceland, and the first
native-born bishop of Iceland, was Isleif (1056 to 1080 A.D.). He
was followed by his son Gissur (1082 to 1118 A.D.).

Gissur and Henricus were both native Icelanders and they
were contemporaries as bishops respectively in Iceland and
Greenland. It is inevitable that they were acquainted.

Icelandic histories of the bishops of Iceland have some interesting things to say about Gissur. When they say that he got
his education at the Sorbonne in Paris, this must be a mistake
because the famous College of Sorbonne was not established until
about a century later. The reference must be to a monastery
school which preceded it. At any rate the Icelanders called Gissur's school "svartiskoli." The meaning is "the black school."

This might have referred to the black garb of the monks but
the circumstances suggest another interpretation. When Gissur
returned to Iceland he was noted for being an expert at carving galdrastafur. The meaning of galdr was magic or sorcery
and "stafur" was the word for runestave, so that the word meant
sorcerers' runes.

It is not known where Henricus, who like Gissur, was from
the southern part of Iceland, received his education or his interest in Norse puzzles. According to Holand he was appointed
bishop by King Sigurd Jorsalfarer (Jerusalem-farer, that is,

crusader) in 1112 A.D. In the previous year the king had returned from a four-year campaign in which he had fought the
Mohammedans in Spain, at various points along the Mediter-
ranean, and in support of Baldwin, King of Jerusalem. Because
of this chain of circumstances, Holand was led to suggest that
Henricus had accompanied the king on his crusade. This would
have given him the opportunity to decide whether Henricus
could withstand the rigors of the post in Greenland.[9]

It is improbable that the Vinland Map and the seven dated
inscriptions in New England represent all of Henricus's cryptographic output. It, nevertheless, leaves him in the position of
the foremost puzzlemaster in volume of output that is known
to date. Gissur seems to have been less fortunate. Not a single
inscription in which he displayed his prowess in making "galdrastafur" has survived.

In Iceland, the native stone is largely volcanic in origin. It
is not suitable either for construction or for carving runes. This
may have restricted the Icelanders to carving their runic inscriptions on wood, bone, or to inscribing them on parchment
or vellum. All of these materials are perishable except under
very favorable conditions.

It is not possible to estimate the total number of runic inscriptions which once existed in Iceland. It is known that entire
books were once written with runic symbols but none have
survived. Today, runic inscriptions of any kind are rare. Weathering and decay have naturally been a factor, but the hand of
man also appears to have played a major role.

The Icelandic scholar Björn Magnússon Ólsen makes some
interesting observations about runic writing in Iceland.[10] The
sagas tell of many persons in late heathen times who *rista runar*,
that is, carved runes. But before the Icelandic language could
be properly written with runes, they must be able to express all
of its sounds. This, Ólsen states, did not happen until a few
years after 1118 A.D. The timing suggests that Henricus had no
choice but to write Legends Nos. 66 and 67 in Latin because
the runic alphabet was not yet capable of it. All of the secret

messages in his seven runic inscriptions in New England contain only two or three simple words (Chapter 9) and the
"text" in SP 3, his longest inscription, which is analyzed in Chapter 12, never has more than two or three translatable words at
a time.

It is an interesting speculation that had the runic alphabet
been ready for such use at the time, Henricus might well have
written Legends 66 and 67 in the Vinland Map with runes
(Chapter 8). Had he done so, his cryptography in the two
legends would certainly have been lost during the translation
while they were being incorporated into the Vinland Map at
Basle in Switzerland in 1440.

Ólsen concluded that runes were used exclusively to write
the Icelandic language until about 1150. A confirmation of the
favor in which runes were held even by educated Norsemen
of the time was provided by a shipwreck in which all hands
were lost off the coast of Greenland. One of the victims was a
bishop. He had scratched an account of their misadventure on
two wax tablets which were hinged together so as to protect
the wax surfaces. These tablets drifted ashore from the wreck.
The year was 1189 and the bishop had written his message with
runes! The tablets are a part of the collection of the National
Museum at Copenhagen.

The Catholic Church had apparently been very tolerant of
the use, by Norwegians and Icelanders, of their native language
and runic symbols. This has been attributed to the fact that it
was largely missionaries from England who helped to establish
the Christian religion in Norway as well as Iceland and Greenland.[11]

One indication of tolerance is the large proportion of runic
inscriptions in Norway which are carved on the interior surfaces of churches. In nearly all instances, members of the clergy
had, apparently, been the runemasters.

This lenient attitude changed abruptly in Iceland in the first
half of the seventeenth century. The belief had become widespread, and was not resisted if it was not actively encouraged

by the clergy, that runes and runic writing were works of the devil. Therefore, it seemed entirely clear that, not only these evil works, but also their practitioners, must be eliminated.

This situation is starkly illuminated in letters which were written by Icelandic scholars in the sixteen-thirties in reply to inquiries from a Danish expert on the Scandinavian perpetual calendars and runic writing. These letters have recently been published in a three-volume edition, in Danish, under the title, *Letters to and from Ole Worm*.[12]

The letters reveal that some scholars were still willing to discuss runes in guarded terms, at least with a foreigner whom they felt they could trust. In 1630, Magnús Ólafsson, a pupil of Árngrim Jónsson of the monastery at Hólar in Northern Iceland, informed Worm that he did not believe that the Icelandic runes will ever be completely understood, but the man who knew most about them (Jón Guðmundsson) had fled after he had been summoned on a charge of runic sorcery.

In the same letter he favored Worm with copies of eight runic alphabets. They reveal a deep involvement of the Icelandic runemasters with secret writing. One alphabet he named *springletur* because the runes are shifted in the alphabet two spaces to the right. (This is a form of substitution cipher. Several examples from about 1300 A.D. in the stave churches of Norway are solved in later chapters of this volume.) A second alphabet he called *villirletur*. This means writing which is designed to confuse the translator. Most powerfully confusing of all was the alphabet which he called *ramvillingar*.[13]

All of this clearly refers to secret writing. It would seem like magic only to those who were not aware that these systems are purely mechanical. There are some modern scholars among them.

In a letter in 1627, three years earlier, Árngrim Jónsson had protested to Worm that he knew nothing about these "powerful" runes. And he continued that: "We still have people who are suspected of sorcery. They will not talk about it." In 1630 he posed this question to Worm: "Now I wish to ask if it is not possible that a runic inscription was used so as to bring fame and reputation for learning by something that it is difficult, or impossible, to understand as it is written?" *This must certainly have been one of the factors which caused Norse cryptography to remain popular with a segment of the clergy over more than three centuries, until the mid-fourteenth century.*

Most revealing, perhaps is a letter which Bishop Gisle Oddsson of Skálholt, one of the foremost scholars of his day, wrote in 1634:

"I know nothing about the runes of our country. That kind of evil, according to His word, has almost disappeared. Perhaps those who were knowledgeable in this art have a bad conscience and have long ago dug down even the memorial carvings [mindesmerker] which were cut into bluffs by a method which is unknown to me. What I saw with my own eyes five years ago, *is now nowhere to be seen*—and *no followers of that kind of signs is tolerated.*"[14] (Italics added.)

The situation in Iceland in 1634 could scarcely be described in more explicit and graphic terms.

It is ironic that, during the same century that "witches" were being put to death in New England, an approximately equal number of Icelanders lost their lives after they had been accused of being interested in runes or merely having knowledge of them. It became worth an Icelander's life to own a runic alphabet or a runic inscription. Under the circumstances, the only safe course was to destroy all traces of them.[15]

What caused this furor against their own native writing with which the Icelanders had been familiar for at least seven centuries? It is difficult to escape the conclusion that this was the "sorcerers' runes" of Gissur, Henricus, and their colleagues which had come back to haunt their cryptographic heirs in later centuries. The Icelandic language has changed very little over the centuries. There has never been a time when almost any Icelander, who had access to a runic alphabet, could not translate a normal runic inscription which was written in Icelandic. When the translation was found to be a harmless message, how could the devil use it for his ends?

Whatever the historical and religious causes for the persecution, the result was not in doubt. It resulted in the virtual disappearance of runic inscriptions in Iceland, and a total disappearance of *books which were written* with runes.

It has been the purpose of this chapter to establish the certainty that much information which once existed about migration of Norse Greenlanders to North America has been destroyed. Essentially, only the two Vinland Sagas survived. They tell of the abandonment of attempts to colonize Vinland. With this as the historical background, historians have been very negative about the possibility of long-term and extensive incursions by Norsemen into the continent and specifically into the United States.

Before closing this discussion it should be pointed out that there was a period of several centuries after 1000 A.D. during which Europe had access to all information about Vinland which reached Greenland and Iceland. To believe otherwise is to assume that it was only the episodes which are related in the sagas which were considered to be of sufficient importance to remember or to transmit to others. Such an assumption would obviously be ridiculous.

Communication between Greenland and Europe was of many kinds and persistent. It included trade in such things as the Greenland white falcons and polar bears which were highly prized all over Europe and mentioned even in archives in Italy. It included large quantities of walrus tusks in the market at Cologne in payment of Peter's Pence. Above all, it included the business of the Church, the comings and goings of bishops and members of the clergy and reports and messages between the bishops, the archbishops and the Vatican about conditions in Greenland. Even in the earliest years, Greenlanders made pilgrimages to Rome. One of the pilgrims was Gudrid, widow of Thorfinn Karlsefni, who, about 1009 A.D., had given birth to Snorri, the first white child who is known to have been born in North America.

This chapter has not been written as a contribution to the

Norse versus Columbus question. That issue was settled decades ago in favor of the Norsemen. The purpose has been to point out that there was no scarcity of information about Vinland in Europe even into the late Middle Ages and up to the time of Columbus. The scarcity of information was a hardship which befell historians during more recent centuries. This vacuum the dated runestones are helping to fill.

CHAPTER 3

Runes of the Norse Puzzlemasters

The Roman Catholic perpetual calendar was the essential tool of the Norse puzzlemasters. The preferred vehicle was their own native runes and their runic alphabets. The priests, monks, and even a nun, who practiced this unique art, were also, undoubtedly, conversant with Latin. It was the official and required language of the Church. The clergy often mixed Latin letters, words, and phrases among their runes.

There was little more difficulty in concealing dates and ciphers from the calendar in a Latin text than in a runic inscription. This is demonstrated by the deft cryptography of Henricus in the Latin legends of V.M. (Chapter 8). Nevertheless, runes had obvious advantages for concealment. Much flexibility was provided by allowable variations in the shape, size, and position of runes even as they were used in normal runic writing. This made deliberate deviations for cryptographic reasons less conspicuous.

Runes also provided relatively great freedom in the way that words were spelled and in grammatical constructions. This was particularly so because there were no written standards for spelling and composition. There were many dialects. Each runemaster must try to spell a word as he knew its sound.

Runologists often call attention to the prevalence in runic writing of magic formulas. They often appear as ritualistic repetitions of runes and bizarre arrangements of symbols that may have no literal meanings. But Norse puzzles have nothing to do with magic even though runologists have often mistaken them for such. Nor are Norse puzzles themselves runic. They are simply embedded in runic inscriptions.

In order to understand why Norse puzzlemasters used runes,

one must also reckon with the remarkable tenacity with which the Scandinavian peoples clung to the use of their native form of writing. Given these preconditions, runes were the obvious choice for Norse puzzlemaking.

The brief history of runes and runic writing which follows adheres to the consensus of scholarly opinion. The only apparent exceptions occur in connection with a few new elements that have their roots in Norse cryptography. However, as noted above, they are not runic and these elements were unknown before Norse dated puzzles and Norse ciphers were discovered.

It is generally assumed that the various Germanic tribes, of which the Scandinavians are one branch, migrated into Europe from an area that lies north of the Caspian Sea. This probably happened about the beginning of the Christian era. During this time they came into contact with people who spoke and wrote the classical Greek and Latin languages. In the process of developing a set of symbols, which could represent the various sounds of their own speech, they assimilated a number of letters from the Greek alphabet. Because the Romans were masters of the then known world, it is not strange that some Latin symbols were also adopted.

Out of these, and perhaps some other elements, a runic alphabet took form. By about 200 A.D., a 24-rune alphabet had come into use. It varied only slightly among the various branches of the Germanic peoples. About this same time they began to move into the areas in Central and Western Europe from which they were later to overrun virtually all parts of the continent. The Scandinavian version of the row of runes will henceforth be referred to as Old Norse or simply by the abbreviation O. N.

The 24-rune alphabet continued in use in Scandinavia until about 600 A.D. During these four centuries the forms of the runes remained essentially unchanged. However, during the three centuries that followed many symbols were abandoned. Others, particularly those which were originally carved with two parallel vertical staffs, were simplified. The reason is believed to have been that it was very laborious to cut symbols into hard stone. The fewer the symbols, and the more simple they were, the better.

It is fortunate that an accurate copy of the O. N. rune-row exists. It was carved on a stone in Sweden which is known as the Kylver stone. A photograph of it is reproduced in *The Runes of Sweden* by Professor Sven B.F. Johnson of the National Historical Museum of Sweden in Stockholm.[1]

FIGURE 1

Three Major Runic Alphabets

Old Norse

Swedish—Norwegian

Normal

By the year 900 A.D. two related, but distinct, 16-rune alphabets were in use. One, which had been developed in Sweden and Norway, is called the Swedish-Norwegian (Sw.-N.) alphabet. It was also used in the islands to the west of Norway and in Greenland and North America. (The Scandinavians called their alphabets the *Futhark* and, later, *Futhork* because the first six symbols had these sounds. Here, they will simply be referred to as alphabets.)

The second of these so-called "younger rune-rows" had its origin in Denmark. Because it was adopted in all Scandinavian countries by about the year 1100, it is usually called the "Normal" alphabet.

The decrease in the number of symbols from 24 to 16 had some undesirable effects. It was no longer possible to express all of the sounds in the Old Norse language. Therefore, some runes had to represent more than one sound. For example, the same rune was used for I and E and for U, V, and W. This defect was not corrected until the late Middle Ages. It was not done by increasing the number of runes but by adding special optional markings, especially points, to the sixteen runic symbols.

Because the Scandinavians had not yet acquired any other system of numbers, runes were used to express numbers as well as sounds. In fact, most early alphabets served this dual purpose. The figure shows that numerical values were assigned to the runes according to their positions in the alphabet.

The O.N. rune-row could, of course, represent numbers up to 24 and the Sw.-N. and Normal alphabets only to 16. It was partly for this reason that O.N. runes were used in some eleventh-century Norse puzzles even though their use in ordinary runic inscriptions had long since been abandoned.

In the Roman Catholic perpetual calendar, which will be discussed in detail in Chapter 4, runes were used to represent its numbers. Such a calendar was called a *runstav* or a *primstav*. Norse puzzlemasters used these calendrical numbers to represent dates in their runic inscriptions. Because they were runic symbols, they were inconspicuous, especially when they also represented a sound value in a word.

One obvious problem, when the Sw.-N. or Normal runes were used, was that there were no symbols for the numbers 17, 18, and 19. These are the last three of the nineteen so-called Golden Numbers in the calendar. Special symbols had to be designed to represent them. They were as follows:

FIGURE 2

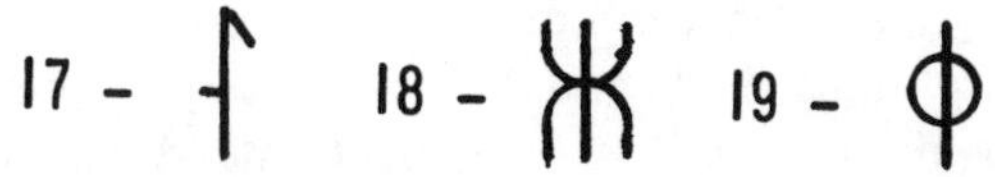

$$17 - \quad 18 - \quad 19 -$$

The table below shows only six of a large number of sets of symbols that were used to represent the Golden Numbers in medieval perpetual calendars. It is a page from an author-

FIGURE 3

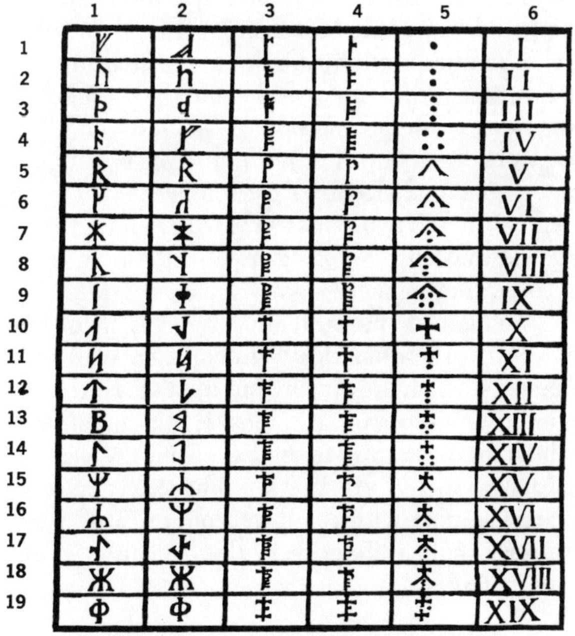

	1	2	3	4	5	6
1					•	I
2					:	II
3					⦂	III
4					::	IV
5					∧	V
6					⟨∧⟩	VI
7					⟨∧⟩	VII
8					⟨∧⟩	VIII
9					⟨∧⟩	IX
10					✦	X
11						XI
12						XII
13						XIII
14						XIV
15						XV
16						XVI
17						XVII
18						XVIII
19						XIX

A page from Worm's *Fasti Danici*

itative work in Latin on medieval Scandinavian primstaves. It was written by a Danish scholar, Ole Worm, and published in 1643 A.D. under the title *Fasti Danici*.[2]

Column I of Worm's table uses a 16-rune alphabet to represent numbers up to 16 with the symbols slightly stylized. To the 16 runes are added the symbols for 17, 18, and 19. In Column 2, most of the symbols in Column 1 are reversed or inverted. Columns 3, 4, and 5 show different versions of the so-called pentathic symbols. The pentathic system of numbers is based on only five digits instead of ten as in the decimal system. In Column 6 the Golden Numbers are expressed in terms of Roman numerals.

The symbols in each of the six columns are *numbers* and, as Worm presented them, were *not* intended to be used as digits in decimal numbers. In such systems numbers can not be multiplied or divided. However, medieval members of the clergy, who had been taught the decimal system in their monastery schools, used the runic and pentathic symbols as digits.

In numerous examples in coming chapters four-digit decimal numbers were built up by placing two two-digit runic or pentathic numbers adjacent to each other. For example, 1012 was stated with the two runes A (=10) and T (=12) and 1010 was indicated by the use of two pentathic symbols for the number 10 written in succession.

An examination of the individual symbols in Columns 3, 4, and 5 shows that the numerical value of each symbol is the *sum* of the elements which are attached to its staff. In the Kensington inscription, the inscription contains eight pentathic numbers. (All of them are used to state, and confirm, the year, 1362 A.D., and the day, Sunday, April 24.) The Kensington pentathic symbols are identical with those in Column 3 of Worm's table except for one slight difference in the formation of the symbol for the number 10:

FIGURE 4

Number	Worm's Column 3	Kensington
 5	Þ	Þ
10	†	φ

There is, of course, nothing wrong with the symbols that are shown by Worm. But, if a half circle represents 5, then 10 could certainly be represented by a full circle. The Kensington symbols are the more logical. Exactly the same pentathic symbol for 10 is used in Henricus's Spirit Pond inscriptions. It had clearly been in use in medieval Scandinavian perpetual calendars.

The Norse puzzlemasters substituted runic and pentathic numbers into the decimal system with a considerable degree of understanding. The question, which remains unanswered, is why they did not use the Arabic digits which must have been known to them. The only case in which the Arabic digits have been found is in a Norwegian perpetual calendar from 1328 A.D. It is illustrated and discussed in Chapter 4.

There is no mystery about the source from which the puzzlemasters acquired their knowledge of the decimal system. It was a French-born Benedictine monk by the name of Gerbert who introduced it into Northern Europe. For centuries the Arabs had nurtured the faltering torch of Western learning and were the leaders in mathematics and science. As a young man Gerbert was sent to study at the famous Arab schools in Spain. He became recognized as the foremost scholar of his day.

By 979 A.D. Gerbert was teaching the decimal system at the Cathedral School at Reims, France. Later, he was the private tutor of the young prince who was to become Otto III, Emperor of the Holy Roman Empire. In 999 A.D. he became Pope Sylvester II.[3]

It is clear that Gerbert had the knowledge, incentive, and opportunity to spread knowledge of the vastly superior decimal system throughout the extensive educational system of the Benedictine Order. He was not one to waste such an opportunity.

It is the Benedictines who are given credit for being the scholars and schoolmasters of Europe during the late Middle Ages. Most of the missionaries who came to Scandinavia received their training in Benedictine schools. They maintained scriptoria in which learned works, including books on science and mathematics by Gerbert, were copied. In this way they built up libraries which could run into many hundreds of volumes. Many promising young men from Scandinavia were prepared for the priesthood in such schools.

These interrelated facts appear to provide an adequate explanation for knowledge of the decimal system among the clergy in Scandinavia even in the early eleventh century. Under the circumstances it would not be surprising if what is now called Norse cryptography had its origin in other lands. The most likely would probably be England.

Another use to which runes were put was to carve two or more in such a way that they blended into a single *symbol*. These were called combined runes (*Bindruner*). The only requirement was that each rune must still be recognizable as a part of the entire symbol.

Runes were sometimes combined to save labor or space in normal inscriptions. But in some Norse puzzles they are found in surprising numbers for purely cryptographic reasons. This can best be illustrated by displaying a total of eleven combined symbols, which involve a total of 23 runes. These combined runes are found in an inscription which has a total of only 86 runic symbols.

FIGURE 5

The Eleven Kingigtorssuaq Combined Runes

LN   ON   NN   TO   TAR   SO   AU   RI   TA   AR   TA

This is the famous Kingigtorssuaq inscription. It was discovered in northern Greenland in 1824 A.D. The original has long been lost but has recently been rediscovered at the National Museum in Copenhagen. Runologists have long been aware of its many non-runic anomalies. They have suspected the purpose of these strange features to be magic and sorcery, but they have not been able to determine their real meaning.

Mr. Mongé proved that they were elements in an ingenious and all-pervasive dated puzzle together with a ciphered message. There is not a hint of magic in the solution.

Those who tried to translate the inscription realized that the last part of the text was missing. The cipher provided the missing part. It was also the cipher which required the eleven combinations of runes in addition to a number of other strictly non-runic features. Any serious student of Norse puzzles would be well rewarded by studying this solution. It is analyzed in full in *Ancient Norse Messages on American Stones*.[4]

In all of Scandinavia there are more than eight thousand runic inscriptions which were carved with one or the other of the three major runic alphabets and their variants and mixtures. Only a little over a hundred use O.N. runes exclusively. To nearly all, if not in fact all, such inscriptions the runologists have assigned dates in the range from 200 to 600 A.D.

The 7th, 8th, and 9th centuries were a period of transition. Only a handful of inscriptions are known from this period. But it produced two long and very significant inscriptions, the Sparlösa and Rök carvings. Both are from Sweden and both use symbols from all of the three major alphabets. Their estimated dates, which are based on runological evidence alone, are set at slightly before and slightly after 800 A.D. respectively.

These inscriptions have, at one and the same time, given the runologists much joy and have furrowed many brows. Good introductions to them are to be found in *The Runes of Sweden* by Sven B. F. Jansson[5] and *Stuttruner* by Ingrid Sannes Johnsen.[6]

Inscriptions that use Sw.-N. runes also number only slightly more than a hundred. While most were carved in Norway and Sweden, examples are found along the shores of the British Isles, on the Isle of Man, the Orkney Islands, Greenland, and in the New England states and Oklahoma. Runologists estimate the ages of inscriptions with Sw.-N. runes from about 900 to 1100 A.D.

The total of O.N. and Sw.-N. inscriptions is only a few hundred examples. Because known runic inscriptions number more than eight thousand, it is clear that the overwhelming number were carved with the Normal runes. It is significant that about 95 percent of all Scandinavian inscriptions were carved after 1000 A.D. All but a few dozen used the Normal runes or a mixture of Normal and Sw.-N.

It is also important to note that Christianity was known and accepted by many Scandinavians before 1000 A.D. This question was recently discussed by a prominent Norwegian church leader, Bishop Fridtjof Birkeli, in an article in *The Norseman*.[7] He stated that, because of long-continued contacts with people in Christian lands, Christianity already had a firm foothold in parts of Scandinavia more than a thousand years ago, that is, before 970 A.D. During the first third of the eleventh century King Olaf Haraldsson, who is better known as Saint Olaf, found that the new religion had progressed in Norway to the point that he could begin to organize the church on a national basis.

These figures show that the increase in the number of runic inscriptions in Scandinavia parallels the acceptance of the Christian religion. The connection is emphasized by the fact that, over a period of three and a half centuries after 1000 A.D., runic *puzzlemasters* were, apparently almost without exception, members of the Norse clergy.

It is a further indication of this close association that medieval Norwegian and Swedish churches were liberally decorated with runic inscriptions, both with and without Norse-type cryptography. Scandinavian scholars have also expressed the opinion that runic writing was largely in the hands of the clergy and that they often derived an income from carving runic inscriptions for the laity.[8]

When one considers the firm control which the Catholic Church exercised during these centuries, such a strong upswing in the popularity of runic writing could not have happened without the benign tolerance of the church authorities. It may, in part, have been a concession to the traditions of the Scandinavians in order to assure their loyalty to the Church and to smooth the acceptance of nagging ecclesiastical regulations. The Norse clergy were selected from among the people and were themselves steeped in their national traditions. They would, therefore, be effective intermediaries.

The intimate connection between the Norse clergy and runic writing is confirmed by a survey which the author made recently of the Norwegian inscriptions that were carved with the 16-rune alphabets. They are all illustrated and discussed in the five-volume work, *Norges Innskrifter med de Yngre Runer* (NIYR).[9] (The recently excavated inscriptions from the wharves at Bergen were not available when the series was completed in 1960.)

The results of the survey are illuminating. Of the approximately 560 inscriptions in NIYR, 68 percent, or about two out of three, are found in or near the medieval churches of Norway. No less than 40 runic inscriptions are reported from the cathedral at Trondheim alone. There are 34 in a single stavechurch, the one at Borgund, which is located on the Sognefjord on the west coast of Norway. It is a further indication of clerical influence that Latin letters, words, and phrases are often interspersed among the runes.

Meanwhile, the attrition to which Norwegian churches, and particularly the stave churches, have been subjected has been very great. Only one in twenty-four has survived.

There is no reason to suppose that the large number of medieval Norwegian churches that have been lost did not have their full share of runic inscriptions. It is obvious from this that the number of church-connected runic inscriptions in Norway was once many times those that are known today. The total must have amounted to several thousand. The incidence of Norse puzzles in these inscriptions is higher than among inscriptions from other sources. Their total numbers must also have been large.

Outstanding examples of church-connected runic inscriptions are those in the stave church which was moved from Gol, in Hallingdal, to the Folk Museum at Bygdøy, near Oslo, in

1885. Thirteen runic inscriptions which are carved on its walls
are illustrated and discussed in NIYR.[10] They are almost totally
cryptographic. Only a few words were intended to be translated. The inscriptions comprise a complex of Norse puzzles by
a nun in 1297 A.D. and a cleric thirty-two years later. They add
further proof to evidence which is already fully adequate about
the extensive use of cryptography by Norse priests.

Naturally, runologists, who attempted to translate such inscriptions, faced difficulties. Since they were not aware of their
true nature, they had a right to expect that no one, not even
a medieval priest, would laboriously carve runic inscriptions
that had no meaning into wood and stone. When, as was often
the case, the only meaning was concealed, attempts at translating the text were futile. Among the thirteen Gol carvings
only one has a translatable text. It is the warning: "Read right
these runes!"

The great Norwegian runologist Magnus Olsen needed no
such warnings in spite of the fact that he did not discover the
true nature of dated puzzles. This is clear from remarks which
he made on various occasions. About a Norwegian west-coast
inscription, which is known as Borgund No. 5, he stated that it
was reasonable to believe that *this runic puzzle* had to remain
unsolved until a specific person who was expected should
arrive, or perhaps the solution must await the later arrival
of some stranger. On another occasion (the inscription was
Urnes stave church No. 20) he said that, in the runic trickeries
of later times, virtually every rune would take part in the sort of
secret writing which we have encountered here.[11] (Italics
added.)

The current ranking Norwegian runologist, Aslak Liestøl,
expressed similar opinions in a discussion of some of the runic
inscriptions which have been excavated from the medieval
wharves at Bergen in recent years: "Some inscriptions may be
relatively easy to read but they contain things which we do not
understand. In others, *which are also easily read*, the orthography

is so bad that it is difficult to make any sense of it."[12] (Italics added.)

Since orthography includes everything which has to do with the shapes and positions of the runes and the spelling of words, this is a very sharp criticism. Many examples in Chapters 5 and 6 show how completely justified it is. Under these conditions, it is obvious how meaningless claims are that any specific runic inscription is not authentic because its symbols, and the spelling of its words, are not what a runologist, for whatever reason, would prefer. Yet some have persisted in such judgments against American runic inscriptions even when they are, relatively speaking, models of acceptable orthography. It is high time that this double standard be recognized for what it is and abandoned. The most bizarre feature of this situation is that dated puzzles in American inscriptions, which are totally obvious, have been brushed aside while, at the same time, it is acknowledged that puzzles which they can not solve exist in Norwegian inscriptions. Meanwhile, no attempt has been made to disprove the existence of the dated puzzles in American inscriptions. To do so is essential if their authenticity is to be successfully disputed. The inconsistencies are clear.

CHAPTER 4

An Indispensable Tool of the Norse Clergy

The history of the 532-year perpetual calendar of the Roman Catholic Church is rooted in the astronomy of the Babylonians about eight centuries B.C. They were among the foremost astronomers of their day. One of their earliest discoveries was that, as viewed from the earth, the motions of the sun and the moon relative to each other occurred in cycles. Fortunately, the cycles coincided, very nearly, with an exact number of years.

The so-called Metonic cycle was known to the Babylonians but it was formulated and applied to the perpetual calendar by a Greek mathematician and astronomer, Meton, during the fifth century B.C. It takes nineteen years for the phases of the moon to occur on the same day of the month as they had nineteen years earlier. The years of the Metonic cycle were numbered in consecutive order. These are the famous Golden Numbers which made the perpetual calendar possible.

It was also discovered that it takes 532 years for *both* the sun and the moon to return to the same relative positions in the heavens as they had 532 years before. It will be noted that 19 multiplied by 28 is 532. Therefore a single luni-solar cycle contains 28 Metonic cycles.

This is the mathematical and astronomical basis for the perpetual Christian calendar. It led to the invention of a special table which accompanies the calendar proper. The Roman Catholic Church named it the Easter Table because, by its use, the date of one of the most important holy days of the church year, Easter Sunday, could be quickly determined for any one of the 532 years.

In 325 A.D., during the reign of the Emperor Constantine, the first Christian emperor of the Roman Empire, a church council, which made many far-reaching decisions, was held at Nicaea in Asia Minor. It was at this council that the perpetual calendar was devised. Presumably, it was of necessity that it was based on the Julian calendar which had been named after Julius Caesar.

This was the calendar which, many centuries later, missionaries brought with them to Scandinavia. Saint Ansgar, who was of German ancestry, was the first missionary to Scandinavia of whom there seems to be a record. He visited Denmark and Sweden during the first half of the ninth century and persevered in spite of great danger to his life and many hardships. During the following century and a half the Scandinavians had a great deal of contact with Christian communities and people, first as raiders but later, and increasingly, as traders and settlers. Nevertheless, as was previously noted, they were not ready to accept Christianity, generally, until about 1000 A.D.

About the same time promising young men began to leave the Scandinavian countries to be trained for the priesthood. It is reasonable to assume that the change from foreign-born missionaries to native-born priests was a relatively slow process. Of course, some of the more accessible districts in Scandinavia were affected much earlier than those that were more remote.[1]

It was pointed out in a previous chapter that runes were a cherished part of the cultural heritage of the Scandinavians. Furthermore, the Roman Catholic Church, whose official language was Latin, had taken a quite benevolent attitude towards continued use of runes and the native language. This was particularly true of the English churchmen who predominated during the early days of Christianity in Norway and Iceland. This background makes it easier to understand the course of the development of the perpetual calendar and the use which was made of it for making dated puzzles in runic inscriptions by a portion of the Norse clergy. In the Easter Table and calendar which are reproduced here, decimal numbers have been substituted for the runes and the pentathic symbols which were normally used to represent the calendrical quantities in the

Scandinavian calendars. The decimal numbers make it more easy to understand and to use but they do not change its operation in the least.

FIGURE 6

The Easter Table

```
DL →   6 5 4 3 1 7 6 5 3 2 1 7 (5) 4 3 2 7 6 5 4 2 1 7 6 4 3 (2) 1
RATI  A.D.
 1.   1140  1  2  3  4  5  6  7  8  9 10 11 12 13 14 15 16 17 18 19  1  2  3  4  5  6  7  8 | 9
 2.   1168 10 11 12 13 14 15 16 17 18 19  1  2  3  4  5  6  7  8  9 10 11 12 13 14 15 16 17 |18
 3.   1196 19  1  2  3  4  5  6  7  8  9 10 11 12 13 14 15 16 17 18 19  1  2  3  4  5  6  7 | 8
 4.   1224  9 10 11 12 13 14 15 16 17 18 19  1  2  3  4  5  6  7  8  9 10 11 12 13 14 15 16 |17
 5.   1252 18 19  1  2  3  4  5  6  7  8  9 10 11 12 13 14 15 16 17 18 19  1  2  3  4  5  6 | 7
 6.   1280  8  9 10 11 12 13 14 15 16 17 18 19  1  2  3  4  5  6  7  8  9 10 11 12 13 14 15 |16
 7.   1308 17 18 19  1  2  3  4  5  6  7  8  9 10 11 12 13 14 15 16 17 18 19  1  2  3  4  (6)
(8.)  1336  7  8  9 10 11 12 13 14 15 16 17 18 19  1  2  3  4  5  6  7  8  9 10 11 12 13 14 (5)
(9.)  1364 16 17 18 19  1  2  3  4  5  6  7  8  9 10 11 12 13 14 15 16 17 18 19  1  2  3 (14) 5
10.   1392  6  7  8  9 10 11 12 13 14 15 16 17 18 19  1  2  3  4  5  6  7  8  9 10 11 12 13 14
11.   1420 15 16 17 18 19  1  2  3  4  5  6  7  8  9 10 11 12 13 14 15 16 17 18 19  1  2  3  4
12.    916  5  6  7  8  9 10 11 12 13 14 15 16 17 18 19  1  2  3  4  5  6  7  8  9 10 11 12 13
13.    944 14 15 16 17 18 19  1  2  3  4  5  6  7  8  9 10 11 12 13 14 15 16 17 18 19  1  2  3
14.    972  4  5  6  7  8  9 10 11 12 13 14 15 16 17 18 19  1  2  3  4  5  6  7  8  9 10 11 12
(15.) 1000 13 14 15 16 17 18 19  1  2  3  4  5  (6) 7  8  9 10 11 12 13 14 15 16 17 18 19  1  2
16.   1028  3  4  5  6  7  8  9 10 11 12 13 14 15 16 17 18 19  1  2  3  4  5  6  7  8  9 10 11
17.   1056 12 13 14 15 16 17 18 19  1  2  3  4  5  6  7  8  9 10 11 12 13 14 15 16 17 18 19  1
18.   1084  2  3  4  5  6  7  8  9 10 11 12 13 14 15 16 17 18 19  1  2  3  4  5  6  7  8  9 10
19.   1112 11 12 13 14 15 16 17 18 19  1  2  3  4  5  6  7  8  9 10 11 12 13 14 15 16 17 18 19
```

It is the Easter Table which makes the calendar "perpetual" over a period of 532 years. In the form that it is illustrated above, it was effective without any change from 916 to 1477 A.D. (The operating range can be moved forward in time by adding 532 years to each of the years in the column at the left end of the table.) The perpetual nature of the calendar resides in the fact that the Easter Table supplies two small whole numbers for each of the 532 years. One is known as the Dominical Letter (or Sunday Letter) for the year (DL), the other is the Golden Number (GN). To serve as a reminder that these numbers apply to the entire year, their identifying symbols are written YDL and YGN. When these two numbers are applied to the calendar proper in ways which will be specified later, YDL immediately reveals which of the days of the year were Sundays. YGN, for its part, points out all of the days of the year which were new moons. This was obviously a great boon to the clergy before the time when new calendars were printed annually. It was critically important to be able to check quickly which days during the current year were Sundays, and the date of Easter

Sunday was counted from the so-called Paschal New Moon which by definition occurred on or after March 7.

Within the rectangular enclosure in the illustration of the Easter Table above, are 19 lines each of which contain 28 year numbers. (28 multiplied by 19 is 532.) However, in place of the consecutive year numbers themselves, their Golden Numbers (YGN) have been substituted. The Golden Numbers are also in consecutive order from 1 to 19 and are repeated 28 times throughout the table.

Since the year numbers are not visible in the table, it becomes necessary to devise a way to find them. This is done with the help of the column of year numbers at the left end of the table. Each number in the column is the first year which appears in its line. For example, the first year number in Line 8 is 1336 A.D. By counting along this line, it will be found that the next to the last position in Line 8 has the Golden Number 14 (circled) for the year 1362 A.D. At the top of this column is the number 2 which is also circled. It is the Dominical Letter for all of the year numbers in the column.

The Scandinavians named the 19 lines in the Easter Table Rati. A year was fully identified, and mutually confirmed, in the Easter Table by stating its Rati, YGN, and YDL. For the year number of the Kensington inscription the values are 8, 14, and 2 respectively. In the Kensington text these numbers are expressed in the following words: At the beginning of Line 1, "8 Goths..."; in Line 11, "...14 days journey..."; and in Line 4, "...2 skerries...". (The translation of the last word as skerries is doubtful but the number 2 is correct for YDL for the year 1362 A.D.)

The calendar proper, which is illustrated on the next page, has twelve months and the same number of days in each as our modern Gregorian almanac. The main difference is that, below the row of numbered days for the months, are two additional rows of numbers. Immediately below the days of the months are the numbers 1 through 7 repeated in normal numerical order throughout the year. They are the Dominical Letters for the

FIGURE 7

The Roman Catholic Perpetual Calendar

```
January │ - 1  2  3  4  5  6·7  8  9 10 11 12 13 14 15 16 17 18 19 20 21 22 23 24 25 26 27 28 29 30 31
     DL │   1  2  3·4  5  6·7  1  2  3  4  5  6  7  1  2  3  4  5  6  7  1  2  3  4  5  6  7  1  2  3
     GN │   3    11    19  8    16  5    13  2    10    18  7    15  4    12  1     9    17  6    14  3
February│ - 1  2  3  4  5  6  7  8  9 10 11 12 13 14 15 16 17 18 19 20 21 22 23 24 25 26 27 28 ·
     DL │   4  5  6  7  1  2·3  4  5  6  7  1  2  3  4  5  6  7  1  2  3  4  5  6  7  1  2  3
     GN │  11 19  8    16  5    13  2    10    18  7    15  4    12  1     9    17  6    14
March   │ - 1  2  3  4  5  6  7  8  9 10 11 12 13 14 15 16 17 18 19 20 21 22 23 24 25 26 27 28 29 30 31
     DL │   4  5  6  7  1  2  3  4  5  6  7  1  2  3  4  5  6  7  1  2  3  4  5  6  7  1  2  3  4  5  6
     GN │   3    11    19  8    16  5    13  2    10    18  7    15  4    12  1     9    17  6    14  3
April   │ - 1  2  3  4  5  6  7  8  9 10 11 12 13 14 15 16 17 18 19 20 21 22 23 24 25 26 27 28 29 30
     DL │   7  1  2  3  4  5  6  7  1  2  3  4  5  6  7  1  2  3  4  5  6  7  1  (2) 3  4  5  6  7  1
     GN │  11    19  8 16  5    13  2    10   16  7    15  4    12  1     9    17  6    14  3
May     │ - 1  2  3  4  5  6  7  8  9 10 11 12 13 14 15 16 17 18 19 20 21 22 23 24 25 26 27 28 29 30
     DL │   2  3  4  5  6  7  1  2  3  4  5  6  7  1  2  3  4  5  6  7  1  2  3  4  5  6  7  1  2  3  4
     GN │  11    19  8    16  5    13  2    10    18  7    15  4    12  1     9    17  6    14  3    11
June    │ - 1  2  3  4  5  6  7  8  9 10 11 12 13 14 15 16 17 18 19 20 21 22 23 24 25 26 27 28 29 30
     DL │   5  6  7  1  2  3  4  5  6  7  1  2  3  4  5  6  7  1  2  3  4  5  6  7  1  2  3  4  5  6
     GN │  19  8 16  5    13  2    10    18  7    15  4    12  1     9    17  6    14  3    11
July    │ - 1  2  3  4  5  6  7  8  9 10 11 12 13 14 15 16 17 18 19 20 21 22 23 24 25 26 27 28 29 30 31
     DL │   7  1  2  3  4  5  6  7  1  2  3  4  5  6  7  1  2  3  4  5  6  7  1  2  3  4  5  6  7  1  2
     GN │  19  8    16  5    13  2    10    18  7    15  4    12  1     9    17  6    14  3    11 19
August  │ - 1  2  3  4  5  6  7  8  9 10 11 12 13 14 15 16 17 18 19 20 21 22 23 24 25 26 27 28 29 30 31
     DL │   3  4  5  6  7  1  2  3  4  5  6  7  1  2  3  4  5  6  7  1  2  3  4  5  6  7  1  2  3  4  5
     GN │   8 16  5    13  2    10    18  7    15  4    12  1     9    17  6    14  3    11 19     8
September│ - 1  2  3  4  5  6  7  8  9 10 11 12 13 14 15 16 17 18 19 20 21 22 23 24 25 26 27 28 29 30
     DL │   6  7  1  2  3  4  5  6  7  1  2  3  4  5  6  7  1  2  3  4  5  6  7  1  2  3  4  5  6  7
     GN │  16  5    13  2    10    18  7    15  4    12  1     9    17  6    14  3    11 19     8
October │ - 1  2  3  4  5  6  7  8  9 10 11 12 13 14 15 16 17 18 19 20 21 22 23 24 25 26 27 28 29 30 31
     DL │   1  2  3  4  5  6  7  1  2  3  4  5  6  7  1  2  3  4  5  6  7  1  2  3  4  5  6  7  1  2  3
     GN │  16  5 13  2    10    18  7    15  4    12  1     9    17  6    14  3    11 19     8    16  5
November│ - 1  2  3  4  5  6  7  8  9 10 11 12 13 14 15 16 17 18 19 20 21 22 23 24 25 26 27 28 29 30
     DL │   4  5  6  7  1  2  3  4  5  6 (7) 1  2  3  4  5  6  7  1  2  3  4  5  6  7  1  2  3  4  5
     GN │  13  2    10    18  7    15 (4) 12  1     9    17  6    14  3    11 19     8    16  5
December│ - 1  2  3  4  5  6  7  8  9 10 11 12 13 14 15 16 17 18 19 20 21 22 23 24 25 26 27 28 29 30 31
     DL │   6  7  1  2  3  4  5  6  7  1  2  3  4  5  6  7  1  2  3  4  5  6  7  1  2  3  4  5  6  7  1
     GN │  13  2    10    18  7    15  4    12  1     9    17  6    14  3    11 19     8    16  5    13
```

individual days of the year so that their identifying symbol is
DDL. Any one of the seven Dominical Letters may represent the
first day of the week. Any DDL does represent Sunday when its
numerical value is the same as the YDL for the year in question.
Thus, we have seen that YDL for the Kensington year, 1362 A.D.,
was 2. Therefore, every day in the year whose DDL is 2 was
a Sunday during that year. It so happens that the Kensington
day, April 24, was one of those days.

The reader may have observed an inconsistency. In this discussion the term Dominical *Letter* has been retained for historical

reasons. As they were normally used, and written, Dominical Letters were taken from some alphabet including the runic. However, Norse puzzlemasters thought of them, and used them, as numbers from 1 to 7 in their dated puzzles. Since this is a treatise on Norse cryptography and has only an incidental connection with normal runic writing, it was thought less confusing if the Dominical Letters were written as numbers.

The third row of numbers in the calendar contains the 19 Golden Numbers. Since they are assigned to individual days, they are identified by the symbol DGN. The nineteen numbers are arranged in a special order which is known as the Dionysian Cycle.[2] Each cycle is distributed over a lunar month which varies between twenty-nine and thirty days. The result is that about one-third of the days of the year have no DGN assigned to them.

It is the function of the Golden Numbers in the calendar to point out the dates of all the new moons during the year. In any given year those days are new moons which have the same Golden Number (DGN) as the Golden Number for the entire year (YGN). The importance of this feature of the calendar is that, even to this day, Easter Sunday and its associated holy days are counted from the so-called Paschal New Moon, the first new moon which occurs on or after March 7.

Unlike the three calendrical details which identify a year from the Easter Table, there was a degree of choice in the way in which a day during the year could be indicated. If the type of calendar was in use in which the months were shown, the number of the month and the day of the month could be displayed. This method is in use even today when, for example, April 17 is expressed as 4/17. The day could then be confirmed by giving its DDL and DGN.

Actually only a few dated puzzles are known which refer to the month. The probable reason is that most Norse puzzlemasters used a distinctive form of the perpetual calendar which was called a *Primstav*. The most unusual feature of the *primstav* was that it omitted the months. The year was divided into only two parts, a summer and a winter season. Summer began with April 14 and ended with October 13. The winter season occupied the remainder of the year. This simplification, and substitution of runes for the more cumbersome Roman numerals, permittted a primstav to be carved in compact form on a stick or slab of wood or even on a piece of bone. Such a calendar was more durable than those from southern lands which were usually written on parchment and often had a page for each month.

Unfortunately, not a single example has survived which was made before 1300 A.D. The earliest of which there is a record was illustrated and described in 1643 by the Danish physician and authority on runic calendars, Ole Worm.[3]

FIGURE 8

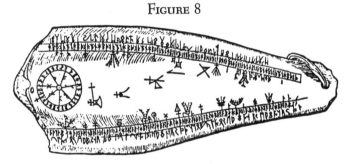

A Fourteenth-Century Norwegian Primstav

The Norwegian *primstav* here illustrated was carved on or about 1328 A.D. on both sides of a piece of bone. The ring at its right end suggests that it was carried suspended by a chain at the waist. The Dominical Letters are located between the two parallel lines at the bottom and top of the figure. They are represented by seven figures of runic type. The most interesting feature consists of the outer rows at both the top and bottom. These are the Golden Numbers (DGN) in their regular Dionysian order and distribution among the days of the year.

Only the winter season which is illustrated here was recorded by Worm. Its first half, which covers the period from October 14 to January 13, runs from left to right along the lower edge. It continues, also from left to right, at the upper edge but with the symbols carved upside down. A careful analysis of the Golden Numbers in this calendar has revealed some interesting facts. They are composed of a form of the Arabic digits and are written as decimal numbers. This is not obvious at first glance because in most cases, in numbers which require two digits, they are combined into a single symbol in the manner of combined runes. The analysis also revealed a surprising number of mistakes. This suggests that the calendar may have been a careless copy, or is perhaps the result of being recopied a number of times.

Some scholars have doubted that the decimal system was used, except on rare occasions, in Scandinavia, even as late as the mid-fourteenth century. This is certainly not so with the Norse puzzlemasters. They used the decimal system with a considerable degree of understanding even as early as the beginning of the eleventh century and with consistency from that time until the fourteenth century.

The *primstav* provided a means for indicating a day of the year which was superior, particularly from the puzzlemaster's point of view, to any other. By this method a single number could identify a day. It consisted of counting the number of days from the last day of the church year back to the day in question. The symbol which is used here to represent this count is ND. In northern Europe during the Middle Ages the last day of the church year was not December 31, but December 24. This made of the following day, December 25, an important double holy day. It was both Christmas Day and New Year's Day. The Roman Catholic Church is presumed to have promoted this arrangement in order to wean descendants of the various Germanic tribes away from the celebration of the pagan feast of the winter solstice.

It was not possible, of course, to state in a Norse puzzle whether a certain number represented an ND, a YGN, or what

else. Had this been done, there would have been nothing to
solve. On the other hand, a puzzlemaster could only use a very
limited number of dates as starting points for counts of ND. He
could not, for example, count from any of the many days of the
saints which are marked in the calendar. To have done so would
have led to confusion and a puzzle which could not be solved.
(This restriction did not hold in ordinary conversation or writing. For example, in many parts of the world the statement "five
days after Michaelsmass" will be recognized as October 4 even
today because the date of Michaelsmass is September 29.)

Besides the last day of the year there were two major breaks
in the year from which counts of ND were occasionally made
in the *primstav* by Norse puzzlemasters. They were April 14,
the first day of summer and October 14, the first day of winter.
Outstanding among such dated puzzles is the Kensington inscription which indicates ND in two ways. ND from December
24 to the Kensington day, April 24, is 244 days. This number
was much too large to represent by the addition of runes so a
special device had to be invented to state it. Three of the nine
lines of runes on the face of the stone are indented to the right
exactly 2, 4, and 4 spaces. The puzzlemaster was apparently
concerned, and justifiably so, that this subtle hint would be overlooked in such a long inscription. He therefore also indicated
twice in the text that ND from April 14 was 10 days by means
of the words "...[we found] 10 men red with blood and dead"
in Line 7; and "...[we have] 10 men by the sea to look after
our ships" in Line 10.

The result of these adjustments of the values of the pentathic
numbers in the Kensington text is that it supplies all of the
calendrical details, Rati, YGN, YDL, ND (two ways), and
DDL. (April 24 has no DGN.) In addition, the year 1362 A.D.
is stated directly as the last word in the text. It does not take a
mathematician to realize that the probability that all this could
have happened by accident is very small. More than this, there
are two numbers in the text which are *not* calendrical indicators.

They are written out in longhand in order not to confuse them with those which state and confirm the date.[4]

It was stated above that a special device to indicate a large value of ND was a necessity. The numerical values of runes could only be added and two runes could only have the sum 48 at the most. But special devices being unexpected, could easily be overlooked. This is the reason that an overwhelming proportion of Norse puzzles have dates that fall in November and December. Fifteen dated inscriptions from the United States are known which were carved in the early eleventh and twelfth centuries. The first twelve have dates in November and December and, of these, five have dates which fell on Advent Sunday in their respective year numbers. The last three were found near Spirit Pond in Maine in 1971. They are all dated October 6, 1123 A.D. and represent the last known cryptographic effort of Bishop Henricus.

The dating of the Kensington inscription has been followed for illustrative purposes in this chapter. A second date, whose calendrical details are also circled in the calendar, may be found useful for review. November 11, 1012 A.D. is the date of the Heavener inscription in eastern Oklahoma. For this date Rati = 15, YGN = 6, YDL = 5, ND = 43, DDL = 7, and DGN = 4.

A good grasp of the operation of the perpetual calendar is essential for a proper understanding of later chapters of this book. The definitions of the calendrical indicators are therefore summarized below:

A. To state and to confirm a year from the Easter Table—
    Rati   The line in which the year is found.
    YGN   It is substituted for the year in the line.
    YDL   Found at the top of the column which contains the year.

B. To state and to confirm a day from the calendar—
    ND.   The count of days from December 24, April 14, or October 14.

DDL   The Dominical Letter which is assigned to the day.
DGN   The Golden Number which is assigned to the day.
(With calendars which show the months, a substitute for
ND was to indicate the number of the month and the number
of the day in the month.)

*   *   *   *

The use of ND was by no means confined to the Norse puzzlemasters. It has a long history which apparently extended over
at least six centuries. The method was not confined to Scandinavia alone. A similar system seems to have been in use in
English perpetual calendars in the early tenth century and in
Scandinavia as late as the sixteenth century. In both cases the
count of ND was facilitated by repeating complete sets of runic
symbols or alphabets throughout the year. During later centuries such calendars were said to be "indexed."

Suppose, for example, that the count of days between two
dates in the calendar is eight full 25-letter alphabets with twelve
letters to spare. Clearly, ND is 212 days. It is equally clear that
a count could be made in this way more quickly and with less
chance for error than by a direct count.

Parts of a perpetual calendar which once belonged to Athelstan, the Anglo-Saxon king (894-940) have been preserved and
are in the keeping of the British Museum. In it the English runic
alphabet of 28 symbols is repeated throughout the year. Athelstan's calendar is also of special interest for another reason. It
shows that the Anglo-Saxons, just as did the Scandinavians,
were still using their version of the Old Germanic runes several
centuries after they had turned to Christianity. This may in part
account for the fact that English missionaries who went to Norway and Iceland took a lenient attitude towards the continued
use of Norse runes and the Norse language. Many scholars have
expressed the view that this more tolerant view produced a
favorable climate for the development of Icelandic literature.

There are also many other striking similarities between English perpetual calendars and those which were in use in Scan-

dinavia. Below is a representation of the first quarter of the year in a so-called English clog almanac. January 1 is at the extreme right. Attached below the date for January 6, which was Epiphany, is the six-armed Jesus Christ cross. This form of the cross, as later chapters will reveal, was one of the symbols around which Bishop Henricus apparently arranged the several transposition ciphers by which he concealed his name.

The age of this calendar is not known. Because it appears to have been printed, it should presumably be dated from the late fifteenth or early sixteenth centuries.

FIGURE 9

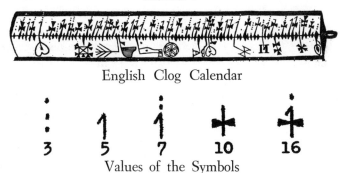

English Clog Calendar

Values of the Symbols

One of the most interesting features of this calendar is that, while it does not use runes to express numbers, it also avoids the use of Latin letters, Roman numerals, and decimal numbers. As did a great many Scandinavian calendars, pentathic symbols represent the Golden Numbers. In spite of the presence of a number of errors, it can be easily determined that the values of the pentathic symbols are as shown below the figure.

Just as in the case of the Norwegian *primstav,* the months are not shown, nor are there any Dominical Letters. However, the same effect was achieved by cutting an extra heavy notch for every seventh day beginning with January 1.[5]

The latest examples in which repeated alphabets for counting the number of days in perpetual calendars are to be found come from sixteenth-century Denmark and Sweden. Since some of the calendars were printed in Germany this suggests that the practice may have been more widespread.[6] While it is certain that not all perpetual calendars had this feature, its use in tenth-century England and in Scandinavia in the sixteenth century implies that it had been in continuous use.

These repeated alphabets suggest an answer to an interesting question. How does it happen that an early eleventh-century puzzlemaster, who must have accompanied a party of Norsemen to Vinland and beyond, was able to use the symbols of the ancient 24-rune alphabet and knew their numerical values? That he did so is proved by the presence of eight dated runic puzzles in Massachusetts and Oklahoma. Symbols from the 24-rune alphabet are mixed with Sw.-N. runes in six. The other two use 24-rune symbols exclusively. Altogether, these eight inscriptions contain thirty-five ancient runes and only seventeen from the medieval alphabet.

The eleventh-century puzzlemaster had an excellent reason for using the ancient symbols. They increased cryptographic efficiency a great deal. This is clearly demonstrated in the solutions of two of the eight inscriptions, Byfield No. 1 and Heavener No. 1, in Chapter 7. (It is also well to note that no hypothetical carver of runic inscriptions in America in recent centuries would have used 24-rune symbols in the unlikely event that he had known that they existed. The runologists have long been firm in the opinion that the ancient symbols were not used in runic inscriptions during the eleventh through the fourteenth centuries. There were good reasons for this opinion but they do not apply to dated puzzles. The ancient runes are only one of several evidences which indicate that the American inscriptions were not carved by rune-happy wanderers in recent centuries.)

The question therefore remains: How was a Norse puzzlemaster able to make use of the ancient runes in eleventh-century America? There seem to be two possible answers. 1) He may have used a perpetual calendar in which the ancient alphabet was repeated in order to count ND. This is not an unreasonable assumption. The ancient alphabet, being longer, would be more suitable for the purpose. Furthermore, in Chapter 14 it is shown that the Narssaq dated puzzle from Greenland, whose year number is 1316 A.D., has carved as a part of its text a Swedish-Norwegian alphabet which was about three hundred years old in the fourteenth century. The alphabet was added for cryptographic reasons. In that respect it is analogous to the use of ancient runes in the eleventh century. 2) As a member of the puzzlemaking fraternity the puzzlemaster may have carried an ancient alphabet with him as a tool of the trade. It would also have been a relatively simple matter to have memorized the alphabet as he probably had memorized his own Swedish-Norwegian runes.

This situation brings into focus a related facet of the same question. Dating of runic inscriptions continued at least from 1009 to 1362 A.D. These dated stones are scattered over a tremendously large area from Scandinavia to Oklahoma and Minnesota. It is difficult to imagine how this could have happened unless centers existed at which Norse cryptography was practiced, its rules and procedures recorded, and copies of dated puzzles preserved. The pages of this volume contain an almost continuous stream of evidences that it was a segment of the Norse clergy who were the puzzlemasters. It follows that such centers were almost certainly located at religious and administrative centers of the Church.

The cathedral and bishop's see at Gardar was very probably such a center. In addition to about a hundred non-dated inscriptions, Greenland has produced three significant dated puzzles which span a period of two hundred years. The earliest is found in the Latin legends of the Vinland Map. Its year number is 1122 A.D. and its author was the same Bishop Henricus who, between 1114 and 1123 A.D., also left seven dated runic inscriptions in New England. They are analyzed in Chapters 8 through 12. The second dated Greenland inscription is the well-known Kingigtorssuaq carving (1244 A.D.) whose elaborately confirmed date is intimately tied to Easter Sunday and Ascension Day. Finally, there is the so-called Narssaq Stick. It was discovered in 1954 near the mouth of Eiriksfjord at the inner end of which Brattahlid, the estate of Erik the Red, was located. The Narssaq carving is dated November 28, 1316 A.D., only 46 years before the date of the Kensington inscription.

These three dated puzzles show that interest in Norse cryptography was alive in Greenland, as it was to an even greater extent in Norway, over the twelfth and thirteenth and into the fourteenth century. Viewed from this background, the three puzzlemasters who account for all known dated inscriptions in the United States were emissaries from homelands which maintained an active interest in their unusual hobby and who, fortunately, chose to practice it in the new surroundings.

CHAPTER 5

Runemasters at Work and at Play

The preceding four chapters seemed to be necessary to lay the groundwork for what follows. This is the first of several chapters in which Norse dated cryptography from both sides of the Atlantic is demonstrated and analyzed. In order to make it as easy as possible for the reader, the examples are of the more elementary types. Yet they leave no doubt of the presence of cryptography. It was carefully planned and, in many cases, brilliantly executed by puzzlemasters who show a great deal of ingenuity and intelligence.

Of the eight runic puzzles which are analyzed here, six are taken directly from *Norges Innskrifter med de Yngre Runer* (NIYR). One is from Sweden and the eighth is from the excavations at Bergen.[1]

In all cases the transcriptions which are used are those that are given in NIYR. When the source offers a translation, or other significant information, this is usually also reported. However, the translations will, in almost all cases, be seen to be mistaken.

1. BUSLABAEN—NIYR, Vol. 2, p. 154

The five runes ISTIL, each of which are repeated six times, are said to constitute a magic formula. The repetitions are interpreted in NIYR as being an attempt to make the magic

FIGURE 10

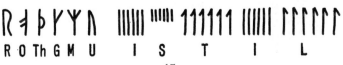

more potent. Six runes, ROThGMU, precede the repeated
runes. These were interpreted to represent the first letters in
the names of six bad men, presumably enemies of the runemaster. By combining each letter with the ISTIL formula as
RISTIL, OISTIL, and so forth, a particularly potent hex was
thrown over each man in turn. The fact that the first letters
of proper names were seldom, if ever, used as initials in runic
writing was ignored. Some meaning must, after all, have been
intended. To the translator, magic must have seemed to be
the only answer.

What had not been noticed was that the first six symbols
are the scrambled runes for the favorite medieval Norse name
GUThORM. The reader can easily sort out the runes for
himself. Even today most persons who are of Norwegian descent
have a relative who is named Gutorm. Because the six runes
spell a well-known name, it is highly unlikely that they represent six names. This is a dated runic puzzle. There is no sign
of magic. Or are we to believe that Gutorm was trying to hex
himself? His name is the only one that appears in the inscription.

There is no doubt that the letters, ISTIL, were, on occasion,
used as a magic formula. However, in this case the letters seem
to have been a decoy to distract the solver from the real purpose
of the puzzlemaster. The fact is that the number 6, repeated
five times, was used in many runic inscriptions in Norway
to indicate the 6th day of the 6th month of a year whose
Rati=6, YGN=6, and YDL=6.

The puzzlemaster had bided his time so as to grasp a rare
opportunity. It so happens that, out of the 532 years in the
Easter Table, one date, and only one, has calendrical indicators
that all have the value 6. The day is June 6, which is the 6th
day in the 6th month, and the year is 1297 A.D. A check in the
Easter Table and calendar will confirm that this is so.

Note that in place of the more usual indicators for the day
which are the ND, DDL, and DGN, Guthorm states the month
and day. He evidently did not use a primstav but the more

conventional RCPC. It is clear that he knew the Easter Table well and used this one opportunity out of 532 years when a complete date could be indicated by the number 6 repeated five times. He did not spell his name as GUThORMR, with nominative R, because he used a formula for transposing the letters in his name that could accommodate only six letters. (See the next solution). However, this may not have been a problem since the use of nominative R may have been discontinued by 1297 A.D.

2. LOMEN CHURCH NUMBER 2—NIYR, Vol. 1, p. 215

Again the five runes ISTIL, this time each repeated three times, follow a group of six runes. The runes spell the name KANUTR (Canute in modern English, Knut in Norwegian. Again, almost every Norwegian will have a relative who bears this name.)

In this case retention of the nominative R was required in order to complete the quota of six runes. It will also be noted that, after he had transcribed the six letters in his name, Kanutr gathered them into three pairs of combined runes. This, however, appears to have been a whim. Perhaps it was another ruse to confuse a potential solver. At any rate, the fact that the runes are combined does not affect the puzzle in any way.

FIGURE 11

Lomen Church Number 2

RT   UA   KN   I   S   T   I   L

Like Guthorm, Kanutr also knew his Easter Table and bided his time. For the year 1199 A.D., YGN=3, YDL=3, and Rati=3 and, of course, March 3 is the 3rd day of the 3rd month in any year. Therefore, the number 3, repeated five times, indicates March 3, 1199 A.D.

Again the magic formula ISTIL has no other function than to serve as a decoy to conceal the date. The same cryptographic effect could have been had by five sets of three vertical lines or by any other five runes each of which were repeated three times.

If there is any reason to question that Buslabaen and Lomen Church No. 2 are dated puzzles, which contain the ciphered names of their puzzlemasters, it is completely dispelled by a significant fact. The runes in both names were transposed by the same formula. It is built around the first five letters PRESB of the word "presbyter" which refers to a Christian priest. What is more, the formula is used in identical fashion in both. Its application is explained in *Ancient Norse Messages on American Stones,* Chapter 6.[2]

The years 1199 and 1297 are the only two of the 532 in the Easter Table whose three calendrical indicators are the same integer. The use of 6,6,6 to indicate the year 1297 is also found among the dated puzzles from Gol stave church (Chapter 6) and the Urnes Church No. 20 which follow in this and the next chapter.

3.   URNES CHURCH NUMBER 20—NIYR, Vol. 4, p. 112

Guthorm was not alone in using the 6-6-6 combination to indicate the year 1297 A.D. Another was the priest Arne who constructed the inscription which is designated Urnes Church No. 20. It was carved on a piece of board which is reported to have been found under the floorboards of the church while

FIGURE 12

URNES CHURCH NUMBER 20

AR N E P R E ST R V IL HA F AI K 6 6 6

repairs were in progress. This cryptopuzzle is analyzed here because it is quite basic.

This inscription uses no points to separate the words. Its transcription is ARNE PRESTR VIL HAFA IK '(KKK). The meaning appears to be "Arne (the) priest will have I."

While the spelling is acceptable, the meaning is somewhat obscure. There is reason to wonder what unfortunate choice of words was forced on Arne in order to satisfy the needs of his cryptogram. It is, however, difficult to accept the translation as given in NIYR: "Arne the priest will have Inga." Inga is a feminine given name and is nowhere to be found in the inscription. On the other hand IK is the correct spelling for "I."

Fortunately, this is an analysis of Norse cryptography. It has no responsibility for the translation of runic texts. They are merely the vehicle, often badly distorted, in which the cryptography is concealed.

The last three symbols are separated from the remainder of the inscription by a short cut which is marked A. The three runes for K each have the numerical value 6 to indicate the year 1297 A.D. in the Easter Table.

There is also a further separation of symbols. The point (marked B) in the third rune from the right distinguishes it from the two that follow. If these three runes were used for their *sound* values the point would change the rune from the K sound to G. But three repeated runes K have no meaning in medieval Norse. Here they have only numerical values. The effect of the point is to distinguish the first number 6 from the two that follow it.

This gives us two numbers, 6 and $6+6=12$. If they represent the day this might be either the 12th day of the 6th month or the 6th day of the 12th month. Which is it? The puzzlemaster gives the answer as clearly as it can be done without spelling it out. The inscription has 19 runes but the first two, the A and R, are combined so that the number of *symbols* is 18. For December 6, which is the 6th day of the 12th month, $ND=18$.

It will be noted that, as is so often the case, the puzzlemaster arranged to deliver a concentrated cryptographic package. The three symbols, which each have the value 6, indicate both the day and the year. It is the prevalence of such apparent coincidences, which are not coincidences at all, which raises the suspicion that many of these dates are carefully selected so they permit spectacular, and yet relatively easy, constructions.

4. NIDAROS CATHEDRAL NUMBER 1—
NIYR Vol. 5, p. 39

FIGURE 13

This inscription contains one of the most simple examples of a transposition cipher. The suggestion in NIYR that this is a part of an inscription which was not completed is mistaken. It is actually a simple transposition of the biblical name Mark (MARKUS).

While any six-pointed figure could be used to distribute the six runes, it is reasonably certain that, in this case, it was a six-pointed star. It can best be represented by two equilateral triangles as is shown in the figure below. The triangle was the ancient symbol for the trinity. When two triangles are superposed in this manner, the six vertices were thought to signify the six major virtues óf God: power, wisdom, majesty, love, mercy, and justice.

The six letters in MARKUS were distributed in the clockwise direction as shown. The puzzlemaster could now choose any one of a number of possible ways to carry out the transposition. He chose the simplest. This was to first pick up, again in the clockwise direction, the letters that were assigned to the triangle which is marked No. 1. He began with the letter S.

FIGURE 14

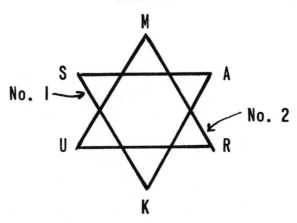

The result was SAK. Next he began with the letter U on triangle No. 2 and picked up the letters UMR. When the two groups of three letters are combined, they read SAKUMR.

This was the order of the runes that were carved on the wall and which is designated Nidaros Cathedral No. 1.

5. KINGIGTORSSUAQ—NIYR, Vol. 2, p. 233

The preceding puzzles have been quite elementary. On the other hand, the Kingigtorssuaq inscription, which was discovered in northern Greenland in 1824, contains one of the most complex and ingenious dated Norse puzzles which are yet known. Its cryptography literally saturates the entire inscription.

The Kingigtorssuaq inscription has always been accepted by the runologists as an authentic Norse carving. It has also been extensively studied, notably by Finnur Jónsson and Magnus Olsen.[3]

There has been general agreement among the runologists that the inscription was cryptographic in nature. It was sensed, because of its numerous unexplained anomalies, that it was exceptional in this respect. In spite of this, no one managed to interpret its hidden meanings. For example, on page 56 of

Volume 3 of NIYR, Olsen made this statement (translated from the Norwegian):

"Furthermore, if one wishes to have an example of exceptional ability and patience in the construction of runic oddities [*bisserier*]—relationships between numbers and such—we can point, among medieval inscriptions, first and foremost to the Kingigtorssuaq inscription from Greenland."

From this statement one might be led to think that it was Olsen, not Mongé, who solved the Kingigtorssuaq cryptography. In connection with Urnes Church Number XX, which was solved earlier in this chapter, Olsen stated (NIYR, Volume 4, page 117) that : "In the runic puzzles [*runekunstlerier*] of later times, every rune may be a part of that form of secret writing which we are dealing with here." The only problem with this was that Olsen never did discover precisely what form of secret writing was present.

Given such acute awareness that many Norwegian inscriptions were cryptographic in content, in whole or in part, one might have expected that the key to the cryptography, namely the Norse perpetual church calendar, would have been discovered. Olsen did, in fact, suggest on several occasions that the numerical values of certain runes represented a date from the calendar. For some reason he never followed up on this idea. On other occasions he seemed to accept the presence of cryptography in some runic inscriptions. For example, about Borgund Stave Church Number 5 (NIYR, Volume 4, page 157) he stated that "... it is reasonable to believe that the runic puzzle [*runegåten*] in Borgund Number 5 had remained unsolved in the expectation that, either a certain person would arrive to solve it [this suggests a coded message], or an unknown visitor would appear [who could solve it]."

Except for the knowledge that they are not coded messages but puzzles, this is exactly what Mongé and the author have postulated about the several dozen dated Norse puzzles that have been solved to date. Mongé solved the date of the Kingigtorssuaq puzzle in 1964 as May 7, 1244 A.D. A part of the solution is a twenty-five-letter substitution message which completes the text. It had been known that a part of the text was missing. The solution accounts for the numerous visible anomalies in the text which had also been well known but which had not previously been explained.

The first line of the inscription gives the names of three men. First named is ELNIKR SIKVATSSONR. Each of the two parts of the name illustrates distinct and striking cryptographic features. Only these will be solved here.

A. The Meaning of ELNIKR.

It is an interesting fact that many of those who have studied this inscription carefully have concluded that ELNIKR is a *confused spelling* of the well known Scandinavian name ERLING even though the rune K does not have the point which would have changed its sound value to G. The runes in the two words are otherwise the same. While this was a perceptive guess, the answer is quite different. ELNI(G)R is exactly the same transposition of ERLING as was SAKUMR of MARKUS in Nidaros Cathedral Number 1. It is no haphazard misspelling.

In the figure, the letters in the name ERLING have been distributed in the clockwise direction beginning at the apex.

FIGURE 15

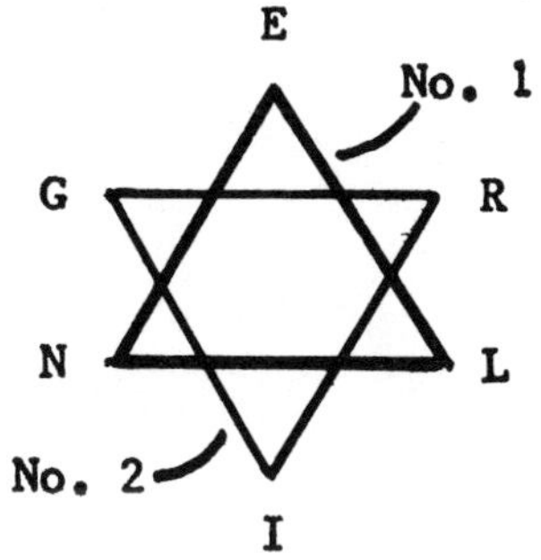

Again, as with Nidaros Cathedral Number 1, the six-pointed star is made up of two triangles one of which is drawn with heavy lines to distinguish it. The puzzlemaster first picked up the three letters E L N from the heavy triangle. To them he added the three letters I G R from the second. Note that the distribution of the six letters, and their subsequent transposition, were carried out in a completely symmetric manner. This is a basic requirement for a transposition cipher.

B.   The Cryptography in SIKVATSSONR.

This is a part of a very ingenious cryptographic arrangement which pervades the entire inscription. The rules for normal runic writing are flouted with abandon, and the cryptographic effect can only be described as startling. Note that the name is cut into two segments by two otherwise superfluous sets of points. In addition, both single and double points are used. In

FIGURE 16

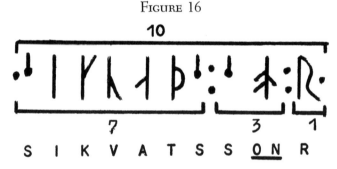

normal runic writing, it is permitted to use single or double points as separators, or no points at all, but they must not be mixed. Finally, the two runes O and N are combined for what will prove to be purely cryptographic reasons. (In Chapter 3 the ten pairs of combined runes in this inscription, and one combination of three runes, are illustrated. This is phenomenal for an inscription which has only 86 runic symbols.)

The reason for mixing the points and combining the two

runes was to permit two successive counts of the same twelve runes (and, of course, all of the runes in the inscription) as a part of a number series in a substitution cipher. It was necessary to count all runes twice because the 86 runes in the text were too few to deliver twenty-five numbers for the desired hidden message.

The first count was of *symbols* from single point to single point (above). In this case combined runes were counted as one symbol. (There were nine such counts in the entire inscription.) The figure delivers one count of 10. Then the count was made between *all* points, single and double, and *each rune was counted* (below). There are three such counts, 7, 3, and 1, in the figure. The entire inscription produced 16 numbers as the result of the second round of counts so that the total was a series of twenty-five numbers.

When these numbers were counted off, in succession, on the so-called substitution alphabet, the result was a hidden message of twenty-five letters. The process would take too much space to reproduce in detail here, but similar substitution ciphers will be found in this and following chapters. The complete cryptography of the Kingigtorssuaq inscription is given in *Ancient Norse Messages on American Stones*.[4]

The hidden message and its apparent meaning are as follows:

— LOSNE   A   ISAN   OIRVAR VALRSLEThN
—a way   through   the [expanse of] ice.   Oirvar Valrslethn[5]

Because of its abrupt and meaningless ending, it had long been suspected that a part of the text was missing. However, no one had managed to find the missing part. By the addition of the hidden message, the text appears to be complete:

"Erling Sigvatsson and Bjarne Tortason and Endridi Osson, on the Saturday before Ascension Day, raised these cairns and cleared *a way through* [or over] *the* [expanse of] *ice. Oirvar Valrslethn.*"

The text now makes good sense. In northern Greenland the

ice may not break up until long after "Saturday before Ascension Day" which in 1244 A.D. fell on May 7. To reach open water, it would presumably have been necessary to make a passage over the expanse of ice. It would be prudent not to read too much into this, however. The text is merely the vehicle for a massive and difficult dated puzzle with an equally difficult and even more extensive cipher added. It is difficult now to detect, and even more difficult to prove, what misspellings and awkward choice of words may have been forced on the puzzlemaster in both the text and the hidden message.

6. VANGE CHURCH (Sweden)

In Chapter 4 it was shown that, as late as the mid-sixteenth century, perpetual calendars were still being printed in Scandinavia. A text from the same century, written in medieval Swedish, shows that the years were also still being expressed in terms of Rati, YGN, and YDL from an Easter Table.

The Vange Church text uses a form of the Latin letters. If the text is a Norse puzzle, no solution has been found but this may be due to inability to read the inscription with sufficient accuracy. The transcription which is used here is taken from *Runinskrifter i Sverige.*[6]

It is interesting to note that, even though the text is written in sixteenth-century Swedish, the words are separated by points as in a runic inscription. It is the fact that several points are missing which suggests that counts of runes for cryptographic purposes had been arranged. The words are as follows:

"Bedin - fyri - jacobs - sial - nikarfua - han - do - faem - daha - fyri - sante - lafranz - dag ta - uar - F - sundahr - ok - M - primstafu - r - i - fimtanda ratu."

The translation is: "Pray for Jacob's soul in Nikarve. He died five days before Saint Lawrence Day. Then F was the Dominical Letter, M the Golden Number, and the Rati was 15."

Saint Lawrence Day is August 10. Therefore, Jacob died on August 5. The calendrical indicators that are stated for the

year are given as Rati=15, YGN=M (=15), and YDL=F
(=1). The year is 1553 A.D. (The reader can extend the Easter
Table which is given in Chapter 4 so that he can check this
year. It is only necessary to add 532 years to each of the year
numbers at the left of the table. The year 1553 A.D. will be
found in Line 15.)

The letters M and F in the text actually represent the runes
M and F. The numerical value of the rune M is 15, and of
the rune F, 1. This shows that the writer of the text was using
a *primstav*, in the mid-sixteenth-century, in which YGN and
YDL were represented by runes.

7. HEDAL NUMBER 6—NIYR, Vol. 5, p. 167

FIGURE 17

Hedal No. 6, in common with three other puzzles which
have been analyzed earlier in this chapter, came about as the
result of another calendrical opportunity. For the year 1215 A.D.
the sum of Rati=4, YGN=11, and YDL=1 was 16. This was
also the number of symbols in the runic alphabet.

An inspection of the photograph from NIYR shows that
the runes were carved in an irregular manner both as to shape,
proportion, and position in the carving. Actually, as with many
other dated puzzles both in Scandinavia and in the United

States, the runes are distributed in a meaningful pattern. This will again be evident in inscriptions by Henricus in New England which are discussed in Chapter 9.

At first glance the inscription seems to consist of the symbols of the 16-rune alphabet but the first symbol is an unusual form of the runic F. This is the only comment about the inscription which is made in NIYR. Actually it is a well-conceived, if rather simple, dated puzzle.

The first four symbols are offset in the upward direction and the last is offset downward from the eleven symbols in the middle section.

Offsets were convenient ways of sorting symbols into groups. As a result they are found in a large number of Norse puzzles. This includes inscriptions from Gol, Bergen, and other places in Norway, Möjbrostenen in Sweden, and inscriptions in the Orkney Islands and in New England.

FIGURE 18

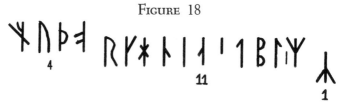

The groups of 4, 11 and 1 runes indicate Rati=4, YGN=11, and YDL=1. The year is 1245 A.D. But there is also more information to be had. If we ignore the offsets, we see two groups of two and three greatly oversized runes as follows:

FIGURE 19

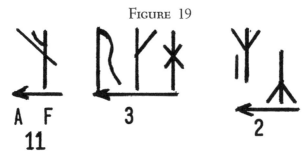

The first symbol faces to the left, that is, it is reversed. This suggests that the two oversized groups of runes are also to be counted from right to left. The result is the number 23. It will appear presently that this represents the 23rd of some month, specifically, November which is the 11th month.

FIGURE 20

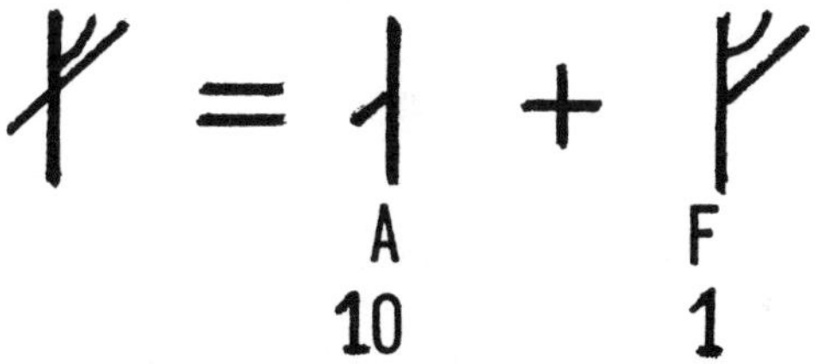

$$\digamma = \daleth + \digamma$$

A   F
10   1

The symbol at the left is not the simple rune F. When it is reversed back to its normal position as has been done above, it is seen to be the combined runes A and F whose numerical values are 10 and 1. The sum of their numerical values is 11 for the 11th month.

Here the use of the runic alphabet as a decoy to distract attention from the cryptogram comes to the fore. The intention was to leave the impression that the first symbol was a carelessly cut first rune in the alphabet, an F.

November 23 was Saint Clement's Day. It is possible that the puzzlemaster used the name Clement. A neighboring inscription, Hedal No. 2, beseeches the deity to bless Clement (not Saint Clement) *and other holy men.* It was quite usual for the medieval clergy to think of themselves as holy.

That the intended day was November 23 is confirmed twice as follows. Note that there are a total of 5 oversized symbols. For November 23 DDL=5. The 5 also serves a second purpose. In the year 1245 A.D. November 23 fell on a Thursday, the 5th day of the week.

Note also that the last two runes are isolated from the remainder of the inscription by a short vertical cut. The two runes, M and Y, have numerical values of 15 and 16 for a sum of 31. ND=31 for November 23!

Such a succession of "coincidences" makes it very probable, as was suggested at the beginning of the discussion, that this combination of day and year was chosen for its calendrical opportunities. The elements of a well-constructed Norse dated puzzle fit together much as the pieces in a jigsaw puzzle. There is no possibility to make them indicate any other date.

8.   BERGEN NUMBER 1 (Norway)

Did a priest from Bergen carve a lewd runic message on Advent Sunday? This was the title of a four-page discussion of a dated puzzle which went out to the mailing list of The Landsverk Foundation on January 20, 1970. The inscription is one of the hundreds that have been retrieved from the ancient

FIGURE 21

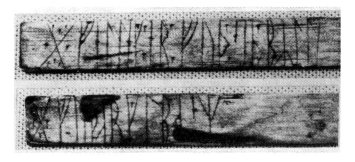

wharves at Bergen. Its two lines of runes are carved on opposite sides of a stick of wood.

In a brochure which was published in 1963 under the title *Runer frå Bryggen,* runologist Aslak Liestøl interpreted the first line of Bergen 1 as pornographic.[7] This interpretation is mistaken. It was his translation which prompted the question which heads this discussion.

The analysis which follows will show that there is not even

a hint of pornography but, instead, a very ingenious, and yet simple, substitution cipher and a hidden date from the perpetual calendar. The cipher reveals the name of the puzzlemaster and the date is Advent Sunday for that year. This again leaves the strong probability that the author was a priest.

Mr. Liestøl recognized that the second line is a partial runic alphabet whose latter portion was confused and, in part, missing. But he discovered no meaning. Taken as a visible text this is correct. However, it is this line that the puzzlemaster used to spell out his ciphered message and, in addition, to state and confirm his day and year. This is quite a burden to place on only eleven runes. Bergen 1 is one of those gems of compact Norse cryptography which can only result from ingenuity and careful planning.

In order to construct this substitution cipher, the number of runes between double points had to be carefully controlled. The figure shows that they form the number series 6-2-3-4-5-11. These are the numbers which are to be transformed into the letters which spell out the message.

FIGURE 22

```
F E L L E G : E R : F U Th : (A) S I N : B Y L L I
    6           2       3           4               5

        F  U  Th  O  R  G  L  B  A  S  M
        I  2  3   4  5  6  7  8  9  10 11
        NUMBER  SERIES:  6-2-3-4-5-11
        THE  MESSAGE:   G U Th O R M.
```

The second part of this type of Norse substitution cipher is the built-in alphabet. This is a consecutive series of runes somewhere in the runic text. When the quantities in the number series are counted off on the runes (or letters) of the built-in alphabet, always beginning from the first rune at the left, the runes (or letters) of the message are spelled out.

It is, of course, the task of a potential solver to locate the built-in alphabet. In Bergen 1 it is the entire second line.

Once the number series and the built-in alphabet have been established, the procedure is very simple. The first number in the series is 6. A count of six letters in the second line ends at the letter G. The next number in the series is 2. It indicates the letter U and so forth. When the six numbers in the series have been substituted in this way, the result is GUThORM.

This was a favorite Norse name which we have encountered before. It is obvious that this cipher could not possibly happen by accident. Several indirect evidences of careful planning will also appear as the solution progresses.

The dating was also accomplished in the "meaningless" Line 2. It will emerge later that Line 1 was merely a warning that the solver should examine the faulty runic alphabet in Line 2 carefully. It is a variation of the admonishment to "Read right these runes."

FIGURE 23

6

F u th o r G l b a s M

5   5

The first five symbols in Line 2 are the first five runes in the 16-rune alphabet. The break comes with the 6th symbol which should have been a K with numerical value 6. It still has the numerical value 6 but when a point is added to runic K, as was done here, its sound value is changed to G. It is clear that the puzzlemaster wished here to call attention to the numerical value 6. This he did by two different methods.

The G is followed by five additional runes. It should be noted that Guthorm could have spelled out the last letter in his name, the M, just as easily if it had been placed in the position that is now occupied by the L. The last number of the substitution series would still have spelled out the letter M in GUThORM.

Obviously, then, the four letters LBAS are fillers. But why? This will become clear later. For now it is enough to know that, as the figure above shows, they allowed the numbers 5-6-5 to be indicated. For the year 1259 A.D. Rati=5, YGN=6, and YDL=5. But this is only a part of the reason for the four fillers, LBAS. (One might say that Guthorm spotlighted the G, with numerical value 6, in a third way. It was the first letter in his name. His construction was possible only because runic K happened to be the 6th letter in the alphabet.)

At this point the four letters LBAS are the only ones in Line 2 for which a direct use has not yet been shown. Do they, in fact, take part in the dating other than as fillers? An examination of their numerical values shows that they do.

FIGURE 24

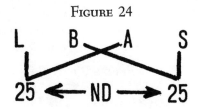

It is seen that the sums of alternate pairs of runes is 25. This is ND for the day and the day is November 30. One need not be surprised that the day was Advent Sunday, the first day of the ecclesiastical year. It is by far the most favored date in Norse dated puzzles. This is evidence that the puzzlemaster was church-connected. It also dispels any thought that the inscription was pornographic.

But why was ND=25 stated twice? The same construction will be found in the Heavener, Oklahoma, dated puzzle from 1012 A.D. in Chapter 6. The answer is that it was not necessary to state ND=25 twice. But it was essential to add two extra symbols on the right side of the G. This made the total 5. The 5 was essential in order to indicate YDL=5 for the year 1259 A.D.

This completes the cryptography. We now return to the translation of the first line. In order to attain the correct series of numbers by his cipher, Guthorm was forced to add to the first word, FEL, the first three runes, LEG, from the second word LEGER. This made it FELLEG. It also left him with the desired number of letters in his second word, ER. The figure shows his original text before the cryptography was built into it and, below, the altered inscription which Guthorm carved on one side of the stick.

The first two words in the original text were FEL:LEGER. In modern Norwegian the words are "feil" which means "faulty" and "ligger" which in this context means "lies" in the sense of "to exist." The runes, FUTh, are the first three symbols in the runic alphabet. It is the equivalent of saying ABC to identify the modern alphabet. The word A has many meanings. In this context it means "in." SIN is the possessive "its." It has the same spelling in modern Norwegian. The nearest meaning for BYLLI is "arrangement." There seems to be no modern counterpart.

FIGURE 25

Guthorm's original text:

FEL : LEGER : FUTh : (A) SIN : BYLLI
 1   2   3   4   5

The inscription as carved:

FELLEG : ER : FUTh : (A) SIN : BYLLI
  1   2   6   4   5   3

The translation, therefore, is "Faulty is the alphabet in its arrangement." Guthorm is clearly referring to his very imperfect alphabet on the other side. The word order is also correct.

Naturally enough, Mr. Liestøl could not translate the first word of the carved text. It is a composite which was made by

Guthorm by moving the first double points three spaces to the right. This changed the count of runes to 6-2-3 etc. from the original 3-5-3-. Only so could the cipher spell his name. Liestøl therefore assumed that the author of the inscription had spelled the word FELLEG incorrectly and that he must have intended to carve the word FERLEGR. This is, of course, an entirely different word. Its meaning is "terrible."

With this erroneous beginning a faulty translation was probably inevitable. As misfortune would have it, the third word, FUTh, could also mean a less glamorous part of the human anatomy. It was this word which led to the pornographic interpretation. Finally, he corrected Guthorm a second time by assuming that he had meant BYRLI, which means bartender, instead of BYLLI. It is not necessary to repeat his translation here but it is important to note that the stem of two words in the carving, FELLEG and BYLLI, were changed into two different words by Mr. Liestøl and a third word, FUTh, was misinterpreted.

There is a problem with the two words (A) SIN which requires explanation. Guthorm required a count of 3 symbols at this point but, as matters stood, he had two words with counts of 1 and 3. His remedy was to combine the A with the S thus:

FIGURE 26

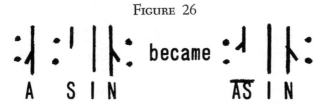

To do this it was necessary to leave the S short so it would not be mistaken for an A after the short slanting cut that characterizes the A had been added. The wood is discolored at all points at which two cuts intersect so that the short slanting cut could easily be overlooked. An examination under a microscope shows that the A is present. This makes a difference only in the cipher. In Mr. Liestøl's translation the A was understood.

CHAPTER 6

A Nun and a Priest at Gol Stave Church

All but two of the eight solutions in the previous chapter were from inscriptions that are listed and discussed in NIYR. The same is true of all solutions that are analyzed in this chapter. These inscriptions were all carved on the interior walls of a single medieval church.

Two of the thirteen inscriptions are omittted because the runologists have not been able to translate them, nor do they seem to contain cryptography. The remainder form an interrelated complex of Norse puzzles which is the subject of this chapter.

Gol stave church stood for many centuries near the inner end of a beautiful valley which is known as Hallingdal and which extends about a hundred miles in a northwesterly direction from the Oslo area. When it was about to be replaced, in 1885, it was rescued by the Swedish-Norwegian king, Oscar II, and put on display at the folk museum at Bygdøy on the outskirts of Oslo. There it still stands.

In this and similar churches the mass was said, and the numerous feast and holy days of the medieval Catholic church year were celebrated. Here, also, were announced the Golden Number and Dominical Letter for the year from the Easter Table so that the communicants could keep track of the Sundays and other holy days that were marked on their runestaves.

The church was also the local administrative headquarters from which the policies and edicts of the Roman Catholic Chuch were made known and enforced. Anyone who doubts that this control was detailed and strict should read the early church laws for the Trondheim and Bergen districts of Norway which are known as the Gulating and Frostating laws.[1]

Under these conditions it is significant that Gol stave church shares a unique feature with virtually all Norwegian churches from the Middle Ages. On its interior walls are carved thirteen runic inscriptions. The record is held by Borgund stave church in Sogn on the west coast which has a total of thirty-four. A simple approximation, based on inscriptions that now exist in the twenty-five churches that still remain, shows that the stave churches of Norway must once have harbored several thousand inscriptions.

In view of the tight control that was exercised by the Church, it seems certain that resident priests, and associated monks and nuns, were responsible for most, if not all, of these runic carvings. This conclusion is also supported by a variety of other evidence. It is significant in this connection that dated puzzles in stave churches are for the most part dated in the last half of the thirteenth and the early part of the fourteenth century. This makes it unlikely that the art of Norse cryptography originated in Norway.

In 1970, Mr. Mongé received from the National Museum of Norway in Oslo a complete set of photographs of the thirteen Gol carvings. They were of excellent quality so that the inscriptions could, for the most part, be easily read. When he had checked them carefully he found himself in full agreement with the transcriptions and transliterations by Mr. Liestøl in NIYR.[2] This is fortunate because they are in almost complete disagreement about the translations.

Mr. Mongé was attracted to the Gol carvings by the difficulty that Mr. Liestøl seemed to have had in translating them. When all of their cryptography had been sorted out and solved, there was a complex of ten related cryptograms. About one half were the work of a nun in 1297 A.D. who used the name ITA, or a variant of it, YThE. The remainder were constructed in 1329 A.D. by TATAI who was presumably a priest. In his puzzles he copied some of Ita's procedures and he often indicated his own year number by adding 32 years to hers. The reason that he did so is not clear.

One of the thirteen inscriptions, Gol XI, contains a challenge to a potential solver: "Read right these runes." Such exhortations, of which there are a number among Norwegian inscriptions, are always accompanied by cryptography. Three examples are: Bergen 1 (1259 A.D.) which was solved in Chapter 5, with its "Faulty lies the alphabet in its arrangement"; Borgund 5 (1313 A.D.) from Sognefjord on the west coast of Norway, which admonishes the solver to "Read right these runes"; and Hettusvein (1328 A.D.) which also came from the wharves at Bergen and which contains the mandate "Read this name he who can."

Gol is separated from Sognefjord and Bergen by rather formidable mountains. However, the fact that the dates in Gol stave church correspond so well with the dates of many west-coast inscriptions must be more than coincidence. Travel through mountain passes and sailing from fjord to fjord was quite routine in Norway. That these four inscriptions all have warnings of the presence of cryptography is further proof that there had been intercommunication of some kind. This is only one of numerous evidences that puzzlemasters learned, and borrowed, from one another. Often the borrowing spanned centuries and thousands of miles.

The latest year number which is known in a cryptopuzzle from Bergen is 1328 A.D. This is the date of the Hettusvein inscription which was just mentioned. Hettusvein contains many features which are also found in the Kensington, Minnesota, inscription which was carved in 1362 A.D. just 34 years later. *The difference puts Hettusvein easily within the lifespan of Harrek, the puzzlemaster who created the extensive Kensington cryptography.*

During these years Bergen was the major port of departure from Norway for Greenland and points beyond. It is, therefore, reasonably certain on historical grounds that the expedition which reached Kensington set sail from Bergen. Further support for this theory is an order in 1354 A.D., of which a copy still exists in the archives at Copenhagen, from Magnus, King of

Norway and Sweden. He ordered a prominent Norwegian from the Bergen area, Paul Knutson, to find and to bring back to the true faith the Norse Greenlanders who had abandoned their homes in Greenland and settled on the American continent. This was the thesis which the late historian Hjalmar Rued Holand researched to the point that it seems credible that the Kensington inscription had been carved by a member of the Knutson expedition.[3]

To this general proposition is now added substantial cryptographic support. The Hettusvein inscription from Bergen, which was carved in 1328 A.D., contains the most extensive Norse cryptography of any that is yet known by a factor of at least two times. Unfortunately, its solution would require too much space to be included in this volume.

The Hettusvein cryptography includes procedures that are also found in four key inscriptions from the western hemisphere. In chronological order they are: 1. The Latin legends in the Vinland Map (1122 A.D.) which were presumably written in Greenland; Spirit Pond Number 3 (1123 A.D.) from Maine and also by Henricus; The Kingigtorssuaq inscription (1244 A.D.) from northern Greenland; and the Kensington carving (1362 A.D.) from Minnesota.

Later in this chapter it will also be shown that in Gol V is found *the same spelling, AHR, for the word "year" as is found in Henricus's Spirit Pond Number 3 and the Kensington inscription.* Norse linguists have objected that this spelling did not come into use until after the mid-fourteenth century. Available evidence now indicates that, at least in so far as Norse puzzlemasters were concerned, this was not the case. AHR goes back at least as far as the early twelfth century.

These striking interrelations imply that Henricus, the superlative puzzlemaster of his day, may have been the chief exponent of this unusual art in the early twelfth century. This suggests that Greenland, and especially the bishop's seat at Gardar after his disappearance in Vinland, may have served as a center for the development, distribution, and preservation of the art of

Norse cryptography. (The west coast of Norway apparently fulfilled a similar function but not until the thirteenth and the
first half of the fourteenth centuries.)

No puzzle from Norway has been solved to date which is
dated before 1100 A.D. On the other hand two inscriptions with
year numbers 1008 and 1015 A.D. are known from Sweden.
These dates correspond with the early eleventh-century inscriptions which span the range from 1009 to 1024 A.D. in the United
States.

These early eleventh-century Swedish and American dated
puzzles have one surprising feature in common. Both groups of
inscriptions use symbols from the ON alphabet several centuries after the runologists believed that ON runes were no
longer used. In so far as normal runic inscriptions are concerned,
the runologists were probably right. In this matter the author
has no right to express an opinion. However, it will be demonstrated in Chapter 7 that ancient runic symbols were certainly
used to construct Norse dated puzzles after 1000 A.D. The
runologists had no knowledge of the work of the Norse puzzlemasters.

There appears to be a simple and natural explanation for the
similarities between the Kensington inscription and a number
of other dated puzzles from the west coast of Norway. These
Norwegian inscriptions are dated one to two generations before
the Kensington date. It is not necessary to assume that it was
the Bergenser Paul Knutson who led the expedition which
reached western Minnesota in 1362 A.D. In any event it was
inevitable that the Kensington party set out from Bergen and
that a large proportion of the Norwegian contingent which took
part was recruited from the west coast of Norway.

We proceed now with the solutions to the Gol puzzles. It
is not possible to analyze all of the Gol cryptography. The
longer and more involved solutions have been omitted. Fortunately, those which use relatively few runes are the most
interesting. They will give the reader a good understanding of
the purpose and significance of these puzzles even though they

contain virtually no translatable text. The numbers which were assigned to them in NIYR have been retained. Because their cryptography was unknown at that time, they are not discussed in numerical order here.

The nun and the cleric who contrived the Gol puzzles often replaced each rune with the rune which precedes it in the runic alphabet. On occasion, they also used more intricate forms of substitution from the alphabet. But they apparently realized that, given patience and persistence, such a puzzle is solved with relative ease. Therefore, they superposed on it other types of Norse puzzles. This double-layered cryptography made it unlikely that anyone but a trained cryptanalyst could have solved them.

Once the solution is known, it is more easy to explain these puzzles by *beginning with the original messages.* One can then proceed through the same steps which led the puzzlemaster to the apparently meaningless series of runes which he carved on the wall.

This chapter, and those that follow, will show many fine examples of Norse-type transposition ciphers. In nearly all cases the puzzlemaster first distributed, in an entirely symmetric pattern, his intended secret message on the arms, or vertices, of a geometric figure. Because they were members of the clergy it is reasonable to assume that the favorite patterns were the various forms of the Christian cross.

When the runes had been distributed, the next step was to pick them up in a scrambled but equally symmetrical order. It is this second step which is the transposition. In order to make the two steps as easy as possible to follow, two separate figures are used. The first shows the *distribution* and the second the *transposition.*

1. GOL NUMBER VI—NIYR, Vol. 5, p. 183

Many of the Gol ciphers appear to be built around a Christian symbol which is known as the Jesus Christ cross. It is a combination of the first letters of the Greek equivalent: I and X.

FIGURE 27

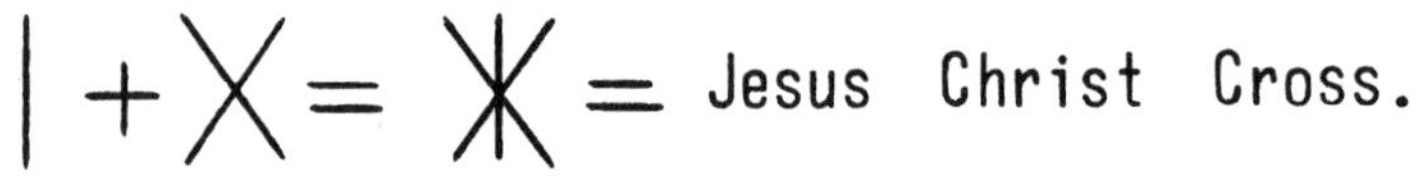

$| + X = X =$ Jesus Christ Cross.

The cryptogrammed portion of Gol VI, which is carved on the wall, is:

FIGURE 28

I N S L I S

We shall discover that these are the transposed letters of the name MATTIA. According to the seventeenth-century Danish scholar Ole Worm this was the correct spelling in medieval Scandinavia for the English name "Matthew."

FIGURE 29

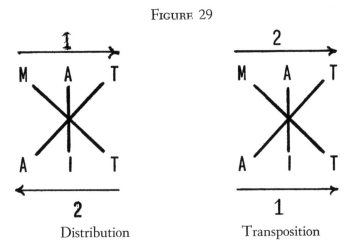

Distribution   Transposition

The nun Ita, for she was the puzzlemaster, distributed the letters MATTIA on the six arms of the cross in the clockwise direction as shown. (They could also be distributed in the counterclockwise direction. The requirement is that whatever is done must be done consistently. If it is done arbitrarily there is no puzzle which can be solved.)

Next she *chose* to scramble the six letters by first picking up the letters AIT as indicated by arrow number 1 and then the letters MAT as per arrow number 2. The result is AITMAT.

Apparently feeling that this one operation was too elementary, Ita next substituted, for each letter, the letter which precedes it in the 16-rune alphabet. The result is the six letters INSLIS. The 16-rune alphabet, which was used in the Gol inscriptions, appears to be a mixture of Sw.-N. and Normal symbols. It is reproduced here for the convenience of the reader in checking this and later substitutions.

FIGURE 30

The Gol Runic Alphabet

It was these six runes that Ita carved on the wall. But she was aware that several persons with the name Matthew are named in the Bible. She must somehow indicate that it was Saint Matthew of whose name she wished to make a cryptogram. The method that she chose was simple but effective. Below the puzzle she carved the runes P A T E R N O S T E R K I E S.

These are the four Latin words PATER NOSTER KI ES but written with runes. KI represents the Latin word Qui because the runic alphabet had no Q. The words represent the first line in the Lord's prayer: PATER NOSTER QUI ES IN CAELIS. The key to the reference is that it was Saint Matthew who stated the Lord's prayer in the Bible.

This Latin sentence is correctly interpreted in NIYR, but no translation for INSLIS is attempted. This is also correct in the absence of knowledge of the cryptography which is the only reason for the existence of any part of Gol Number VI. However, NIYR missed the reason for the addition of the Latin sentence which was to indicate that it was the name of Saint Matthew which had been ciphered.

2.   GOL NUMBER II—NIYR, Vol. 5, pp. 178-80

This cipher is actually less difficult to solve than Gol VI even though it involves a total of twenty runes. The inscription which was carved on the wall was:

FIGURE 31

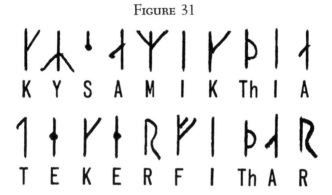

A transposition cipher can distribute a message in any one of a number of ways. Here it is clear that the choice of method was made so the resulting scramble of runes *seems to have* a meaning. The purpose was to distract attention from the cryptography. Note how effectively the first seven runes, KYS A MIK, serve this purpose.

Mr. Liestøl translated the three words as "kiss me." This is acceptable. Ita must have been pleased to have managed her deception so well. But the remainder of his translation seems very far-fetched. It is: "Kiss me, for I have it difficult!" In the solution which follows, it is evident that Ita had nothing of the sort on her mind. Her original text is shown in Figure 32.

FIGURE 32

(K K K) Y Th E R I S A
A F (I) T M (I) E Th A R

Of the twenty runes in the message, five were inserted in order to state the year and day. They have been enclosed in parentheses. When they are omitted, the message reads: "Ythe carved after Methar." It is probable that Methar was a departed friend of Ythe but this can not be proved from the puzzle.

In this cipher Ythe distributed her message, three runes at a time, by weaving alternately out and in along the six arms of the cross. The order and direction is indicated by the six arrows 0, 1, 2, 3, 4, 5. The first three runes, KKK, were placed on the vertical upper branch, the next group of three, YThE, on the adjacent branch to its right, and so on in the clockwise direction.

This takes care of eighteen of the twenty runes. The two that remain were placed above and below the intersection of the arms

FIGURE 33

Gol Number II

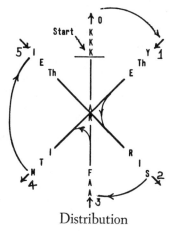

Distribution

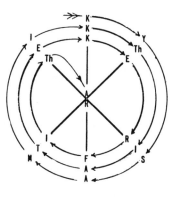

Transposition

of the cross as shown. It will be noticed that complete symmetry and consistency are maintained.

The rest is straightforward. Begin with the K at the top of the figure. Move from arm to arm in the clockwise direction. When the six outer letters have been picked up, continue with the second and third row until the six arms have been swept bare. Then proceed inward as indicated by the arrow to pick up the last two letters Λ and R. This is the order in which the runes are carved in the wall.

It was noted above that this inscription is also dated. Ythe made use of the fact that for the year 1297 A.D. Rati=6, YGN=6, and YDL=6. This is the meaning of the three repeated runes KKK. They could have no other meaning and this is only one of several puzzles in which use is made of this peculiarity of the calendar.

The two remaining parentheses contain the runes for I in the words AF(I)T M(I)EThAR. Note that they have between them the two runes T and M. The four runes indicate the day in this way:

FIGURE 34

(I)   T   M   (I)
9   12   15   9

The numerical values are as shown. Let us first tentatively assume that the 12 and 15 represent the 15th day of the 12th month, that is, December 15. That this was the intention is proved by the two runes for I of the numerical values 9. For the day December 15, both ND and DDL have the value 9. This confirms the date, December 15.

It is clear that Ythe inserted the two runes for I in order to state, and confirm the day. She knew that this made misspellings of AFT and METhAR but she also knew that this would be understood.

3. GOL NUMBER I—NIYR, Vol. 5, pp. 175-78

This puzzle is similar to Gol No. II but it has only eleven runes and it is not dated. Ita's message in this case was SANKTI MARIA.

If this were uncorrupted Latin it should have read SANCTA MARIA. This is, however, a Norse runic inscription and there is no doubt about the runes which are carved on the wall. It is possible that Ita felt that a fourth rune, A, would have confused the cipher. Hence the I.

A completely symmetrical distribution of SANKTI MARIA was attained by attaching runes only to the ends of the four slanted arms *the first time around* but on all of the six arms during the second circuit. Again the distribution proceeds in the clockwise direction. The first letter, S, is at the upper right arm.

Again Ita clearly chose a system for picking up the runes that would suggest the possibility of translating the scrambled text.

FIGURE 35

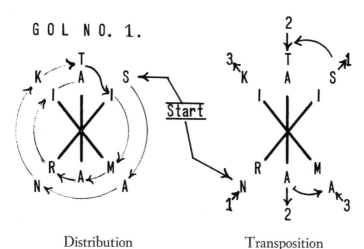

Distribution   Transposition

The transposition proceeds as is indicated by the three numbered arrows. The result is the eleven runes that are carved on the wall: N R I S T A A A M I K .

MIK has the meaning "me" and one of the accepted meanings of A is "owns" so that A MIK is properly translated as "owns me." But by some involved reasoning Mr. Liestøl concluded that NRIST is the word KRIST. This also assumes that this profane spelling of KRISTUS (Latin, Christus) would have been permitted in a medieval church. Both propositions appear to be questionable.

Another difficulty is the fact that the A is repeated three times. This makes the translation "Christ owns, owns, owns me." Here, Liestøl had no choice but to assume that the repetition was to emphasize the idea of belonging to Christ.

It was demonstrated above that the inscription is a transposition cipher by which the letters in SANKTI MARIA were scrambled. The vague appearance of a textual meaning then becomes only a deceptive screen whose function it was to cover up the cryptography.

4. GOL NUMBER VII—NIYR, Vol. 5, pp. 183-84

This was the fourth, and last, of Ita's ciphers. Its message is that "Ita wrote 4." Because the rune 0 has numerical value 4, her original seven-rune message was ITA RIT O. However,

FIGURE 36

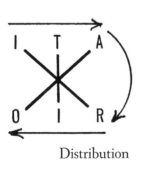

Distribution

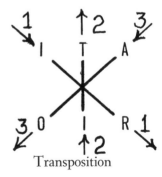

Transposition

symmetry of distribution on a six-armed figure could only be attained by reducing the number of runes to six.

Ita knew that the message would still be understood if she dropped the rune T, thus: ITA RIT O became ITA RI O.

The transposition was carried out in the same way as in Gol VI. The six runes were distributed in the clockwise direction. The order of the transposition is indicated by arrows 1, 2, and 3 in the figure at the right.

The result is IRITAO. In this case also, Ita must have felt that the transposition cipher alone was too simple. Therefore, she superposed on it the same substitution cipher as in Gol VI. This consisted in substituting for each rune the symbol that precedes it in the runic alphabet. The result was the six symbols that she carved on the wall:

FIGURE 37

N   O   N   S   I   Th

Mr. Liestøl concluded that the six runes were the Latin words NON SIT and he suggested the translation "It shall not be." While this is acceptable Latin he does not explain why the rune Th was used instead of a T. Of course, from the point of view of probabilities, it is impossible that Mr. Mongé's solution could appear through a double layer of cryptography, had it not been so planned.

In analyzing the Gol solutions, Mr. Mongé found that only two persons had constructed all of the cryptopuzzles. The nun, Ita, or Ythe, apparently constructed her four runic puzzles in the year 1297. She dated Gol II December 15, 1297.

Thirty-two years later, in 1329, a cleric whose name was Tatai followed with another four puzzles. One, Gol V–A, B, and C is actually a complex of puzzles. Parts of them tie in with other nearby carvings.

In the cryptographic work of Tatai one fact stands out. On many occasions, and in many ways, he based his dates on the year 1297. He did so both directly and by calling attention to the span of 32 years between the two dates. The date August 25, 1297, seems to have had a very special significance for him. This may have been his date of birth, the day on which he said his vows, or some other outstanding event in his life. Whether the correspondence between the ciphers of Ita and Tatai means that they were friends, or colleagues, is not known.

A representative sample of the work of Tatai will be presented here. The more extensive and intricate ciphers must be omitted because they are not necessary for the purposes of this volume.

5. GOL NUMBER V C–NIYR Vol. 5, pp. 180-82

It was mentioned above that Gol V is a complex which includes several ciphers. In NIYR it is separated into three parts, A, B, and C. Part A is by far the longest. It has a total of sixty-one runes. Part B has six runes and part C has seven. The former is carved below, and the latter above the line of runes in part A and are cryptographically connected with it. Only part B has a translation. It reveals the name of the puzzlemaster, Tatai.

Gol V C is particularly interesting because the word AHR, which means "year," is spelled in the same way that it was spelled in 1123 by Henricus in Spirit Pond No. 3, and again in 1362 by puzzlemaster Harrek in the Kensington inscription. Philologists have been critical of this spelling in the Kensington carving. It appears to have longer antecedents than have been suspected.

As usual, we shall begin with Tatai's original message in Gol V C. It stated the date, and nothing else, as in Figure 38 on the next page.

The numerical values of the last three runes are added. The runes in the original message are such that they cannot be

FIGURE 38

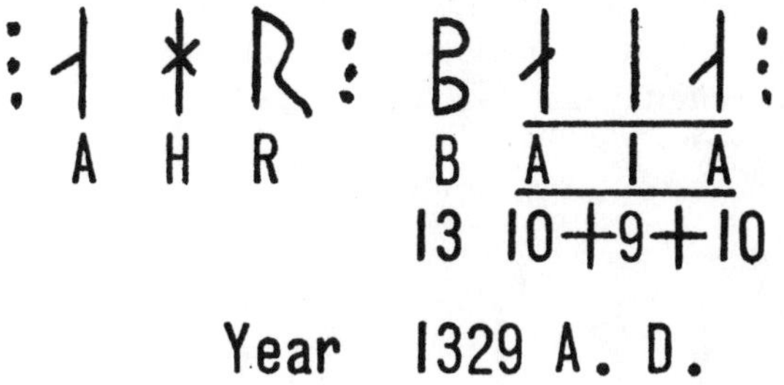

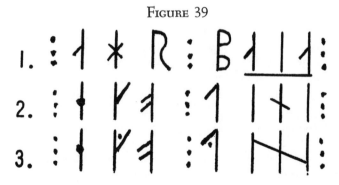

combined because they would blend into a single rune A. But *they were combined as they were carved on the wall.* Therefore, the addition to 29 is proper. The message is AHR 1329 which means "Year 1329 A.D."

This is a substitution cipher. For each rune the one which is immediately to the left of it in the alphabet is substituted. In the figure below, Line 1 shows the original message. In Line 2 the substitution has been made and in Line 3 the last three runes are combined. This was the inscription which Tatai carved on the wall.

FIGURE 39

Note also that, after his substitutions in the alphabet, Tatai made significant changes in two runes. He added points to the third and fifth runes. These were thirteenth- and fourteenth-

century innovations which changed the sound of the K to G
and the T to D. These points were not shown in the runic alphabets so that it was a conscious choice on the part of Tatai. The
correct transliteration of Gol V C is therefore:

FIGURE 40

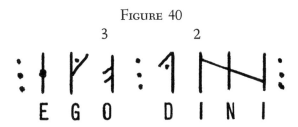

The reader will notice that the substitution cipher in Gol
V C had no need for the two points. They were added for
another purpose. Here we see that Tatai also tried to mislead
the solver into believing that a translation was possible. The
words EGO DINI have a Latin ring. Mr. Liestøl assumed that
two letters were omitted and that the two words should be
read EGO D(OM)INI. This he translated as "I am the Lord's."
Why two essential runes should be omitted for no apparent
reason was not explained. The cipher shows that they do not
belong, and that the two extra letters do not belong.

Gol V C is the ciphered year 1329 A.D. In other parts of
his cryptography Tatai associated Ita's year number, 1297 A.D.,
with his own by indicating one or the other year number together with the difference between them which is 32 years.
Whether he did so because the earlier date was important in
his own personal life, or to tie his own cryptography in with
Ita's, is not known. In Gol V C he used the same procedure
by combining the last three runes in his inscription. This
formed two groups of 3 and 2 *symbols* which, written as a
decimal number, gives 32.

6. GOL NUMBER IV–NIYR, Vol. 5, p. 180

In this cryptopuzzle, Tatai duplicated the principal details of Ita's four ciphers. He apparently did this to demonstrate his familiarity with her work.

1. He used the Jesus Christ cross which she used in all four of her transposition ciphers. This is an assumption but is very probable.

2. He used the same substitution system as Ita had employed in Gol VI and VII.

3. He showed his awareness of the subject matter of Gol II (Sankti Maria) by choosing an associated date, which was the *Day of Assumption of Saint Mary.*

4. He indicated Rati=7 for his own year 1329 in Gol IV by limiting the number of runes to seven. (Ita had done the same in both Gol VI and VII by limiting the number of runes to six. For the year 1297 Rati=6.) Nevertheless, in Gol IV he made it clear that his own year was 1329 by indicating only this year number.

As it is carved, Gol IV reads as follows:

FIGURE 41

This inscription certainly justified Mr. Liestøl in his translation, "Halbiork." Except for the conspicuously missing rune for A, and the missing point in the rune for K to give it the sound G, it is the correct spelling for the female name Halbjorg.

Again, as we shall see, this is a cover for the hidden cryptography. As was true in Gol V C, Tatai did not begin with a translatable message but with a set of runes which state and confirm the date, Tuesday, August 15, 1329 A.D., from the calendar. They were the seven runes whose equivalents in Latin letters and in numerical values are shown in Figure 42.

FIGURE 42

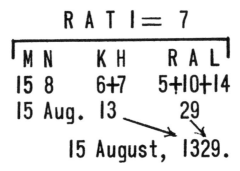

The figure shows that the indicated date is August 15, 1329 A.D. There are three groups of runes. This has a double significance: 1. For August 15, DDL=3. 2. In 1329, August 15 fell on a Tuesday, the third day of the week.

FIGURE 43

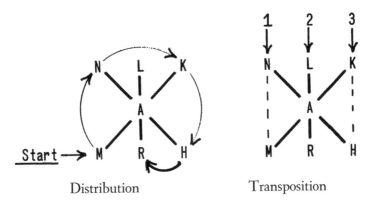

Distribution   Transposition

It remains now to show how these seven runes were converted into the seven runes that spell HLBIORK which were carved on the wall. The answer is that Tatai distributed them on the Jesus Christ cross as Ita had done in Gol I. The first four runes were placed clockwise, at the extremities of the two slanted arms beginning with the M at the lower left. The last three were distributed along the vertical arm beginning at the lower end. (See the figure.)

Now the transposition is carried out by taking the letters as indicated by the three vertical lines 1, 2, and 3. This gives NM LAR KH.

The next step was to substitute for each rune the one which is to its left in the 16-rune alphabet. The result was what Tatai carved on the wall. (The L came before the M in the fourteenth-century alphabet.)

FIGURE 44

H L B I O R K

Tatai was not yet done with showing that he knew Ita's cryptographic procedures well. He constructed four cryptopuzzles—no more, no less—and all were transpositions, presumably on the Jesus Christ cross. They are numbers IV, V-A, VIII, and X. In two of the four, Gol IV and VIII, he, like Ita, substituted for each rune the symbol to its left in the 16-rune alphabet.

We have now covered approximately one half of the cryptography in the Gol inscriptions. The remainder are no more difficult but they are interrelated and therefore more difficult to explain. Among them are Gol V-A, V-B, VIII, IX, X, and XI. Gol V-A, VIII, and X are almost identical. Each delivers the date, August 25, 1297 A.D. They also indicate the lapse of 32 years to Tatai's own year, 1329 A.D. Gol IX is tied into Gol V-A. In Gol XI, Tatai stated in the visible text his admonition: "Read right these runes." This warning remained ineffective, however, over nearly six and a half centuries, until Mr. Mongé heeded it in 1970.

In Norway, as in other countries, monks and priests often adopted the names of saints. This appears also to have been the

case with Ita and Tatai. Saint Ita was the seventh-century
founder of the monastery at Hy Connall near Limerick in Ireland. Saint Tathai was a fifth-century Irish monk. The Book of
Saints, which was compiled by the Benedictine monks of Saint
Augustine, lists both these names and the various spellings
under which they were known.[4]

The Gol cryptography was selected for presentation here
because of its very high concentration. No other group of cryptopuzzles furnish such a large and coherent mass of dovetailing
proof that Norse ciphers exist, in most cases unsuspected, in
large numbers of Scandinavian runic inscriptions.

There has been no intention, in this and the preceding chapter, to deny the competence of runologist Aslak Liestøl in his
own field. That question has nothing to do with the subject of
this volume. Nor do the solutions in these chapters imply criticism because he, and other runologists and experts in the medieval Norse language, failed to discover Norse dated puzzles. It
is no accident that it took someone with the special training and
talents of cryptanalyst Alf Mongé to solve this unusual and unexpected art of the medieval Norse clergy.

*Under these conditions it has been little less than shocking
to find, during the past few years, runologists and linguists called
on to act as if they were experts in a field which is foreign to
them. It has, if possible, been even more surprising that some
have been willing to assume the mantle of critics under these
conditions.* This has added an element of confusion but it will
not affect the outcome.

CHAPTER 7

Ancient Norse Runes in Medieval Inscriptions

The extensive use of Old Norse runes in dated inscriptions in the United States, which were all carved after 1000 A.D., is interesting and historically very significant. Up to the present, nine early eleventh-century dated carvings are known. One is from Massachusetts and eight from Oklahoma. Of these, seven use a mixture of O.N. and Sw.-N. runes. Altogether, there are about twice as many O.N. as medieval runic symbols.

Such a preponderance of O.N. over 16-rune symbols after 1000 A.D. is contrary to the long-held opinion of runologists which they based on normal runic writing. They have consistently dated inscriptions with O.N. runes alone from 200 to 600 A.D. while those which are mixed also with Sw.-N. and Normal runes have been dated as late as 850 A.D.

The nine American inscriptions contain a total of 35 O.N. runes against only 17 from the Sw.-N. alphabet. With only one exception, all are easily read. This is as might be expected because they were carved by knowledgeable puzzlemasters. It is also a fortunate circumstance that the climate of Oklahoma causes relatively little weathering and the inscriptions are all carved on hard, weather-resistant rock.

It is significant that no runologist has ever suggested that the Oklahoma symbols are difficult to read or that they are not runes. As an example, the Danish runologist Dr. Erik Moltke agreed, in a letter which is dated April 4, 1970, that the eight symbols of the Heavener No. 1 inscription from Oklahoma are runes in these words: "Av disse er de sex av Dem citerte tegn regelmessige urnordiske runeformer, mens nr. 2 og nr. 8 med ligeså stor sikkerhed er vikingetidsformer efter den svensk-

norske futhark." (Of these, six of the symbols which you cite are
regular Old Norse runic forms, whereas numbers 2 and 8 are,
with equal certainty, forms from the Swedish-Norwegian alphabet.)

At the same time, Dr. Moltke was strenuously resisting the
idea that Heavener Number 1 is an authentic medieval inscription. He based this opinion on the supposition that it had been
carved in modern times. But he advanced no proof of any kind.
What is worse, he totally ignored the existence of the beautifully executed Norse-type dated puzzle which the inscription
contains. This made his argument invalid on two counts.

The only other serious attempt, which has ever been made
to disprove the medieval origin of Heavener No. 1, also conceded
that the Heavener symbols are authentic runic forms and it also
ignored the hidden date from the Norse medieval calendar.
This argument was presented in 1968 by Mrs. Birgitta Wallace,
Swedish-trained archeologist with the Carnegie Museum in
Pittsburgh. It will be discussed as a part of the solution of the
dated puzzle of the Heavener inscription later in this chapter.

This chapter will demonstrate that cryptopuzzles are found
in Scandinavia which were carved after 1000 A.D. and which use
O.N. runes exclusively. It is interesting to note that they were
also carved during the very same years that a Norse puzzlemaster constructed dated inscriptions in Massachusetts and
Oklahoma. Only two such Scandinavian inscriptions are known
to date but a thorough search would undoubtedly disclose others.
The discovery and solution of Norse dated puzzles constitute
research into a hitherto unknown field. Much remains to be
done.

In the last half of the chapter are solutions for two of the
eleventh-century dated inscriptions from the United States.
They are Byfield 1 and Heavener 1. Not only are they fine examples of the Norse puzzlemaker's art. They also demonstrate
the considerable cryptographic advantage which is gained by
mixing O.N. and Sw.-N. runes. No other reason for this use
was necessary.

1. NORRA VANGA (Sweden)

Norra Vanga is as elementary as a dated puzzle can be made. The first four runes indicate a year from the Easter Table by giving its Rati, YGN, and YDL. These are, of course, mutually confirming quantities. It also gives ND for the day but there was no opportunity to include DDL and DGN to confirm it.

The inscription was carved as a mirrored image as it is represented in Figure 45 below. It will be noticed that the calendrical indicators for the year and the day are in the order that they appear in the Easter Table and calendar: Rati=15, YGN=2, YDL=3, and ND=24. The indicated date is November 30, 1008 A.D.

FIGURE 45
(As it was carved)

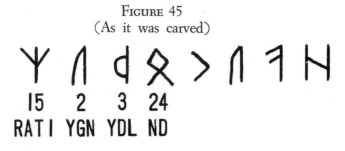

15 2 3 24
RATI YGN YDL ND

By carving the inscription as a mirrored image of itself, the significance of the last four runes was obscured. When it is reversed back to its normal condition, these runes, which are now the first four symbols in the inscription, are seen to be the well-known medieval Norse name HAUK whose meaning is "hawk."

FIGURE 46
(Reversed back to normal position)

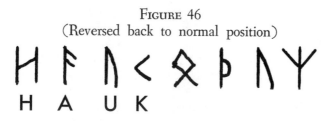

H A U K

It might be objected that, in 1008, the nominative R should have been used so as to make the spelling HAUKR. Had this been done, however, the last four runes would have been spotlighted as not belonging to the name. A Norse puzzlemaster-colleague would at once have suspected that they were a part of a cryptogram. As it was arranged, the last of the eight runes was an R. This invited the assumption that this was nominative R at the end of a name which included all of the runes.

This is another example of deception to keep the puzzle from being too easy to solve without hiding it so well that it can not be discovered. In the absence of nominative R after HAUK, and because only O.N. runes were used, the runologists who tried to translate the inscription were led to believe that HAUK-OThUR was a single ancient name. It was suggested, for example, that THUR might be another spelling for the Norse god Thor. However, so far as is known, no such name as HAUK-OThUR has previously been known from the fifth century A.D.

These assumptions caused the inscription to be dated at about 400 A.D. In the absence of knowledge of the presence of the dated puzzle it is difficult to see how a better interpretation could have been made.

It was by no means required that nominative R be used with the name HAUK in 1008 A.D. In her recent book *Stuttruner* Ingrid Sanness Johnsen, among others, states that nominative R began to be omitted a long time before the eleventh century.[1]

One more comment should be made. A check in the Easter Table shows that, for the year 1008 A.D., YGN=2 and YDL=3 whereas for the following year the numbers are reversed, that is, YGN=3 and YDL=2. Hauk, if that was the runemaster's name, gave his calendrical indicators in the order that they appear in the Easter Table for the year 1008 A.D.

Having stated the case for the existence of a Norse dated puzzle, and the name of the puzzlemaster, it is only fair to say that this is not a completely confirmed date. There are, for example, no values for DGN and DDL to confirm the date November 30. Hauk, if indeed he was the author of the inscription, presented his puzzle on a "believe it or not" basis. No complete dated puzzle does so.

In the case of the Norra Vanga inscription, it is possible that there was no puzzlemaster whose name was Hauk and that no puzzle was, in fact, arranged. The alternative is that these elements fell into place in this precise manner by pure chance. A close examination of the probabilities on both sides seems to weigh strongly in favor of the existence of a dated puzzle together with the name of its author, Hauk. It is important to note in this connection that Hauk could not have added the missing confirmations for his date from the calendar without destroying his puzzle by making its presence entirely obvious. Then there would have been no puzzle. The watchword in this case had to be simplicity.

2. MÖJBROSTENEN (Sweden)

If the cryptographic nature of Norra Vanga can be thought of as slightly ambiguous, this can not be said of a well known inscription which is known as Möjbrostenen. It is pictured and discussed by Sven B. F. Jansson of the National Historical Museum in Stockholm.[2] The transliteration which is used here is his. The photograph shows that the runes are reversed but the entire inscription is not mirrored.

This beautifully carved inscription is important in several respects.

1. Its cryptopuzzle exhibits the *earliest known use of a transposition cipher since classical times.* This was a transposition device which was called a scytale. The historian Plutarch made the scytale famous in his accounts of the Peloponnesian naval commander Lysander. The episode will be discussed in connection with the transposition ciphers in Legend 67 of the Vinland Map which are analyzed in Chapter 8.

2. The only other known eleventh-century Scandinavian inscription that uses the ancient runic symbols is the eight-rune HAUKOTHUR which was analyzed above. How many more exist remains to be seen. However, the two establish the fact that

FIGURE 47

O.N. runes were used in runic inscriptions after 1000 A.D.
This is very important for a proper understanding of eleventh-
century American cryptopuzzles.

3. The decimal system is used in the same way as it was used
in dated puzzles centuries later. It was known and used by nearly
all Norse puzzlemasters. This included the cleric who constructed the early eleventh-century dated inscriptions in Massachusetts and Oklahoma.

4. Möjbrostenen shows no church connection. The warlike
stance of the mounted warrior suggests war or the hunt. It is
conceivable that its author may have been a nobleman who had
been educated in a Benedictine monastery school or had a Benedictine priest as a tutor.

The transcription shows that, as carved, the runes are reversed.
It will appear later that all runes have numerical values but
that nine runes also deliver a secret message.

FIGURE 48

Transcription

There are 10 runes in Line 2 and 15 in Line 1. This indicates the year 1015 A.D. in typical fashion. Full confirmation of the year will appear later. However, to make certain that the year was not misunderstood, it is stated a second time as follows: When the second rune in Line 1 is reversed back to its normal position, it is seen to be an N. Its numerical value is 10 in the 24-rune alphabet. Immediately above it is the O.N. rune R with numerical value 15.

Again the indication is 1015 A.D. This is the only use which is made of the rune R. It takes no further part in the solution. This is the reason that it could not be carved within Lines 1 or 2 but must still be paired with the rune N.

The ND is also indicated directly by the two lines. The runes in the two lines are adjusted so the *sum of their numerical values* is 201. This is ND for June 6. We shall see later that DDL=3 is also given for June 6 (The date has no DGN). The information is also provided that June 6 is the 6th day of the 6th month.

These numbers 10, 15, and 201, denote entirely conventional verifications of the year and day. In addition, the date, June 6, 1015, is pinpointed by different, equally conventional calendrical details in the puzzlemaster's basic transposition setup. The cipher also includes his name and a one-word statement to the effect that he constructed the cryptopuzzle on this date.

The transposition cipher in Möjbrostenen is a gem of logic and organization. As was the case with Norra Vanga, there were

excellent cryptographic reasons for reversing the runes. The
purpose in this case was to indicate that the count which was to
establish the basic pattern of the transposition cipher was to be
made in reverse.

In the figure which is entitled The Six Cycles, the runes have
been reversed back to their normal positions. A count backwards
from the last rune in the inscription, the F, establishes the pattern. Every fourth rune is an A six times in succession.[3]

FIGURE 49

The Six Cycles

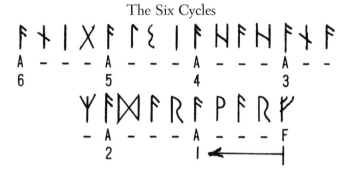

Having helped to establish the basic transposition pattern, the
rune F has served its purpose and drops out. The next task is
to discover how the puzzlemaster distributed the remaining
18 of the 24 runes. It is clear that this must be in groups of
six runes so that there were a total of four groups of six runes
each.

It turns out that the distribution is the simplest that could be
arranged. In the figure whose title is Distribution, the runes
which precede the six runes A are numbered 1. They are the
runes GIHRRR and they form the first of the four lines in the
transposition. Likewise, the runes, which are in the 2nd and
3rd position ahead of the runes A, are numbered 2 and 3.
They become the second and third lines in the transposition.
Of course, the runes A must now be numbered 4 and form
the fourth line.

FIGURE 50
The Distribution

ᚠᚼᛁᚷᚠᛚᛤᛁᚠᚻᚠᚻᚠᚼᚠ
4 3 2 1 4 3 2 1 4 3 2 1 4 3 2

ᛦᚠᛥᚠᚱᚠᚹᚠᚱ
1 4 3 2 1 4 3 2 1

The first nine runes in the transposition contain the only ciphered message in the inscription. They read GIHRR RISA which means "Geir wrote (these runes)." Geir was a favorite medieval Scandinavian name which means "spear." Its most common spelling was GEIRR in which the last rune was nominative R. In Norwegian inscriptions it is often spelled GAEIR or GAIR. In Sweden it was often spelled GIR. This is the spelling that is used in Möjbrostenen except that the silent rune H was inserted and the nominative R added.

FIGURE 51
The Transposition

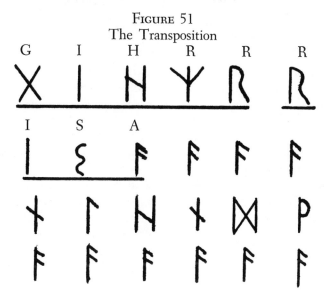

G	I	H	R	R	R

I	S	A			

It will be shown later that nine runes were needed in this part of the pattern. This is all the explanation that is needed for the presence of the H. There is, therefore, no reason for rejecting the spelling GIHRR in the Möjbro inscription.

FIGURE 52

The Nine-letter Message

G I H R R   R I S A.
"Geir wrote."

The word RISA presents no problem. It is one of more than a dozen different ways in which the word was spelled. This spelling is found in several other runic inscriptions. The meaning is "wrote."

It was noted above that the year 1015 A.D. is indicated twice. For this year Rati=15, YGN=9, and YDL=2. These numbers are neatly indicated in the transposition pattern. YGN=9 is represented by the number of runes in GIHRR RISA. The remainder of the pattern has 15 runes for Rati=15. The two parts, which have 9 and 15 runes, indicate YDL=2.

Note further that after GIHRR RISA 3 runes remain in Line 2 of the pattern. There are also 6 runes in Line 3 and another 6 in Line 4. These are the numbers that indicate for the date, June 6, that it is the 6th day in the 6th month and that its DDL=3.

This completes all confirmations of the date June 6, 1015 A.D. It is not too much to say that this was an inspired performance by Gihrr, the puzzlemaster.

Let us return briefly to the sum of the numerical values of the twenty-four runes in Lines 1 and 2 which indicate ND=201 for June 6. Actually this was not very difficult. Note that most of the 24 runes can not be changed because they perform specific functions. The remainder could be selected by the puzzlemaster with the sole objective of causing the sum of the 24 runes to total 201.

The basic reason that the runologists assigned Möjbrostenen to about 400 A.D. was that it uses O.N. runes exclusively. This reason has now been shown to be mistaken. Another reason, which has been advanced to support the 400 A.D. dating, is that the style of the horse, the rider, and the dog below the inscription is more typical of the fifth century than of the eleventh. This is a criterion which would seem to be very difficult to substantiate. On the other hand, there appears to be no way to overthrow the evidence of Geir's cipher.

The argument in favor of the 400 A.D. dating also assumes that the inscription and the figures below it were carved at the same time. This is a natural assumption but, since geologists can not date cuts in stones with any degree of precision, it could probably not be proved. But Geir's cryptopuzzle proves that the inscription was cut in 1015 A.D. regardless of the age of the figures.

3. BYFIELD NUMBER 1 (Massachusetts)

It was mentioned at the beginning of the chapter that nine dated runic puzzles from the early eleventh century have been discovered and solved in Massachusetts and Oklahoma. All use O.N. runes, some exclusively, but most have O.N. runes mixed with symbols from the Sw.-N. alphabet. Their dates fall in the narrow range of years from 1009 to 1024 A.D.

The earliest which is yet known is Byfield 1. Its date is November 24, 1009 A.D. It is carved on a large granite boulder which is located in Byfield, about fifty miles north of Boston.

FIGURE 53

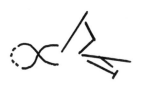

The Merrimac River flows eastward to the Atlantic in the extreme northeastern corner of Massachusetts. About fifteen miles upstream lie three small contiguous areas which are known as Byfield, Groveland, and West Newbury. Located within these areas, and separated by distances which do not exceed five miles, are a number of runic inscriptions. In Chapter 1 it was reported that they were discovered in the years from 1930 to 1948 by Strandwold, Pearson, and Bjorndal with the assistance of local residents such as the late Lawrence M. Rogers of Byfield.

This work resulted in a series of very good photographs of inscriptions from this area. It was among these photographs that Mongé discovered three dated puzzles. One of these is Byfield 1. The other two were constructed by Bishop Henricus about a century later.

The cryptographic procedures that are used in Byfield 1, and in four major dated Oklahoma inscriptions are as similar as their different dates would permit. It is therefore very likely that all were the work of the same runemaster. These similarities will become apparent by a comparison of the Byfield 1 and the inscription which is known as Heavener 1 which is solved later in this chapter.

This inscription was carefully examined by the author in 1969 and again in 1971. It is carved on hard granite and is easily read except for the O.N. rune O at the left. Here the stone has been fractured so that some of the upper part of its loop is missing.

This is the only symbol of the early eleventh-century inscriptions, which there has been any reason to question. However, it was transcribed as the O.N. rune O by the Strandwold-Pearson team in the late 1930's. This was about thirty years before anyone could have had any knowledge that the O was essential for a solution of its dated puzzle. Enough of the loop remains to show that its sides curve inward. This suggests that the symbol could not be the O.N. rune G but can only be the rune O.

To one who is conversant with Norse-type cryptography, the

most persuasive reason that the symbol must be an O is that it completes the solution of a very deftly constructed dated puzzle. If the rune is not an O, no solution is possible.

Norse dated puzzles rely heavily, for their effectiveness, on geometry. This appears as changes in the relative positions of single runes and groups of runes, gathering runes into groups, changing their sizes and shapes, combining and reversing them and many other procedures.

In Byfield 1, reliance is also placed on geometry. The first rune at the lower right was shortened and underlined. It, and its neighbor, are the two Sw.-N. runes that state the year. At the left is an O.N. rune which states the day. The two O.N. runes at the top of the inscription confirm this day. The runes all point towards a common center. They were carved so as to be read from the lower right in the counterclockwise direction.

It will also be recalled that many, in fact most of the Norse runic puzzles from Scandinavia that were solved in Chapters 5 and 6 had no translations. All early eleventh-century American dated puzzles, including Byfield 1, are of this type.

The actual solution of this puzzle presents no problem. It was possible, perhaps by the deliberate choice of a convenient date, to fully state and confirm the day and year by the use of only five runes. For the solution it is desirable to lay out the symbols in a straight line.

FIGURE 54

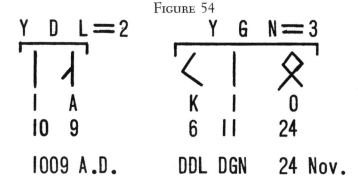

This inscription was carved in three groups of runes, two Sw.-N., two O.N., and a single O.N. The first Sw.-N. rune is an I. It was cut only two-thirds as long as the O.N. rune I at the top of the carving, and it is underlined. This made it possible to distinguish them. Only so could their numerical values and their groupings be determined correctly. The solution depends totally on such distinctions. The shorter underlined rune comes, of course, from the shorter alphabet. Such indirect evidences of careful planning, which are very numerous in Norse puzzles, are persuasive. The probability that they were accidents is very small.

The same puzzlemaster, or someone who must have been a close associate, also underlined two runes for I in the Tulsa, Oklahoma, inscription which was carved in 1022 A.D. He thereby called attention to the fact that they belonged to each other in the dated puzzle even though they were separated in the inscription. Underlining was a convenient technique which is found also elsewhere.

The second detail which needs to be explained is how the Sw. N. runes of numerical value 10 and 9 can indicate the year 1009 A.D. Why not 1090 A.D. or 910 A.D.?

This illustrates a difficulty in expressing decimal numbers with runes (or pentathic numbers). There was no rune whose numerical value was zero. Therefore the zero must be understood. The problem and how it was solved by the Norse puzzlemasters were discussed in Chapter 3.

The reason that the year is not 1090 is that the confirmations for the year are YDL=2 and YGN=3. This confirms the year 1009 and rejects 1090. The puzzlemaster grouped two Sw.-N. and three O.N. runes for just this purpose. (This also excludes the year number 910 A.D.)

A price had to be paid for using only five runes in this setup. No place could be found for the ancient rune R whose numerical value is 15. Therefore Rati=15 for the year is omitted. But it was not necessary to state the Rati in this case. The year had already been stated directly by the Sw.-N. runes of numerical value 10 and 9. Therefore, the YGN and YDL simply confirm the year.

In the process of stating the day, the puzzlemaster again paid a price of sorts for his compact arrangement. He could not use runes to indicate that ND=30 for November 24. That would take two extra runes and destroy his plan for a compact five-rune puzzle. His O.N. runes K and I have numerical values of 6 and 11. For November 24 DDL=6 and DGN=11. The 24 indicates the 24th day of one of the twelve months. Only November 24 has a DDL=6 and DGN=11. The puzzle is, therefore, complete and leaves no ambiguity. (The number 24 is so large that it can not be a DL or a GN. It must either be an ND or a day of the month. The DDL=6 and DGN=11 show that it represents the 24th day of November.)

The reader will realize that, simple as this puzzle seems, it is a gem of ingenuity. Five runes are normally not sufficient to indicate a fully confirmed day and year. Many features, without which the puzzle would have failed, provide indirect proof that it took the close attention of an experienced puzzlemaster to produce this result.

One final comment. In four similar dated puzzles in Oklahoma, Sw.-N. runes state the year, and O.N. runes confirm it, in just the same way as in Byfield 1. O.N. runes are also used in the same way to state and confirm the day. This clearly goes far beyond mere coincidence. The only reasonable explanation seems to be that the same puzzlemaster constructed all of them.

4. HEAVENER NUMBER 1 (Oklahoma)

The penetration by 1012 A.D. into what is now known as the southwestern states presents another intriguing phase of the history of the Norsemen in North America. That they reached and lived in what is now Oklahoma must be considered proved unless, and until, it is demonstrated that eight dated puzzles do not exist. Up to this time, five years after the solution of the Heavener dated puzzle was first announced, there has

FIGURE 55

been a peculiar reluctance to even make the attempt. The Heavener 1 solution is only one good reason. Until their existence is disproved, it is irrelevant to propose that a wandering, rune-happy Scandinavian had carved the inscriptions in recent times. Not even the runologists, to say nothing of foot-loose amateurs, had any knowledge of dated puzzles until *Norse Medieval Cryptography in Runic Carvings* was published in 1967.

The massive Heavener runestone has eight large runic symbols which are carved at breast height on its ten-foot-wide by twelve-foot-high vertical surface. During modern times, it was apparently first known to Choctaw Indians. They were one of the so-called civilized tribes who were moved into Oklahoma Territory in the 1830's. The inscription was repeatedly observed by white hunters and others beginning some time before the turn of the century. However, the location was fairly inaccessible and the inscription was overgrown with lichen so that it was apparently lost and rediscovered several times.

In 1928 the stone was shown to Gloria Farley, a native resident of Heavener. It was then known as "Indian Rock." She continued to be interested in the inscription but did not realize, until years later, that the symbols were runic. During the past twenty-five years or more she has supplied the motivating drive in Oklahoma to determine the origin and to establish the authenticity of the Heavener carving and to discover new inscriptions.[4]

These efforts have succeeded beyond all expectations. Of course it took on an entirely different aspect when the solution of the hidden date in the Heavener carving, November 11, 1012 A.D., became known in September of 1967.[5] Two years later solutions for Poteau 1 and Tulsa 1 were also published.[6] Their cryptographic procedures match those in the Heavener carving as closely as their different dates would permit. The last of the five major dated cryptopuzzles in Oklahoma was made known to Mr. Mongé and was solved in 1971.

The photograph of the Heavener symbols is marred by the presence of lichen which partially obscures the cuts. However, they are large and cleanly cut into very hard sandstone and are correctly formed and easily read. In the transcriptions which are shown below there are two Sw.-N. and six O.N. runes. The latter are drawn with heavier lines in order to distinguish them.

This is a very compact puzzle in which both the indications for the day and the year make use of all eight runes. Therefore, the solution can be diagrammed more easily by separating the confirmations for the year from those for the day.

A.   Indications and Confirmations for the Year

FIGURE 56

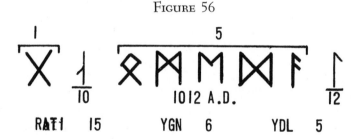

Just as with Byfield 1, the procedure is simple but effective. One Sw.-N. rune was used to separate the O.N. runes into two groups of 1 and 5 symbols. The Sw.-N. runes have numerical values 10 and 12. Together they indicate the year number 1012 A.D.

A check in the Easter Table shows that, for the year 1012 A.D., Rati=15, YGN=6, and YDL=5. All these indicators are confirmed. The two groups of 1 and 5 runes deliver the decimal number 15 in exactly the same way as the year number was indicated. This is the Rati. Five O.N. runes are isolated in one group. This is the YDL. There are also a total of 1 plus 5=6 O.N. runes which represent YGN.

The indication of the day is done with equal finesse. This time the Sw.-N. runes take no part and are left out.

B.   Indications and Confirmations for the Day

FIGURE 57

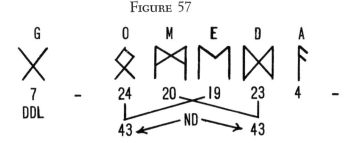

Alternate symbols of the four interior O.N. runes add up to 43. Because this is too large a number to represent DDL or DGN it is reasonable to assume that N.D.=43. If so, the day is November 11. That this is the intended date is confirmed by the first and the last O.N. runes. Their numerical values are 7 and 4. A check under November 11 in the calendar shows that, for this date, DDL=7 and DGN=4.

We now have the day and year confirmed from the perpetual calendar in every way that the calendar provides. One question may occur to the reader. Why was it necessary to state ND=43 twice?

The answer is that it was not necessary but let us have another look at the confirmations for the year. There are five O.N. runes in the second group. If ND=43 had been stated only once, there would have been only three. Then all the confirmations for the year would have been incorrect.

Such indirect evidences that the arrangement of the symbols

was carefully planned by the puzzlemaster are very persuasive. It may be particularly effective with those who may not realize that the probability is for all practical purposes zero that the construction of the puzzle could have happened by mere chance.

A review of this solution will emphasize to the reader what a gem of organization and precision it is. With only eight runes nothing is left out. Each rune is involved twice and there are no loose ends.

The date is also one which was entirely appropriate for a medieval priest. It was Saint Martin's Day, a favorite in Scandinavia. November 11 was also the first day of fast before Advent Sunday. The Heavener inscription is not alone about the year 1012 A.D. A cryptopuzzle at Church Hill, about sixty miles west of Heavener, uses the same cryptographic methods. It is dated ADVENT SUNDAY, November 30, 1012 A.D.

The Poteau inscription, which was discovered about 15 miles north of Heavener, is also dated November 11, but five years later. Somewhat more than a hundred miles to the northwest is the Tulsa inscription. Its year number is Advent Sunday another five years later, December 2, 1022 A.D. It is clear that this Massachusetts and Oklahoma puzzlemaster must have been a priest.

The Tulsa date was more difficult to cryptogram. A total of ten runes were required. Of these, five were combined into two symbols with three and two runes respectively. As a result the inscription has only seven *symbols*.

It is entirely clear that the high efficiency of Byfield 1 and the Oklahoma cryptopuzzles was made possible by two features. One was the fact that both O.N. and Sw.-N. runes were mixed. How effective this could be was demonstrated in the solutions of Byfield 1 and Heavener 1.

The second important element that promoted efficiency was the fact that the runes were used only for their numerical values. This can easily be seen from the transliteration of Byfield 1, and its four associated cryptopuzzles in Oklahoma, which are given below.

INSCRIPTION		DATE	TRANSLITERATION
Byfield	No. 1	November 24, 1009	A I O I K
Heavener	No. 1	November 11, 1012	G A O M E D A T
Church Hill		November 30, 1012	T S I A O K K I G I
Poteau	No. 1	November 11, 1017	G A O I E A (17) Th
Tulsa	No. 1	December 2, 1022	GI (S A S) (K I) S S I

Anyone who is even slightly familiar with the Norse language will know that these jumbles of sound values are not Norse. (The two groups of letters in parenthesis were runes that were combined for strictly cryptographic reasons.)

The number 17 which appears in Poteau 1 is an interesting feature. As it is carved on the stone it is the symbol for the Golden Number 17. It could only have come from the Easter Table of the puzzlemaster and it shows that the symbols in his table were runic.

This is illustrated in Column I of Worm's table of sets of Golden Numbers which was reproduced in Chapter 3. It is the symbol which is used in Column 1 for Golden Number 17. The presence of this symbol in an inscription which is dated 1017 A.D. seems to prove that calendars, in which runes had replaced Roman numerals or other types of symbols, were in use in Scandinavia by the early eleventh century. The presence of English runes in King Athelstan's calendar in the first half of the tenth century indicates that the custom was more widespread than in Scandinavia alone.

On the other hand, the calendar could not have been a primstav in which the months were left out. This is shown by the fact that, in Byfield 1, November 24 was not stated as ND=30 but as the 24th day of a month which was identified as November and confirmed by DDL and DGN.

Bishop Henricus also used the corresponding special symbol for Golden Number 19 in his Popham Beach dated puzzle which bears the date Advent Sunday, November 29, 1114 A.D. It can be concluded from this that the Golden Numbers in his calendar were expressed with runes. (See Chapter 9)

CHAPTER 8

Bishop Henricus Sails to Vinland

In October, 1965, after seven years of intense study and research, Yale University published a scholarly work, *The Vinland Map and the Tartar Relation*. The coauthors were R. A. Skelton, Superintendent of the Map Room, British Museum; Thomas E. Marston, Curator of Medieval and Renaissance Literature at the Yale University Library; and George D. Painter, assistant keeper in charge of incunabula at the British Museum. The introduction was written by Alexander Orr Vietor, Curator of Maps, Yale University Library. Each is recognized as an authority in his own specialty.[1]

The volume will henceforth be referred to as VMTR. It deals *inter alia* with the discovery and interpretation of the earliest known map of Greenland and Vinland, or more correctly, outlines of these areas. The original of this map, and two adjacent legends, which are labeled Numbers 66 and 67 in VMTR, were fitted into the northwest corner of a world map which has become known as the Vinland Map (VM).

It was determined in VMTR that the various sections of the Vinland Map were copied and combined from several sources. By painstaking research, it was found possible to prove that VM had been composed, and drawn in 1440 A.D., probably in connection with a church council at Basle, Switzerland. The authors concluded that the Greenland-Vinland portion of VM, including Legends 66 and 67, had been derived from an original Scandinavian source. However, surviving historical documents could not supply the answers to some critically important questions, among them the following:

1. What Scandinavian had managed to draw the outline of Greenland, such as it appears in VM, with such surprising accuracy?

127

2. What Scandinavian could have had sufficient knowledge of the northeastern shores of North America so that he could locate its two major features, Hudson Bay and the St. Lawrence estuary?

3. Who wrote Legends 66 and 67 in their adequate but sometimes misspelled, and not very elegant, medieval Latin?

4. At what time, indeed in what century, were these elements brought into being?

To these questions, this chapter, and the three which follow, provide definite and apparently final answers. Many supplementary facts will also be revealed which have a bearing on the long-hidden ministry of the Icelander, Eirik Gnupsson, in the Vinland of the early twelfth century.

At some point in his career, Eirik had adopted the name Henricus. It was he who was the author of Legends 66 and 67 in VM and also, very probably, the outlines of Greenland and Vinland and other parts of VM. In 1112 A.D., he was appointed by King Sigurd Jorsalfar of Norway to be bishop of Greenland and Vinland. It was the custom at that time for the temporal power to appoint and for the Church to consecrate. The consecration took place during the reign of Pope Paschal II.[2]

Jorsalfar is a composite title which meant "the Jerusalem traveler." From 1107 to 1111 A.D. Sigurd had led a considerable force against the Mohammedans in support of Baldwin, King of Palestine.[3] The historian Hjalmar Rued Holand has expressed the belief that Eirik must have accompanied the king on his crusade. This would have given him the opportunity to assess Eirik's qualities as a dedicated man of the church and as someone who would be able to withstand the rigors of the post in Greenland.

Legends 66 and 67, and the hidden date and ciphers which they harbor, were certainly the work of Henricus. So, very probably, were the outlines of Greenland and Vinland even though it is possible that they may, at least in part, have been made with the assistance of his associates such as an experienced ship's captain or navigator.

The legends tell of a long visit to Vinland. In Legend 67 Henricus was speaking of himself in the third person. Two ciphers in Legends 66 and 67 also reveal religious sentiments which are in every way worthy of a dedicated bishop. A third cipher, in an integrated group of three, is the hidden autograph of the name Henricus. The ciphered date, taken as always from the Norse perpetual church calendar, is August 23, 1122.

Seven dated runic puzzles by Henricus, which are spread along a three-hundred-mile-long shoreline, prove that the Vinland of which Henricus speaks in VM was centered in New England. Their solutions are presented in Chapters 9, 11, and 12.

Henricus is the latinized form, not of his given name Eirik, but of Henrik. The implications are strong, as will be evident later, that he chose this name for its extraordinary cryptographic qualities.

Henricus had presumably returned to Greenland by 1122 A.D. But Chapters 11 and 12 will show that, in the following year, he had again returned to Vinland. This is the only conclusion that can be drawn from three runic inscriptions that were discovered in Maine in June of 1971. They have been referred to in previous chapters as Spirit Pond 1, 2, 3.

After this brief introduction to the ramifications of the Henricus story, we are ready to examine his cryptography in VM. As a note of caution the reader is reminded that, as has been all of the cryptography which has been discussed up to this point, these are puzzles, not coded messages. For the latter the intended recipient is provided with a prearranged system for deciphering the message. A puzzle must adhere to a general set of rules. Of these, the potential solver was presumed to be well aware before he attempted to solve it. However, there were no specific instructions as to the procedure which was followed.

In order to construct his cryptography the puzzlemaster might need to adjust the numbers of words in each line, the number of letters in each word, and even to use incorrect spellings of some words. Whether he used these and a variety of other procedures, depended on his cryptographic repertoire and the specific message that he wished to convey. There was a trend over the centuries from the compact early eleventh-century dated puzzles, whose plain text had no meaning, to more elaborate constructions that were concealed within longer runic inscriptions. Among them were at least two Latin texts, Legends 66 and 67 in VM.

FIGURE 58

Northwest Corner of the Vinland Map

The northwest corner of the Vinland map, which is shown here, is reproduced from VMTR. Greenland is at the upper center. Vinland, which has indentations for Hudson Bay and the Saint Lawrence estuary, is at the left, and Iceland, Ireland, and parts of England and Scandinavia at the right.

Transcribed from the script into Latin letters, Legend 66 reads as shown in Figure 59.

The substitution message in these three lines can be explained without any preliminaries because the reader has seen an identical construction as a part of the "pornographic" cryptopuzzle

FIGURE 59

Legend No. 66

```
V I N I L A N D A     I N S U L A
        9                     6

A     B Y A R N O         R E P A
I         6                   4

E T   L E I P H O   S O C I J S
2         6               6
```

from Bergen in Chapter 5. Because the largest number of letters in any one word is 9, the substitution alphabet must contain 9 letters in order to be able to spell out the message. In this case the alphabet is the first nine letters in Line 3: ET LEIPHO S . . . . This is established by the fact that, used as an alphabet, these nine letters spell out an intelligent and appropriate message. No amount of trying will discover another nine letters which can do so.

The procedure is routine. The series of numbers which Henricus established by adjusting the counts of letters in the nine words was: 9 - 6 - 1 - 6 - 4 - 2 - 6 - 6.

The ninth letter in the alphabet is S, the sixth is P, the first is E and so on. The message is: S P E P E T P P .

At first glance these eight letters appear unpromising but this is so only because there are two abbreviations. The eight letters separate into three parts which each represent a Latin word: SPE PET. PP.

SPE is no problem. It is the ablative case, singular, of the word SPES, which means hope. The meaning is "By hope . . ." or "Because of hope . . . ." Catholic historians say that the translation "Because of faith . . ." is also acceptable in this context.

We now must be aware that, as will appear presently, the

message of Henricus consists of three parts. Each part must have eight letters, no more and no less. The reason is that the third part is his own name which has eight letters. The second and third parts are an acrostic and a telestic at the left and right ends, respectively, of Legend 67. Its eight lines can only deliver one letter from each.

Because Henricus could use only eight letters, the letters PET and PP are abbreviations. The three letters, PET are the base of the Latin word PETO. This is the first person singular, present tense, and means "I seek" or "I beseech."

So far the translation is "Because of hope I beseech . . . ." What then does the PP signify? Henricus well knew that, without some assistance, this abbreviation might become a stumbling block. Therefore, he provided a perfect hint. In Line 6 of Legend 67 he suddenly, and for no apparent reason, broke into a series of abbreviations. The line reads as follows: ". . . spaciosa vero et oppulentissima et postmo anno p. ss. nrj." These are the only three words which are abbreviated in Legends 66 and 67 of VM. On page 140 of VMTR they are interpreted to represent the words PATRIS SANCTISSIMI NOSTRI and the translation is "our most blessed father [Pope Paschal]." This interpretation is undoubtedly correct.

The abbreviation which attracts our attention here is ss. for SANCTISSIMI with the meaning "most blessed" because the last word in SPE PET. PP., namely the pp., is of exactly the same form. Just as SANCTISSIMUS is the superlative for the adjective SANCTUS, PATRISSIMUS is the superlative for the adjective PATRIUS which has the meaning "fatherly." As they are used, SANCTISSIMI is in the genitive and PATRISSIMUM is the accusative case but this has nothing to do with the abbreviation which is identical in the two cases. In the context in which it is used as the abbreviation pp., PATRISSIMUM, with the meaning "most fatherly," clearly refers to the deity. The translation therefore becomes, "Because of hope, I beseech the Almighty." This is a sentiment which is worthy of a dedicated bishop and, as will appear presently, fits perfectly with the two other eight-letter parts of the hidden message.

Anyone who is disturbed by the unceremonious dropping of the O from PETO should consider this. In Gol VII, whose solution is given in Chapter 6, the word RIT was abbreviated to RI for exactly the same reason. The nun Ita could use only six runes and her message had seven. Such abbreviations are common also in normal runic inscriptions. Given a suitable context, a runologist will not hesitate, for example, to interpret the single rune M as MIK and translate it as "me." The isolated abbreviations P. SS. NRJ, shows that Henricus was a master at the art. Typically, these same abbreviations also take part in additional cryptography. They indicate, and confirm, the date August 23, 1122 A.D. This reduced the possibility that some of the cryptography might remain unnoticed.

The omission of the ending which would have indicated the person and tense of the verb PET leaves them to be determined from the context. Since Henricus signed his name to the message in part three, he was clearly speaking of himself. Therefore PET was abbreviated from PETO which is the first person singular, present tense.

What awkward choices of words Henricus was forced to use in order to attain the correct number series in Legend 66, can not now be determined. Did he actually believe that Leif and Bjarni discovered Vinland together, as he says in the legend, or was this a departure from the truth in order to complete his cipher? There is no way to judge this but it seems unlikely that Henricus, who lived only about a century after these events happened, and who was an educated and well-informed man, did not know what the writers of the sagas nearly two centuries later seem to have been in no doubt about—that Leif's was an independent expedition.

One thing is certain. No historian can put the least faith in this statement as evidence. Nor should linguists assume that Henricus did not know that the proper latinized spelling of Vinland was VINLANDA, not VINILANDA as it is spelled in

Legend 66. This misspelling was forced upon him because he needed nine letters and VINLANDA had only eight.

Most of the cryptography in VM is actually concentrated in Legend 67. An acrostic is built into the left ends of its eight lines and a telestic in the right ends. An acrostic or a telestic bear powerful internal evidence of their individual existence. In Legend 67 the proof goes far beyond this to the point of absolute certainty.

These are not simple ciphers in which the message is delivered by the first or last letter of *successive* lines. The selected letters come from the lines in an irregular pattern. When, however, the order of selection is identical for the acrostic and the telestic, this is virtually impossible unless it was so arranged.

In addition to this, Henricus used the ultimate device for guaranteeing that these are arranged ciphers; he used a *key word*. It was the function of the key word to *dictate* the order in which the letters were to be selected from the eight lines. With the use of a key word, which in this case was the eight-letter name of a person who was famous in antiquity for his association with transposition ciphers, it became certain that a puzzlemaster, in this case Henricus, had arranged the ciphers.

The Text of Legend Number 67

No. of
words.

11 VOLENTE DEO <u>P</u>OST LONGU ITER AB INSULA GRONELANDA PE<u>R</u>
    MERIDIEM AD

 9 RELIQUAS <u>E</u>XTREMAS PARTES OCCIDENTALIS OCEANI MARIS ITER
    FA<u>C</u>IENTES AD

11 AUSTRU INTE<u>R</u> GLACIES BYARNUS ET LEIPHUS ERISSONIUS SOCIJ
    TERRAM NO<u>U</u>AM UBERRIMA

 8 VIDELIC<u>E</u>T VINIFERA INUENERUNT QUAM VINILANDA INSULA
    APPELLAUERUNT <u>H</u>ENRICUS

10 GRONELAND<u>E</u> REGIONUMQ FINITIMARU SEDIS APOSTOLICAE EPIS-
    COPUS LEGATUS <u>I</u>N HAC TERRA

15 SPACIOSA VERO ET <u>O</u>PULENTISSIMA IN POSTMO ANNO P. SS. NR<u>J</u>.
    PASCALI ACCE<u>S</u>SIT IN NOMINE DEI

11 OMNIPOTETI<u>S</u> LONGO TEMPORE MANSIT ESTIUO ET BRUMALI POSTEA
    VERSUS GRO<u>N</u>ELANDA REDIT

8 AD ORIENTEM HIEMALE DEINDE HUMILLIMA OBEDIENCIA SUPERIORI VO-
LUTATI PROCESSIT. (Partial ninth line.)

In the eight complete lines of Legend 67 above, the number of words in each is marked at their left ends. This number of letters is counted from both ends of each line and the last counted letter is underlined. These underlined letters, selected in the order which the key word specifies, deliver the two secret messages. It is of considerable interest that two ciphers in the text of the Kensington inscription are of the same type. The source of this similarity will become clear in later chapters.

Later on it will be shown that the key word requires that the letters be selected from the lines in the order 4-8-7-1-5-2-3-6. When this is done the two series of letters result which are shown in the table below. This can easily be checked in the text above.

FIGURE 60

The line number:	4	8	7	1	5	2	3	6
Left (acrostic):	E	T	S	P	E	E	R	O
Right (telestic):	H	E	N	R	I	C	U	S
	E	T		S	P	E		E	R	O

The message that emerges from the acrostic, at the left ends of the eight lines, is the second part of Henricus's three-part message. It consists of three short words in basic Latin: ET SPE ERO. They translate directly as, "...and because of hope [or faith] I shall become [saved]."

The first and second parts of the message, taken together, now read, "Because of hope, I beseech the Almighty, and because of faith I shall become [saved]." The word saved is quite clearly called for from the context but only eight letters were available to him. In spite of this severe limitation, Henricus managed to make his meaning clear.

The third part of the message is his own autograph. Henricus built the three-part message around his own name. This he also did in each of his seven dated runic puzzles in New England. At the same time, his use of various forms of the Christian cross almost amounted to a mania. It seems certain that he chose the name Henricus because it lent itself so well to the style of cryptography which he used.

It was this restriction to eight letters for each part of the message that forced him to abbreviate PETO and PATRISSIMUS in the first part and to leave out a word which meant "saved" or "blessed" in the second part.

Henricus also appears to have used a procedure which is typical of Norse puzzles that are concealed in longer texts. This was to set out signals that suggest the nature or location of the most important part of the puzzle. In this case, an extra letter was added to *three words* that form the names of two neighboring countries. Iceland and Ireland. so that they also have *eight letters*. This correlates with the *three parts of Henricus's message*, each of which has *eight letters*.

FIGURE 61

Correct Spelling		As Misspelled	
Islanda	(7)	Isolanda	(8)
Ibernia	(7)	Ibernica	(8)
Irlanda	(7)	Ierlanda	(8)

R. A. Skelton discussed the proper spellings of these three names in VMTR. He stated that no latinized spelling Isolanda had ever been encountered and that Ibernica, whether associated with Iceland or other islands, was known in maps only as Ibernia.[4] Likewise Ierlanda was an unknown spelling and was assumed to be a corruption of Irlanda.

To summarize, the known forms of the three words contained

seven letters. The spellings that are used in VM had an additional letter inserted in each case. The spelling that resulted,
which now has eight letters, was unknown from any other
source.

It can not be proved, of course, that these misspellings were
deliberately made as a guide to locate and confirm the cryptopuzzle in Legends 66 and 67. However, the theory has much to
commend it over and above the improbability that these are
mere coincidences. Similar signals occur in many other Norse
puzzles which are built into long texts. Again the Kensington
puzzle is an example. They obviously serve a useful purpose
once they are discovered. In addition, this is the only explanation for their presence which makes any sense.

These misspellings, assuming that they were deliberately
made, have an interesting consequence. They imply that the
Scandinavian original of VM included outlines also of Iceland
and Ireland (and perhaps, but not necessarily, Scotland and
England). These countries like Greenland, are surprisingly
well drawn. It could be conjectured from this that the original
(except for the outline of Vinland) was drawn by someone
who had learned the elements of mapmaking, perhaps in England, and who was familiar with the contours of the islands
to the north and west including Greenland. If so, this may well
have been Henricus himself. This matter would seem to deserve
the attention of experts in cartography.

We have already noted misspellings and abbreviations in
Legend 66. There are also misspellings in Legend 67 which
were required by its two ciphers. For example, the spelling of
Greenland, as it appears in Line 1, is GRONELANDA. This is
apparently the accepted spelling. But in Line 5 it is spelled
GRONELANDE for a very good reason. Henricus needed an
E in the 10th letter of this line and he arbitrarily changed the
A into an E. Likewise, the next to the last word in Line 3
should have been spelled NOVAM. But Henricus needed a
U in the 11th space from the right hand end of the line. He
changed the spelling to NOUAM.

The right-hand end of Line 7 presents a very interesting situation. Here the 11th space from the right end should have an N. Actually the N is in the 12th place. But it would have been in the 11th place if GRONELANDA had been misspelled GRONELADA with the second N omitted. The VM copy apparently corrected Henricus's misspelling!

Is there anything to suggest that the original was GRONE-LADA? The answer is, yes. The caption of Greenland, which is located very close to Legend 67 in the map, is also misspelled GRONELADA. Here is apparently another of the signals which was used in Norse puzzles to warn the potential solver of the presence of some cryptographic feature. Why, then, is the word, nevertheless, spelled correctly in Line 7? This can be explained very simply in a way that throws an interesting light on the performance of the scribe who had received the assignment to copy Legends 66 and 67 into the Vinland Map.

It must be assumed that the scribe who drew VM at Basle, Switzerland, knew the correct spellings of at least some of the misspelled words, such as Vinilanda, Gronelande, Gronelada, nouam, Isolanda, Ibernica, and Ierlanda. Yet, except in a single instance, he copied the words exactly as Henricus had misspelled them. The single exception is the word GRONELANDA in Line 7. This word he appears to have inadvertently altered back to its correct spelling whereas Henricus, most certainly, had spelled it as GRONELADA.

The author would suggest that someone who is expert in such matters should examine the title of Greenland carefully. It looks as if the scribe had almost completed copying the name as GRONELANDA before he realized that the original was GRONELADA. On the other hand, he seems to have suffered his only discernible mental lapse by spelling GRONELANDA *correctly* in Line 7 but not the way that it was spelled in the original.

We have seen that the numerical *key* which read out the Norse-type acrostic-telestic in Legend 67 was 4-8-7-1-5-2-3-6.

This order of selection of letters from the eight lines resulted in the two eight-letter Latin messages ET SPE ERO and HENRICUS.

It is important to demonstrate exactly how Henricus chose this order of the lines for reading the acrostic and telestic in the eight lines. Mr. Mongé was able to reconstruct the KEY WORD which dictated this order. This is like bolting and barring a door which is already locked. As a result, there is not the slightest chance that the cryptography does not exist. The key word is LYSANDER. The very appropriate nature of this key word will presently become apparent.

The *key*, which is the series of numbers 4-8-7-1-5-2-3-6, was developed from the *key word* as follows. The letters of the key word, LYSANDER, were first rearranged in the order in which they occurred in the Latin alphabet which Henricus was using. They were then numbered thus:

FIGURE 62

A	D	E	L	N	R	S	Y
1	2	3	4	5	6	7	8

When the eight letters are now again arranged in the order by which they spell Lysander, carrying their assigned numbers with them, the series of numbers is the *key* which Henricus used for his ciphers:

FIGURE 63

L	Y	S	A	N	D	E	R
4	8	7	1	5	2	3	6

Considerable search has not produced another Latin eight-letter name or word which generates this same numerical key. While it is possible that one exists, this is extremely unlikely. But even if there is another possible key word, this does not affect the acrostic and telestic of Henricus's message. It would also be very unlikely that any other key word could have the same prestige as Lysander. This is an important consideration in choosing a key word.

The implications of the name Lysander as a key word are far-reaching. He was the famous Spartan statesman and naval commander who vanquished the Athenians during the Peloponnesian War in the sea battle at Aegospotami in 405 B.C. Five hundred years later the great historian Plutarch made him the best known among those who used the ancient Spartan cryptographic *device* which was known as the *scytale*. This is one of the very few which have been invented for constructing transposition ciphers mechanically.[5]

FIGURE 64

Scytale

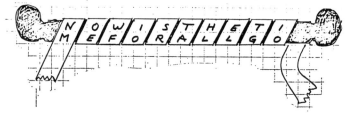

An example of the scytale is shown in the figure. Two identical cylinders were prepared. One was given to the one who was to receive and read the message. The other was retained by the sender. When a message was to be transmitted, a narrow strip of parchment or leather was wound around the cylinder. When it was wound at the correct angle, no space remained between turns. The message was then written as is shown in the figure. When the strip was removed and wound into a roll, only someone who had a matching cylinder could read it.

About Lysander, Plutarch told this dramatic story. He was personally given such a roll to carry to naval headquarters at the Hellespont. When he wound the strip on the cylinder and read the message, he found to his horror that it condemned him to death for misconduct!

By the use of LYSANDER as his key word, Henricus, in effect, said that he was familiar with the art of cryptography from ancient times. How else is he likely to have known about Lysander? He must certainly have known about the scytale because this transposition cipher device is historically associated with Lysander. This must have been the reason that he chose the name LYSANDER as the key word for his transposition cipher. He could scarcely have done better.

The tremendous burden that the key word put on Henricus in constructing his coordinated double cipher is clear. Each line had to deliver two specific letters which must occur the same number of letters from its two ends. What problems this posed in choice of words and sentence structure can easily be imagined. Misspellings were a last resort and were, in a sense, an admission of failure to find the right word or phrase.

It is of considerable interest in the history of cryptography over the world that Legend 66 represents the *earliest known use of a mono-alphabetic substitution cipher with variants*. In this case the single variant consisted in the fact that both the numbers 1 and 4 in the transposition alphabet deliver the same letter E to the cipher message from the substitution alphabet, *ET, LEIPHO S*...

No less surprising is the use of a transposition key in Legend 67 which was generated by the key word Lysander. The use of a key word was, until recently, thought to have been a relatively modern invention.

A final note on the ciphers in Legends 66 and 67. When one considers the superb skill which was shown by Henricus in the construction of his VM cryptopuzzle—which is equal to that which was shown by his puzzle-oriented successors—it is hardly surprising that modern cryptographers have hitherto been totally unaware of the existence of such concealment cipher systems. They have never been mentioned in historical accounts of the ancient art of cryptography.

This lack of recognition was most surprising in a review of *Norse Medieval Cryptography in Runic Carvings* by David Kahn, author of *The Codebreakers,* which appeared in the March, 1968, issue of *The American-Scandinavian Review.* Mr. Kahn concentrated on such irrelevant things as what he conceived to be the "arbitrary" methods of the present author and he dutifully quoted Mr. Liestøl on the utter worthlessness of the work of Mongé and Landsverk. As criticism, these are meaningless generalizations and the real issues were missed by both.

The Codebreakers purported to be a history of cryptography from its early beginnings. One would presumably have the right to expect that Kahn would be well informed about cryptography throughout the ages. Yet, in his review, he completely failed to recognize that Norse cryptography is certainly one of the great discoveries in the field in modern times.

The day and year number of VM are also hidden in Legend 67. They might have been overlooked entirely had not Henricus taken steps to spotlight them. In Line 6, the abbreviation SS, which provided the clue to the interpretation of part one of his ciphered message, is only one of a series of three abbreviations. Taken together with a word which belongs with them, they are ANNO P. SS. NRJ. The original phrase before it was abbreviated was ANNO PATRIS SANCTISSIMI NOS-TRI, and the translation, as it is rendered in VMTR, is "...in the year of our most blessed father...." Henricus was here referring to Pope Paschal II who died in 1117 or early 1118 A.D.

It is notable that these are the *only* three abbreviations in the texts of Legends 66 and 67. There is nothing to indicate that these words had to be abbreviated in so far as the text is concerned. Furthermore, the first two are very drastic abbreviations which can only be interpreted from the context in which they occur.

The secret lies in the fact that the numbers of letters in this four-word phrase form another numerical operating key, 4-1-2-3 as follows:

FIGURE 65

A N N O	P.	SS.	NRJ.
4	1	2	3

The question is what the key was intended to operate on. A way to proceed is often to see what part of the text has, as yet, taken no part in the cryptography. In this case there is the very conspicuous *partial ninth line* in Legend 67. Of the last two words, VOLUTATI PROCESSIT, the first two letters are in Line 8. The remainder appear in Line 9 as LUTATI PROCESSIT. This was no accident.

The acrostic and telestic each contain eight letters. They therefore require only eight lines. This suggests that the partial ninth line performs a special function. Such is, indeed, the case.

In Line 8 the last two letters, VO, which are a part of a word, were counted as a word for the purpose of the telestic. To be consistent, the same must therefore be done with the remainder of the word in Line 9. According to this logic, Line 9 has two words. We therefore count two letters from each end of Line 9 according to the system which was used with the first eight lines.

FIGURE 66

L U T A T I   P R O C E S S I T
2   11   2

The result is the three numbers 2-11-2 which have digits 2-1-1-2. To this sequence we now apply the operating key from the abbreviations in Line 6 thus:

FIGURE 67

OPER. KEY:	4	1	2	3
SEQUENCE :	2	1	1	2

When the operating key is now transposed to the normal order just as was done in the case of the key word, Lysander, we have:

FIGURE 68

OPER. KEY: 1   2   3   4
SEQUENCE :   1   1   2   2

$$= 1122 \text{ A.D.}$$

We have noticed previously that a puzzlemaster usually tried to use the same setup to indicate both the day and the year. This was also done by Henricus in VM.

What day does the key 4-1-2-3 indicate? It is August 23. For this day ND=123 and DDL=4 (August 23 has no DGN). Therefore, all possible confirmations of the day from the calendar are stated. This even includes the day of the week. In the year 1122 A.D., August 23 fell on a Wednesday. This is the 4th day of the week. This confirmation is also included in the key.

The full date is Wednesday, August 23, 1122 A.D. It is, of course, possible that this was the date that Henricus landed on his return to Greenland—or some other memorable day. However, as is so often true, this date develops from the calendrical indicators with a perfection which could scarcely be improved. Therefore, it is perhaps more likely that this is another "opportunity date"[6] whose numbers from the calendar fell into place in a particularly simple and satisfactory manner.

The interpretations of Legends 66 and 67 were the cause of considerable comment among the authors of VMTR. On page 139 R. A. Skelton transcribes Legend 66 as VINLANDA INSULA A BYARNO REPA ET LEIPHO SOCIJS. He rendered the translation as "The island of Vinland, discovered by Bjarni and Leif in company."

There appears to be an error in this transcription. An examination with a magnifier reveals that the spelling of the first word in Line 1 is VINILANDA. The I after the N is an intrusion. It was necessary to increase the length of the word from eight to nine letters. This permitted the transposition cipher of Legend 66 to call out the required S as the first letter in its secret message. With eight letters in VINILANDA, the indicated letter would have been O.

This is clearly a complete and satisfactory explanation for the misspelling. Mr. Skelton called attention to the fact that the word was also spelled VINILANDA in Line 4 of Legend 67. This is apparently another signal whose purpose it was to confirm that the spelling with the extra I in Legend 66 was intentional.

The word SOCIJS in Line 3 of Legend 66 also attracted attention but in this case on historical grounds. Mr. Skelton correctly comments on page 140 of VMTR that "None of the Icelandic accounts of Leif's voyage of discovery states that Bjarni accompanied him. The legend in VM, if it faithfully reproduces a genuine record, accordingly authenticates Bjarni's association with the discovery of Vinland and adds the information that he sailed with Leif."

In the same connection George D. Painter states on page 251: "Perhaps, however, the unusual and probably erroneous statement that Bjarni and Leif were companions is more naturally explained as a conflation by the compiler (of VM), rather than as already present in his source."

In the absence of knowledge of the cipher in Legend 66 these statements appear entirely logical. However, we now know that the one all-important task with which Henricus was struggling was to deliver his secret message. If this could be done so that a reasonably accurate text remained, so much the better. But under these circumstances no reliance can be placed on the text as historically accurate.[7]

It seems certain that the compiler of VM did an almost perfect job of copying Legends 66 and 67 exactly as they appeared in his source. His may have been a copy of a copy, etc. However, no matter if the transmission from Henricus to VM happened in one or more stages, the result speaks highly of the dedication and accuracy of those scribes who had a hand in copying it. A single error in a critical place could easily have made impossible the solution of any one of the several parts of the cryptography in VM. The next four paragraphs are directly quoted from Mr. Mongé on this point.

"Speaking in general terms, until a solution has been obtained it can never be stated with any degree of certainty that a suspected inscription actually is a cryptopuzzle. Yet, when this task is finally accomplished, *only* the secret text and its cryptographic relationship to the plaintext is revealed. It is next to impossible to reconstruct the puzzlemaster's exact line of reasoning in the step by step procedure involved in the changes he must have been forced to make before he arrived at his final version.

"There is every reason to believe that the puzzlemaster was always compelled to compromise to a considerable extent, and that he at least had to make certain that his puzzle-solving colleagues would *understand* his *secret* text. The plaintext was of much lesser importance unless his principal idea was *to leave no clue whatsoever* to indicate that a cryptopuzzle was present.

"In either of the two Norse-type concealment ciphers in Legend 67, however, we can usually determine from a close study of the plain and secret texts why conspicuous anomalies were unavoidable, or at least why specific words were shortened, lengthened, or otherwise misspelled. This applies to both plain and secret texts.

"We can also often determine the *cryptographic* reasons why a specific word or expression of more or less uncertain application to the existing situation was used and relevantly positioned in the plaintext instead of a now unknown, possibly synonymic word or expression which, perhaps, would have clarified a seemingly ambiguous statement. But it is extremely unlikely that we can ever identify the unknown word which was replaced. This may conceivably be the difficulty with the Latin word SOCIJS in Legend 66."

Based on the logical assumption that Henricus's initial as well as eventual intention was to write SPE PET. PP. as the first part of his three-part secret message, we need only point out a few more obvious cryptographic necessities. Legend 66 reads:

FIGURE 69

V I N I L A N D A   I N S U L A

A   B Y A R N O   R E P A

E T   L E I P H O   S O C I J S

Any change in the order of the words, or in their individual lengths, would have produced a different sequence of cipher numbers. This would have eliminated the cipher message. On these matters Mongé continued as follows:

"If, for example, BYARNO and LEIPHO were exchanged, no P would have been available in the built-in alphabet, ET LEIPHO S, to furnish the four P's in SPE PET. PP. Nor could the E in PET. have been delivered. Furthermore, in Line 3, a final six-letter word was needed to provide the second P in PP. The first letter of this word must also be an S so that the 9th letter in the built-in alphabet would be S. It is this letter that delivers the S in SPE. It may have been impossible to find any other six-letter word than SOCIJS for this last word in Line 3."

"Note also that the message SPE PET. PP. contains only four different letters, namely, S-P-E and T. The other four letters of the message are repetitions of E and P. These repetitions lessened the difficulty in indicating specific letters which were needed for the message."

In constructing the cipher in Legend 66 the situation was sufficiently difficult to force the use of an awkward and certainly also misleading plaintext. Unavoidable byproducts were historical implications which are at odds with respected historical sources. This must surely have been known to Henricus because the writers of the sagas do not appear to have been confused in these matters one and two centuries later.

CHAPTER 9

In the Sign of the Cross

In the summer of 1969 Mr. Sigvald Stoylen of Minnetonka, Minnesota, visited at the home of Alf Mongé at Santa Rosa, California. He was already quite familiar with the methods that were employed in Norse dated puzzles. After a brief discussion of them, he wrote three words that appear in the rectangle.

FIGURE 70

"Is it not true that a medieval Norse puzzle does not differ very much from this?" he asked. "The story goes that many years ago the U.S. Post Office received, and, believe it or not, promptly delivered, a letter which was addressed in this way. The solution reads JOHN (under) WOOD (and over) MASS. The man's address was John Underwood, Andover, Mass."

While the story is probably fictitious, this is, indeed, a fine illustration of an important characteristic of Norse puzzles. Despite its simplicity it compels the solver to discover *that which is hidden within its own arrangement.*

In previous chapters, and in the course of the present chapter the reader will discover similar subtleties. In this respect particular attention should be paid to the Newport Tower cryptopuzzle. In that case the rune U in HENRIKUS is represented in a shadowy manner which resembles the "under and over" feature in Stoylen's analogy.

The east coast of the United States harbors a treasure of runic inscriptions. The story of their discovery was discussed at some length in Chapter 1. These inscriptions are, for the most part, carved on large boulders or on solid rock surfaces.

In recent years Mr. Mongé has proved that five of these inscriptions, excluding the recently discovered Spirit Pond stones, are dated puzzles. One of the five is Byfield 1 whose solution was analyzed in Chapter 7. The other four were constructed by Bishop Henricus in the years from 1114 to 1118 A.D. They are the subject of this chapter.

The late Magnus Bjorndal generously made his glass negatives available for the analysis of these cryptopuzzles. They are excellent photographs which had been made by Malcolm Pearson a quarter century earlier. It soon became apparent that each of these inscriptions contained the eight runes that spell Henrikus (of course with a "k"). Statistically, it is for all practical purposes impossible that these things could happen, and be repeated, by pure chance.

Fortunately, also, Henricus used the same *pattern* to transpose the letters in his name in each inscription. The pattern was built around a form of the Christian cross so that it involved some of the most basic symbolism of the Roman Catholic church. Without these guides the solutions would have been much more difficult.

This is by no means the end of such helpful evidences. The name HENRIKUS itself is one of them. It is not a latinized form of his own given name EIRIK, which would have been EIRICUS, but comes from quite a different name, HENRIK. It so happens that the name HENRICUS had exceptionally convenient properties for facilitating the cryptography which Henricus had in mind. This will become obvious as the solutions proceed.

Except for the fact that they use runic symbols, these dated puzzles have little in common with normal runic inscriptions.

The runes that spell the name Henricus are distributed in each inscription according to the same transposition pattern. Adjustments are made to the pattern in order to accommodate the four different dates. These arrangements, which were clearly carefully planned, prove that these are Norse-type dated puzzles. By the same token, they are authentic medieval inscriptions.

FIGURE 71

FIGURE 72

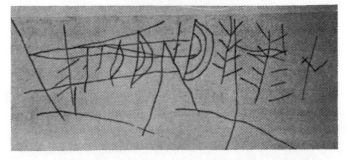

There are a considerable number of Scandinavian, and especially Norwegian, runic inscriptions which make use of spacing and arrangement of the runes in the same manner. The runes may be carved in different sizes and they may be distorted in order to serve cryptographic needs. Two examples are shown above. The inscription in Fig. 71 is known as Bratsberg Church No. II (NIYR II, p. 185). Fig. 72 is Storhedder I (NIYR III, pp. 48-50). The two inscriptions are from neighboring districts in Telemark and Setesdal in southern Norway and they are, to judge by their similar symbols, related.

These carvings depart very far from normal runic inscriptions. No translations are proposed by Mr. Liestøl in NIYR but he suggests that they must be examples of magic. If they were intended to deliver a hidden date or message, Mr. Mongé has not been able to solve them.

Even more outrageously unconventional are two inscriptions which are carved on opposite sides of a wooden paddle, parts of which are shown below. It was excavated from the ancient wharves at Bergen. These inscriptions also make use of non-linear distribution of runes, different dimensions of runes, unusual combinations and repetitions. To the runes are added patterns of non-runic marks. No translations or cryptographic solutions have as yet been accomplished.

FIGURE 73

FIGURE 74

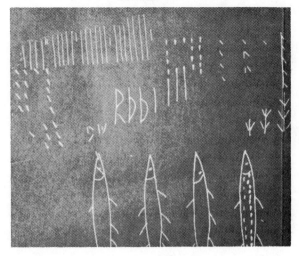

It was apparently out of Christian devotion, as well as cryptographic convenience, that Henricus made use of several forms of the Christian cross. One example is his substitution of the Greek cross for the first letter of his name. As a result his name began "with the sign of the cross." He made this substitution both from Sw.-N. and O.N. runes as follows:

FIGURE 75

Henricus was apparently very preoccupied with this universal symbol for Christianity. In his four early New England inscriptions crosses were very much in evidence both visibly present and implied. In three of the four he introduced the Sw.-N. rune M, which also has the shape of a cross. It served two purposes. It was convenient for separating the runes in the inscrip-

tion into four quadrants and it also carried its normal sound
value M. With this addition all letters were present not only to
spell HENRIKUS but also RUNEMUNK, that is "rune monk."
This is an obvious reference to his cryptographic avocation.

One famous Christian emblem which Henricus used in each
of the four inscriptions was the symbol that represents the
benediction "In this sign—the cross." In Latin the words are
IN HOC SIGNE—CRUS. In Norse, the last word was spelled
KRUS. The emblem whch presented this benediction used
the first letter of each word as follows:[1]

FIGURE 76

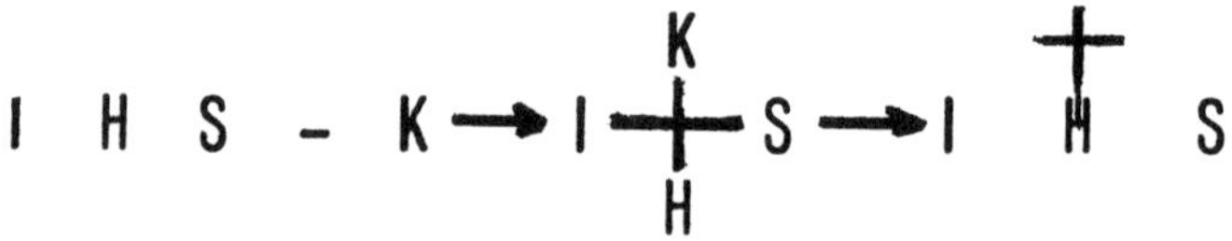

In each of the four cryptopuzzles the basic secret message was
the name HENRIKUS. The first step was to transpose the eight
runes into two groups of four runes each.

FIGURE 77

NAME	HENRIKUS
Ist.	H I K S
2nd.	E N R U

It will be noted that the two groups anagram into

FIGURE 78

I H S – K and R U N E

These two groups set the tone for the cryptography of Henricus in the four inscriptions. From these two groups he extracted

four pairs of runes in which each pair had a rune from each group. This was the basic transposition pattern. The four runes HIKS were always placed in the same fixed position. This is shown in the chart below. Each diagram represents the basic setup for one of the inscriptions. The designations are B 3 for Byfield No. 3; NT 1 for Newport Tower No. I; B 4 for Byfield No. 4; and PB 1 for Popham Beach No. 1.

FIGURE 79

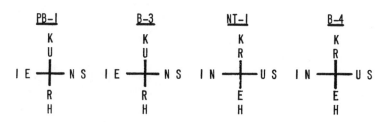

It will be noticed that, while the letters HIKS always have the same position, the letters RUNE are distributed so as to obtain the needed sequences of four pairs of runes. The objective was to state and confirm a day and a year as logically and understandably as possible. For each date the symbols, RUNE, had to be distributed differently.

After Henricus had selected his four final transposition patterns, he had to make a number of geometric adjustments before the carving of the inscriptions could proceed. Single runes and groups of runes had to be shifted relative to the remainder of the carving. Some runes had to be offset in a certain direction, others were combined. Special symbols, such as the rune M, were introduced not only for their sound values but also as convenient separators of parts of the inscriptions.

In each inscription the year is indicated in the same distinctive way. A rune of numerical value eleven represents 1100 A.D. On opposite sides of it are runes, or combined runes, whose value is the number of years after the year 1100 A.D., thus:

FIGURE 80

The Year:	1114 A.D.	1116 A.D.	1118 A.D.
Indication:	14 -11- 14	16 -11- 16	18 -11- 18

Because this system is used in each of the four carvings, there is no question about which year is meant. There is also another confirmation of the year in each case. Advent Sunday is a movable holiday. Therefore, an indicated year, and Advent Sunday for that year, must be a matched pair. In B 3, B 4, and PB 1 the date is Advent Sunday for the indicated year. In NT 1 the date is the second Sunday in Advent. It is clear that Henricus matched the days with the years.

As was noted above, these cryptopuzzles depend on detailed geometric adjustments of the runes after the specific transposition pattern for each had been selected. In order to make it as easy as possible for the reader to follow these manipulations, four pages of charts are supplied, one for each inscription. Each page has six charts which are labeled A to F. They illustrate the following features of each solution:

A. The transcription of the carving.
B. The runes labeled (O.N. runes drawn heavily).
C. The transposition pattern.
D. The indication for the year.
E. Any message other than "Henricus."
F. The indication for the day.

1.   BYFIELD No. 3 (B 3)

Because PB 1 and B 4 are very similar and can be taken together, the inscriptions are not taken in chronological order. Byfield No. 3 will be discussed first. It is perhaps the most representative and will be analyzed in detail. Only special features will be covered in the other three. The charts will be useful to follow the features which all have in common.

The important points of the solution of B 3 are these:

FIGURE 81

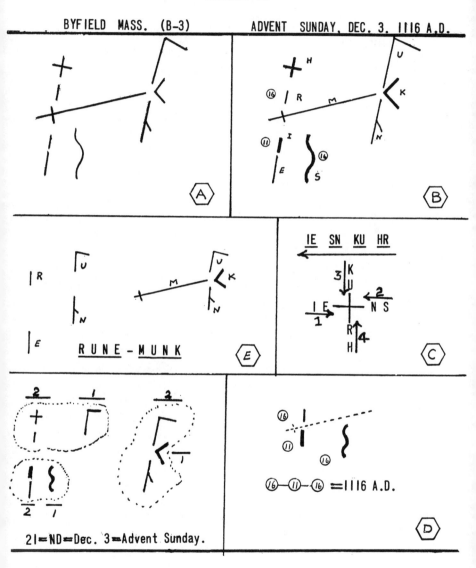

BYFIELD MASS. (B-3)

ADVENT SUNDAY, DEC. 3. 1116 A.D.

RUNE - MUNK

IE SN KU HR

21═ND═Dec. 3═Advent Sunday.

⑯—⑪—⑯ ═1116 A.D.

1. The inscription contains only the eight runes in HENRI-KUS—plus the special rune M. (See chart B)

2. The IHS-K and RUNE transposition pattern here gives, by pairs, the sequence IE-SN-KU-HR (C). Henricus used O.N. runes for IHS-K and Sw.-N. runes for RUNE (B).

3. The extra rune M serves three functions:
   a. It has the desired shape of a cross.
   b. Its vertical staff and its cross-arms serve as separators.
   c. It provides the missing rune to spell RUNEMUNK. (E).

4. The year 1116 A.D. is identified by 16-11-16. (D)

5. The date is given three times as ND=21 (F). This is December 3 and was Advent Sunday in 1116 A.D.

6. There are no less than five crosses, both visible and indicated:
   a. The Greek cross which Henricus substituted for the O.N. rune H in his name (B).
   b. The extra rune M (B, E).
   c. The invisible, yet essential, cross around which the groups IHS-K, in O.N. runes, and RUNE, in Sw.-N. runes, were distributed (C).
   d. The verbally expressed cross which is the last word in the benediction IN HOC SIGNE—KRUS.
   e. The runes that spell out the word MUNK are adjusted so they indicate a cross (E).

Most of the manipulations of the runes in B 3 are easily observed and were obviously carefully planned. Others are inferred not only from the construction of B 3, but because the same features are present in the other inscriptions.

2.   Newport Tower No. 1

Were it not for one distinctive special feature, this crypto-puzzle is quite routine and undistinguished. All dates are not equally difficult to cryptogram. Some present unique problems. In NT 1 the U in the transposition pattern which Henricus

Figure 82

NEWPORT TOWER, R.I. (NT- I). 2nd Sunday in Advent. Dec.10, 1116.

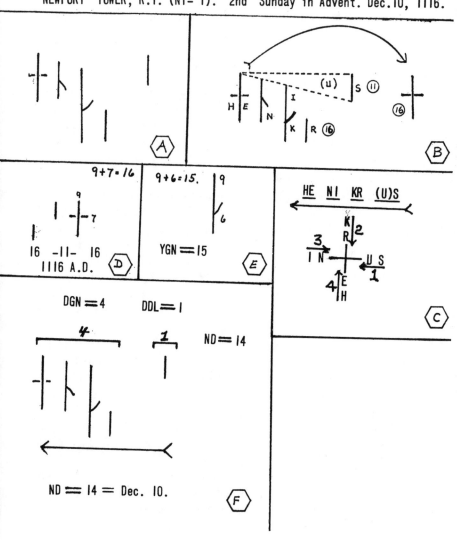

had selected threatened to block the display of the 16-11-16 sequence which was needed to indicate the year 1116 A.D.

Before this problem is attacked it is necessary to note that the first symbol is a combined rune which consists of the Sw.-N. runes H and E as follows.

FIGURE 83

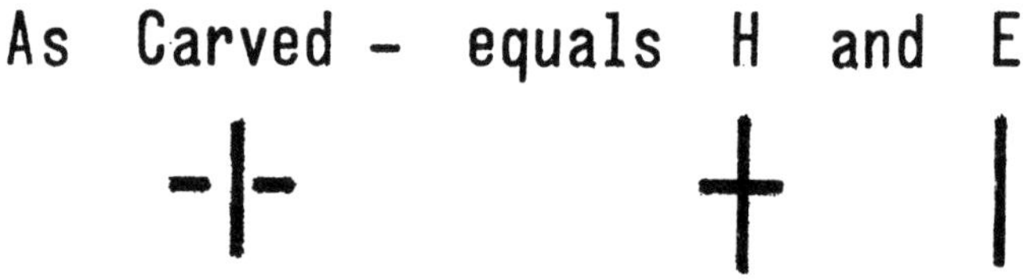

As Carved — equals H and E

When the crossbar does not intersect the staff, the rune is an E. When it is cut across the staff, it becomes an H. The sum of H and E is 16. To indicate the year as 16-11-16, the combined runes H and E must be cycled around to the right (B). But the sequence of runic pairs which Henricus was using shows that the U is in the way (C). It is the H-E, the S, and the R, whose numerical values are 16, 11 and 16, which form the 16-11-16 pattern. Unfortunately, the U lies between the S and the R in the pattern. It had to be removed.

There is a second reason that the U had to be physically removed. ND=14 is indicated by one rune and a group of four runes (F). This would become either 24 or 15 if the U were not removed depending on with which of the two groups the U was placed.

Here we have one of those John Underwood, Andover, Mass., situations with which this chapter was introduced. The U is not present in the carving but is indicated by carefully adjusting the vertical offsets of the remaining symbols (seven runes but with two pairs of runes combined) (B). Relative to the first symbol the three that follow it are moved downward so their upper ends form a uniform slope. The S is left at its normal height relative to the first symbol so that it forms the base of the U.

This is the crux of the NT 1 puzzle. In other respects it develops in a quite normal way. A single rune and a group of four runes indicate ND=14 for December 10 (F). This is the second Sunday in Advent for the year. It is cycled from right to left as is the entire sequence of pairs of runes as indicated in C. But the two groups of runes also serve other purposes. For December 10, DDL=1 and DGN=4.

This shows that, except for the U that had to be removed, NT 1 was relatively easy to cryptogram. It may properly be suspected that NT 1 was another "opportunity cipher." Even if this is so Henricus still managed to associate the day with Advent Sunday. It is the second Sunday in Advent.

3. Byfield No. 4 and Popham Beach No. 1

These two cryptograms are so similar that they can be discussed at the same time. The main difference between the two is that in PB 1 the symbol for Golden Number 19 is used to express YGN=19 for the year 1118 A.D. The GN was taken directly from the Easter Table of his primstav.[2] It eliminated the necessity for introducing two runes which together would have numerical value 19.

In both cases the rune M is carved in its normal upright position so that, in both, the total message is HENRIKUS RUNEMUNK. The M also served other useful purposes. All runes that spell the name HENRICUS are *below* the horizontal arms of the M whereas all that are added in order to effect the dating are *above* them. This is the rune T, with numerical value 12, in B 4 and the rune L with numerical value 14 (together with Golden Number 19) in PB 1.

The vertical staff of the M also performs a separating function. In B 4 there are 2 runes to the left of it and 3 to the right. This states ND=23 in the same way that is done in each of the four inscriptions. The date is Advent Sunday, December 1 for the year 1118 A.D. Similarly, in PB 1 a group of 2 runes and of 5 runes indicate ND=25 which is Advent Sunday November 29, 1114.

FIGURE 84

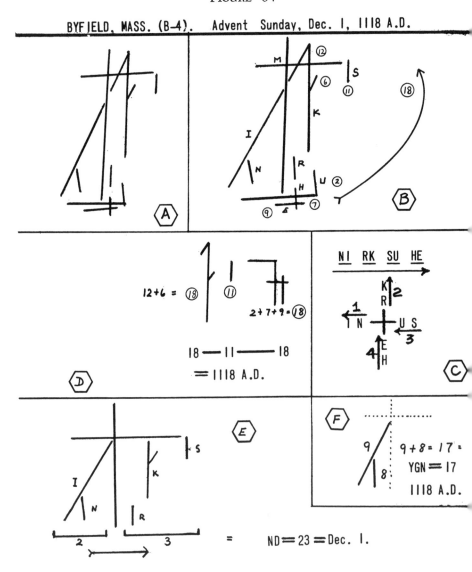

BYFIELD, MASS. (B-4).   Advent Sunday, Dec. 1, 1118 A.D.

FIGURE 85

POPHAM BEACH, MAINE. (PB-I). Advent Sunday, Nov. 29, 1114 A.D.

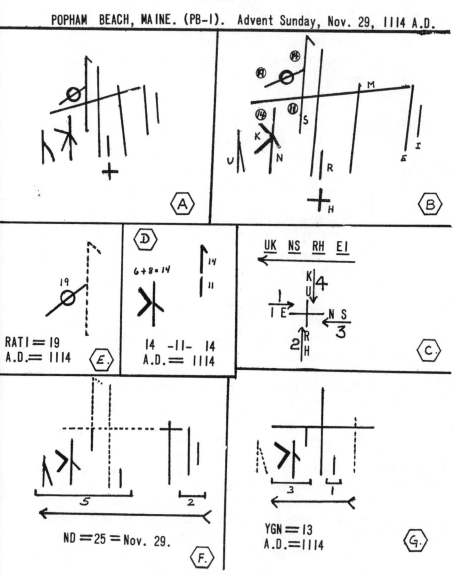

(In PB 1, as in NT 1, the progression of the sequence of four pairs of runes that form the transposition pattern, again goes from right to left as does, therefore, the entire solution (Compare C in all four).

The ND was attained in both cryptopuzzles by making some adjustments. In B 4 the group of combined runes, E, H, and U of total numerical value 18 (for 18-11-18) had to be shifted to a position below the staff of the M so as not to interfere with the indication ND=23 (B). The shifted group is a part of the indication 18-11-18 (D). Likewise, in PB 1, the Greek cross, which replaced the rune H, had to be moved below the level of the runes which give the indication ND=25. The H is, nevertheless, close to the R with which it belongs in the transposition pattern.

Finally, in PB 1, the O.N. rune and the Sw.-N. rune N are combined (B). Their combined value provides the 14 in 14-11-14 (D). But the two runes are counted separately in the count that gives ND=25 (F). This option to count *symbols* or *runes* when runes are combined is always open in Norse puzzles. Examples in which both options have been used in the same cryptopuzzle have been illustrated in previous chapters.

These cryptopuzzles are obviously highly organized in their geometric arrangement. They do not at all resemble a normal runic inscription in which the runes are in regular lines which are read from left to right. Actually, a large proportion of the puzzle element in cryptopuzzles consists of violations of this rule by offsetting the runes up or down, right or left; by shifting their relative positions; by varying their sizes and shapes; by variable spacings or variable separation with points; by combining the runes, and many other devices. Of such maneuvers these four puzzles have an abundance.

There is no miraculous key to a prompt understanding of the intricacies of cryptopuzzles such as these. However, the same can be said for modern ciphers. Anyone who is inclined to think otherwise would do well to compare the simple transposition ciphers of Henricus in these four puzzles with the transposition systems that are discussed in Sections IV to VI of Colonel W. F. Friedman's *Military Cryptography*, 1935 edition. It was on material such as this that Mr. Mongé "cut his eyeteeth" in cryptography. The same Colonel Friedman was then his mentor.

Henricus did not refer to the month of the year in his dating of VM or in his four cryptopuzzles which were analyzed in this chapter. However, in his SP 1, 2, and 3, whose solutions are discussed in Chapters 11 and 12, he does refer to October as the 10th month and October 6 as the 6th day of the month. This shows that Henricus also used the more conventional type of calendar in which the months and days were shown. The Golden Numbers and presumably the Dominical Letters were, however, written with runes.

CHAPTER 10

"Let Some Other D--n Fool Dig Them Up!"

In mid-1971 an important discovery was made a few miles inland from the Atlantic coast of Maine and west of the Kennebec River estuary. The site is about fifty miles due south of Augusta, the state capital. The find consists of three stones on which are carved more than three hundred Norse runes. There is also an outline map and a representation of a variety of objects.

Historically, these inscriptions are, without a doubt, the most important Norse artifacts that have ever been recovered on the North American continent. Their discovery also brought in their wake an unusually interesting chain of events. Fortunately, because of the nature of the artifacts, they will not have any permanently harmful effect on the determination of their authenticity.

Discoveries of this kind are, by their very nature, almost always made by someone who has no knowledge of runes or runic inscriptions. Such was also the case in this instance. The finder is Mr. Walter L. Elliott of Quincy, Massachusetts, a carpenter by trade and, among other things, a collector of Indian artifacts in his spare time. He is also a native of Maine and was raised in the area in which the stones were discovered.

On June 3, 1971, Mr. Elliott was hunting arrowheads along the banks of the Morse River just below a small body of water which is known as Spirit Pond. The find was made on a low ledge close to the point at which Morse River drains the pond. Actually, Morse River is a misnomer. It is a narrow and shallow tidal estuary which empties into the Atlantic, a distance which is slightly more than a mile in a generally southward direction from Spirit Pond.

Mr. Elliott reported that the stones were lying in a cluster,

166

partly covered with gravel and soil, and obscured by grass and weeds. A steep rise behind the ledge suggests the possibility that the stones may have tumbled onto the ledge as the result of erosion. However, there is at present no evidence which can throw light on the history of the stones after they were carved.

Mr. Harold Brown, Curator of Bath Marine Museum, which is located about ten miles north of the site, was the first person to whom Elliott showed the stones. He states that, when he first saw them, the stones were still partly covered with dirt and sand. He also noticed that a part of the inscribed symbols, and the neighboring areas of the stones, were covered with a fine growth which he calls rockweed.

We shall return to the stones and their significance later after some interesting events have been told which happened subsequent to the discovery.

Because of the solid proof of their authenticity, which is inherent in the cryptography which is hidden in these inscriptions, the character and reliability of Mr. Elliott is of less importance than is the case with most discoveries of artifacts. It would seem, nevertheless, that a few items which are relatively important should be a part of the record.

The actions of Mr. Elliott have always been open and honest in spite of considerable emotional strains to which the course of events subjected him. This the reader can judge for himself as the story unfolds. In addition, reputable witnesses have volunteered strong endorsements of Elliott's reliability.

In a letter which is dated August 19, 1971, Harold Brown of Bath Marine Museum made these unsolicited comments:

"... I believe Mr. Elliott to be a completely honest person. His family is well-known and highly respected in our area."

An equally favorable report, also unsolicited, came from Mr. Lester Oliver of nearby Popham. He is 73 years of age and is a retired member of the Coast Guard. He is described by Mr. Winthrop Stowell, whose preliminary report on the Morse River-Spirit Pond topography is referred to later in this chapter, as a highly respected member of the community whose comments and opinions are deemed reliable. The land on which the stones were discovered had been in the possession of the Oliver family until Lester Oliver sold it to the State of Maine recently. Mr. Oliver stated that he was "well acquainted with Mr. Elliott and his father and uncle, that they were sound, reliable people and not likely to be party to a fraud or deception in such a matter."

When Mr. Brown first viewed the stones he informed Elliott that the symbols appeared to be runic and that, if this is so, they were very important. He advised Elliott to seek expert help. Elliott tried to do just that but the results were surprisingly unsatisfactory. Despite the fact that he strongly dislikes writing letters, he is reported to have sent letters which told of his discovery to about a hundred persons and institutions in a vain effort to enlist their interest and assistance. Among them were a number of museums. He also brought the stones personally to museums. Among them was the Peabody Museum at Harvard University. At no time did he receive any meaningful attention or assistance.

To say that Elliott's experience has been typical in this field is not to explain it and certainly not to excuse it. It is reminiscent of a similar experience which Mr. Mongé had after his monumental discovery of Norse dated puzzles. In 1966 he made up a report of about thirty pages with a dozen or so of his earliest solutions. He mailed copies to eighteen scholars who were active in the field of the Norse language and history and who, presumably, should have been interested. About six weeks later he mailed a second report with some additions.

The result of this effort was a solitary reply from the author. We have worked as a team ever since that time. It has been an unusually productive division of labors.

It was at this juncture that Elliott mailed a letter with information of his discovery to the Landsverk Foundation with the request that, if possible, the inscriptions should be translated. Even a cursory examination showed that a translation, if any existed, would be piecemeal. On the other hand, the partial transcription, which Elliott originally provided, showed evidences of the presence of cryptography.

When an urgent request was made to him on behalf of the Foundation to make the stones available for examination and transcription, he reluctantly complied. A transcription reached Mr. Mongé during the last half of August. He promptly determined that the inscriptions were heavily laden with cryptography, that their author was Henricus, the first bishop to Greenland and Vinland, and that the date, which together with the name was repeated in many different parts of the inscriptions, was October 6, 1123. There were also repeated references to a sailing of 34 days and 68 days, the latter number apparently including the return journey.

At this point the author must make a confession. For many years he has been hampered by deficient eyesight. When he undertook to transcribe the inscriptions, he overlooked a considerable number of quite short and inconspicuous cuts which later turned out to be cryptographically significant. Some of the cuts were attached directly to several runes. Others overlined runes so as to identify them for special cryptographic purposes. As a result Mr. Mongé was unable to solve some parts of the cryptography with which the inscriptions abound.

After the errors in the transcriptions had been revealed, the first reaction was that the stones should have been sent to Mongé. He would probably have discovered the missing cuts. More mature reflection, however, shows that this would have been a mistake. As the only person who can solve, to say nothing of construct, such complex Norse puzzles, he would have been accused of "finding" such cuts as he needed them.

As matters now stand, Mongé has not yet seen the stones. The missed cuts have been gradually revealed over many months by persons from the New England area who have been asking for a translation of the visible texts which, in fact, does not exist. They could not possibly have known that the main thrust of the *cryptographic procedures* was concealed in these obscure and almost invisible cuts.

Some of the cuts were eventually discovered by Mongé himself in very fine photographs which were later provided by Richard O. Card. He is a Boston banker who also undertook to guide Mr. Elliott in the tribulations which resulted from his discovery of the three runestones.

This is written to put the record straight. It precludes any possibility that anyone, who could remotely be suspected of being able to construct this very sophisticated cryptography, had the opportunity to do so.

The three stones have been named Spirit Pond Numbers 1, 2, and 3. (SP 1,2,3). One of the most interesting features of these inscriptions is found on one side of SP 1. It was Mr. Harold Brown who first called attention to the fact that it contains an outline map of the area in which the stones were discovered. And it is just as interesting that, over the spot on the map where the stones were discovered, the same name is carved as the sagas give to one of Thorfinn Karlsefni's camps more than a century before Henricus reached the shores of Vinland. On the map are also the runes VINLAND and the year number 1011 A.D. Actually, the year numbers 1010 and 1011 are carved on the Spirit Pond stones a total of four times.

The great historical significance of these interrelated details is that the historians believe that Thorfinn Karlsefni and his party attempted to establish a permanent colony in Vinland during the same years. Karlsefni's Hóp was a landlocked tidal estuary as is Spirit Pond.

Several months passed before Mr. Mongé was certain that he had discovered and solved all of the cryptography in the three *transcriptions*. Meanwhile, no translations were forthcoming other than a word or two scattered here and there. Their function was quite obviously to distract attention from the secret messages.

This lack of a translation was not acceptable to Elliott. Because he did not know, or believe, that many dated puzzles both in Scandinavia and the United States can not be translated, he became progressively more frustrated and demanded that the stones be returned to him promptly. Because they were presumably his property, this was done.

About this time the State of Maine learned that the stones had been discovered on state land and were, by law, state property. Thereupon, its legal division demanded their return. Elliott had spent much time and a substantial sum of money in his campaign to learn what the inscriptions were and their significance. By this time he had also been offered a sum of several thousand dollars for the stones by persons who could have no idea how valuable they really were.

When the state threatened to prosecute him in order to force the return of the stones, Elliott's frustration overcame his better judgment. He wrapped the stones carefully in a plastic bag and buried them near the site at which they had been discovered. Then he dashed off a telegram to Mr. John Briggs, historian of the Maine Park and Recreation Commission, and informed him of what he had done. A careful search of the area convinced Mr. Brown of Bath Marine Museum that the stones were well concealed and might never be rediscovered.

The climax came when Elliott, still in high dudgeon, returned to his home, called a press conference and announced: "Now let some other damn fool dig them up!" This made a fine headline for a UPI article which saw wide distribution.

Thus Mr. Elliott had his "revenge" but, predictably, not for long. His action was displeasing to virtually everyone and this, probably, included Elliott himself. Persuasion, and the threat of prosecution, caused him to change his mind in the early part of February, 1972. He recovered the stones and turned them over to the state—but not without conditions. He requested that the stones be on display at Bath Marine Museum at least three months each year. He also demanded a sum of money as repayment for his outlay and efforts. Since the state could not use taxpayers' money to pay for property already owned, the money had to be raised privately.

As a result of this settlement, Elliott did what he had said that he intended to do from the first. He presented the stones

to the museum authorities in Maine. Whereupon everyone presumably was happy. In a letter to the author on February 4,
1972, Mr. Elliott expressed his relief: "Now that I have been
able to get out of hiding, so to speak, from reporters and people,
I write to say I hope I haven't offended you and Mr. Mongé
during this whole situation." He had not, but his actions had
concerned us and many others considerably.

Mr. Winthrop M. Stowell is president of the Freeport, Maine,
Historical Society. After a preliminary investigation of the Morse
River-Spirit Pond area he made these observations:

"The site at which the stones were discovered is situated at
the west end of the dam at the outlet of Spirit Pond. It contains
considerable water at low tide due to a natural ledge barrier.
During a few years of the early 1800's there was a dam which
consisted of two rows of quarried granite about fifteen feet
apart. Between them was an earth fill which is now completely
washed away.

"The shore of the lake at the spot where the stones were discovered is characterized by a ledge embankment topped by a
thin layer of soil from a foot to eighteen inches thick which
extends from the tide line to about 15 feet inshore. There the
ledge again crops up and rises, rather steeply, to a height of
about 30-50 feet with no topsoil and only a clump or two of
juniper."

These two paragraphs roughly define the terrain in the
immediate area where the stones were discovered. Whether this
was the exact location where they were carved and originally
deposited is, of course, not known. However, the site of the discovery is near the center of the outline map of SP 1. This spot
is marked HOOB and below it is the word VINLAND and
the year 1011 A.D. The conclusion seems to be that Henricus
knew that about 112 years earlier this had been Karlsefni's
camp, which the sagas call Hóp.

The outline map covers an east-west distance of only about
five miles. Therefore, it is reasonable to assume that any habita-
tion sites, anchorages, or graves should be somewhere in the

neighborhood. It is of course possible that the Karlsefni party wintered over in the area, and that no Norsemen had occupied it until Henricus rediscovered it over a century later but this does not seem likely. The much more probable assumption is continued occupancy. Whether one or the other happened will considerably affect the prospects of discovering additional artifacts.

In this connection it is interesting to see what *The Saga of Erik The Red* has to say about the site which is there called Hóp. This was the second and most southerly of the two permanent camps which Karlsefni established in Vinland. To it he took a portion of his expedition. The remainder, including his wife Gudrid and their son Snorri, remained at their first camp which was called Straumfjord.

"Karlsefni sailed southward along the coast and Snorri and Bjarni and the rest of the crew went with him. They sailed for a long time and in the end they got into a river that came from the up-country and fell first into a lake and from there into the sea. There were big banks of gravel at the mouth of the river, and it was impossible to get up the river except at high tide. Karlsefni and his men sailed into the river mouth and called the place Hóp."[1]

Offhand, this is not a bad description of Morse River even today. The observations that are recorded in the sagas are believed to have been made in 1010 or 1011 A.D. The three sections of SP 3 end with AHR 1010, AHR 1011, and AHR 1011. Ahr was the word for "year." These all testify that Henricus believed, when he constructed his Spirit Pond cryptopuzzles in 1123 A.D., that this had been Karlesfni's Hóp.

The exact classification of the stones on which the Spirit Pond runes are carved must await examination by geologists. However, a superficial inspection suggests that SP 1 and SP 2, which are dark blue in color, are very fine grained igneous rocks whose surfaces have been smoothed either by glacial action or by water. They are quite hard. SP 3 is bluish-gray in color, is sedimentary in origin, and distinctly layered to the extent that a slight amount of jarring could easily shatter it. The stone would probably be classified as shale.

Naturally, it is the width, depth, and shapes of the cuts that form the runes which are of the greatest interest. They will undoubtedly be examined with great care now that the stones are again available for study. A few preliminary observations which it was possible to make while the stones were in the possession of the Foundation will be recorded here.

For runic inscriptions the cuts are unusually fine, being about .020" to .030" wide and a little more than one-half as deep. The bottoms of the grooves are rounded and their surfaces are quite smooth. No evidence of the use of a punch or a chisel can be observed. This seems to imply that they were scraped out with a relatively dull point or edge. With the softer material in SP 3 this may have been quite easy. It would have been more tedious with SP 1 and SP 2.

The grooves have a patina which, in many places, seems to be as deep as on neighboring areas. (In some spots the patina has been worn off the surface but is still present in the grooves. This presumably happened in more recent times.)

Geologists are usually very reluctant to estimate the age of a cut by its weathering and patina because, in any given case, the conditions of exposure are often not well known. In the case of the Spirit Pond stones the history of the exposure is entirely unknown. Therefore, a reasonably accurate estimate of the age of the inscriptions on that basis may not be possible.

Examination of the grooves under a microscope confirmed the shape of the grooves. It also revealed a considerable residue at the bottom of the grooves of what Mr. Brown called rock-weed. Parts of its branched stems, which are about one-tenth the width of the grooves (about 0.003") still cling firmly to the bottom of the grooves.

One thing appears to be reasonably certain. The grooves are so fine and the weathering so slight that the stones must have been protected from the elements most of the time after their inscriptions were carved.

There are several ways by which this might have happened. The most obvious is that the stones were deliberately buried in the ground or were covered with debris and soil which was windblown or deposited by water. The first seems unlikely in view of the fact that a runic cryptogram was not made to be concealed. Quite the contrary. But, of course, neither were the Dead Sea scrolls written in order to be hidden in caves. That was presumably brought on by subsequent unfavorable events.

Except for those that are extremely durable, artifacts must be covered or, with the passage of time, they will be destroyed. Geologists say that, when a stone surface has been covered by soil, erosion and weathering are extremely slow. This could account for the slight weathering, especially of SP 3.

There is another possible theory, however, which is intriguing. Runic inscriptions were sometimes mounted, for protection, in small piled rock turrets which are known as cairns. Two very interesting examples are known.

The first is the carved inscription which the early French trader Sieur de la Vérendrye found mounted in a cairn in, or near, a Mandan Indian village along the Missouri in North Dakota, in 1738 A.D. This stone was later lost in France and has not been recovered. However, Jesuit scholars studied it in Quebec and said they thought it was Tataric. Since the Tatars of Asia Minor and the Germanic people both borrowed much of their alphabet from the Greeks, the two alphabets are quite similar. In La Vérendrye's time no one was aware that the Norsemen could have been anywhere near the Missouri River. After the Kensington inscription was discovered in 1898 there has been speculation that the La Vérendrye inscription may have been runic. Recent evidence strongly supports the view that Norsemen did, in fact, reach parts of the Dakotas. This question is discussed in Chapter 15.

The second inscription that had been mounted in a cairn has, in addition, intriguing similarities to the Spirit Pond carvings. The Kingigtorssuaq cryptopuzzle, which has been discussed previously, was carved in 1244 A.D., 121 years after Henricus constructed his puzzles in Maine. It was discovered in northern Greenland in 1824 A.D. and brought to Copenhagen for study.

At the site of the Kingigtorssuaq find was the rubble from three cairns which had apparently been used as navigational signals. It was concluded that the stone had been mounted in one of the cairns.

FIGURE 86

Copy of the Kingigtorssuaq inscription. From Grønlands Historiske Mindesmerker. Volume 3, pl. 9, 1843.

Figure 86 is a reproduction of a carefully drawn sketch which was made of the Kingigtorssuaq inscription in 1843 A.D. A comparison with photographs of SP 1 and 2 on pages 186 and 193 respectively in Chapter 11, and the sketch of the inscription on SP 3 on page 205 of Chapter 12, is interesting. It shows that, in all cases, the grooves of which their runes are formed are very narrow. For example 37 runic symbols and five spacer points occupy only 3½ inches in line 2 of the Kingigtorssuaq carving. The inscription has been generally accepted as authentic. It had long been reported to have been lost but has very recently been rediscovered by the National Museum[2] of Denmark at Copenhagen. This opens up the possibility to arrange to have it compared directly with the Spirit Pond carvings. It might be possible, for example, to determine whether they had been carved by the use of the same techniques. Such an examination would be particularly interesting since the Spirit Pond and Kingigtorssuaq inscriptions were, according to their dated cryptograms, carved in 1123 and 1244 A.D., respectively, only 121 years apart.

Other intriguing questions which such an examination might answer are whether the grooves on the Kingigtorssuaq stone are similar to their Spirit Pond counterparts in other respects such as their depth, cross section, smoothness and evidences of toolmarks.

Both runemasters were quite certainly Greenlanders at the time that they cut their inscriptions in northern Greenland and Vinland. It appears to be appropriate at this point to suggest again that Henricus, the most prolific puzzlemaster who is yet known, certainly kept a file of the most effective procedures which could be employed in making Norse puzzles. That the same procedures are found over the entire domain of the puzzle-masters, even though they are often separated by centuries, could only have happened if records of Norse cryptography were made and preserved.

What could have been a more logical place for such a repository than Gardar, the site of the bishopric? It was the special mission of Henricus to establish the bishopric in Greenland. The prize items in his file on cryptography may well have been his Vinland map cryptopuzzles. His records, including notes and copies of his work in Norse cryptography, must certainly have been brought to Gardar when the bishopric was established there.

These circumstances establish the probability that the rune-master of the Kingigtorssuaq cryptopuzzle had available to him a record of the cryptographic efforts of Henricus. A part of the record may have been copies of SP 1, 2, and 3 with their unusually narrow grooves. Only by the use of such narrow grooves could the Kingigtorssuaq inscription have been carved on such a small stone. The same is true, of course, of the Spirit Pond carvings.

CHAPTER 11

A Twelfth-century New England Mapmaker

Three outline maps which are shown on page 179 are of the Phippsburg area of Maine within which the three Spirit Pond stones were discovered in 1971. At the right is the Kennebec River estuary. The scale of each map has been adjusted so they are approximately the same. At the upper left is a copy of the outline map which is carved on one of the stones, Spirit Pond No. 1. Below it is a reproduction of a map of the area which was made by the explorer Champlain in 1604 A.D. An outline tracing of a recent map of the same area by the Geological Survey will be found at the upper right.

It was Mr. Harold Brown, Curator of Bath Marine Museum, who first called attention to the fact that Spirit Pond No. 1 contains a map of the area within which the Spirit Pond stones were discovered. There can be no doubt about the correspondence of the main features in spite of the faulty dimensions of SP 1, and the changes in topography which 850 years may have brought about. Long Island is situated in its correct position in the Kennebec River estuary. Morse River and Spirit Pond are also correctly placed even though they are drawn, as is the entire map, with little regard for accuracy in detail.

In his SP 1 outline, Henricus did not observe the modern convention about the orientation of maps. As it is represented here, the outline of SP 1 has been rotated 90 degrees in order to have north directed upward. This causes the four runes HOOB, which are carved over the spot on the map at which the stones were found, to read vertically down.

Except for the map itself, it can not now be known what

178

FIGURE 87

Three Maps From The Phillipsburg, Maine, Area

• Site of find.
• Spirit Pond.
• Morse River.
• Popham Beach.
• Atkins Bay.
Kennebec
  Estuary.
Long Island.

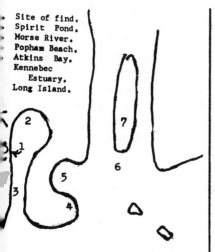

From Spirit Pond No. 1.
(1123 A.D.)

From the Geological Survey.
(1959 A.D.)

Champlain's Map.
(1604 A.D.)

Vinland
without the
"pen - squiggles".

Greenland and Vinland—from VM.
(1122 A.D.)

opportunity Henricus had for becoming acquainted with the
area which he represented on SP 1. In the case of the Champlain map it is known that it was drawn from only one point of
observation. This may have shut off parts of the landscape from
view. The report also indicates that visibility was hampered by
persistent fogs. These things may explain the total absence, near
the left-hand edge of the map, of Morse River and Spirit Pond.
Henricus may have suffered from similar handicaps.

Both the Champlain map and SP 1 show serious errors in
proportions. Curiously, this is, in both cases, most evident in
their central areas. In the Champlain map, Atkins Bay extends
too far to the south so it almost cuts Popham Beach off from
the mainland. In SP 1, the error goes in the opposite direction.
Popham Beach is shown too small and does not extend far
enough to the east and north. As a result, Atkins Bay could not
be located in its correct northeast to southwest orientation between Popham Beach and Spirit Pond.

There is a great deal of difference in the techniques that
must be used in cutting a map into stone, such as was done in
the case of SP 1, and drawing a map on parchment or paper.
In a stone carving the fine details must necessarily be omitted.
However, there is also grave doubt whether Henricus was interested in details. The SP 1 map was almost certainly only a
backdrop for, and distraction from, the very extensive cryptography which is hidden in SP 1, 2, and 3.

At the lower right of the page is a tracing of the outlines of
Greenland and Vinland as they appear in the Vinland Map. The
outline of Vinland is like the outline map in SP 1 in one basic
respect. This is the lack of detail in both. (There is a deceptive
element here which, once it is removed, makes the similarity
clear. This is the arbitrary squiggles which characterize the
entire coastline of Vinland. That they are arbitrary, and have
no relation to the contours of the coasts which they purport to
represent, is evident from the west side of the outline. This is
a fictitious boundary. Yet it is drawn with the same wavy pattern as is the east coast. The squiggles, which could easily be

drawn with a pen on parchment, have no relation to the geography.

Only crude and badly distorted representations of Hudson Strait and Bay and of the Saint Lawrence estuary, all supplied with arbitrary squiggles, indicate that the mapmaker had any familiarity with the northeastern shores of North America. It has, therefore, been assumed that he drew an outline of Vinland because he knew that it was there, either from personal observation or from the accounts of others. On the other hand, it has also been assumed that he knew so little about the details of the shoreline that he could not even identify Helluland, Markland, and Vinland as separate entities.

This view is now known to be incorrect. By the time Henricus returned to Greenland in 1122 A.D. and constructed his VM cryptopuzzle, he had coursed the shores of Vinland, in New England, several times. His mission was of such a nature that he would have become well acquainted with its major features. He may have sailed directly from Greenland to southern Labrador but he must have sailed outside or inside Newfoundland and had followed the coasts of Nova Scotia and northern Maine on his way to Vinland. They may have been counted as a part of Vinland as may, in fact, Newfoundland and Labrador.

Henricus was certainly familiar with many major features of what he identified, but only by inference in Legend 66, as Vinland. We seem here to come back to the same principle which applies to cryptopuzzles in general. The text and extraneous features are merely vehicles for hiding the cryptography and for serving as decoys. Henricus was probably only mildly interested in drawing a meaningful map of Vinland. But he needed a prop which could serve as an excuse, and support, for his cryptographically loaded Legend 66. The lack of meaningful details was, in all probability, intended as a gentle hint that here may be more than meets the eye.

It is not difficult to imagine the feelings that motivated the puzzlemasters in this respect. The puzzles must be constructed and concealed so they were not too easy to discover and solve.

On the other hand, if they were too well hidden, they may never have been found. This dilemma could, of course, never be entirely overcome. It could only be met by a compromise.

The outline map of SP 1 is presumably also not a map in the conventional sense. It provided a fitting framework for Henricus to state, in a secret message, that he had sailed 34 days, October 6, 1123 A.D. It also identified the area as Karlsefni's Hóp. Taken together, this is a weighty historical burden for one small stone to carry.

These conclusions must be reconciled somehow with the accurate detail with which Henricus drew his outline of Greenland. The explanation may be quite straightforward. By the time Henricus constructed his VM cryptopuzzle, the details of the shores of Greenland had been well known to the Greenlanders for more than a century. It may well be that an "official" map of Greenland was in existence. If not, competent navigators, who knew the coastline of Greenland intimately from long association with it, may have helped to draw the outline. In Chapter 8 it was also suggested that Henricus himself may have been familiar with the elements of the mapmaker's art.

The five inscribed surfaces on Spirit Pond 1, 2, and 3 were conceived as a three-in-one multipart cryptopuzzle. Their puzzle nature is clearly evident throughout the whole of the inscribed texts.

At least as early as 1114 A.D. Henricus had been aware that his eight-rune latinized name, but spelled with a K, offered exceptional opportunities for creating a unique, highly personalized trademark for his runic puzzles. His first known puzzle which used this trademark was PB 1 (see Chapter 9). This stone is located at Popham Beach where the Kennebec estuary joins the Atlantic about two miles due east of the Spirit Pond site.

In Chapter 9 attention was called to the fact that, by arranging the letters HIK-S in a clockwise direction around the ends of the Greek cross, the following figure results (see Figure 88 on next page):

FIGURE 88

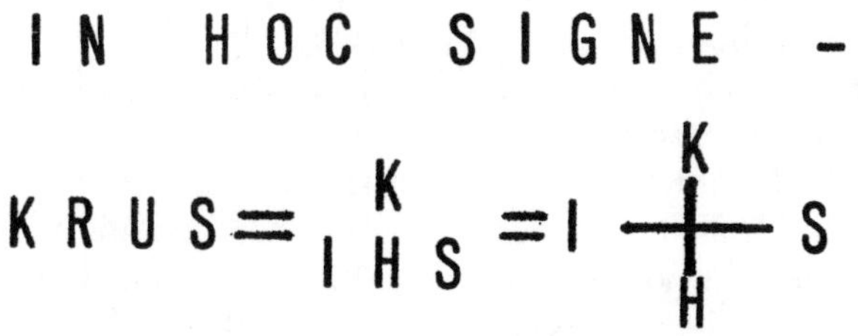

I N   H O C   S I G N E   –

K R U S $=$ $\dfrac{K}{I H S}$ $= I \;\dfrac{K}{\underset{H}{\vert}}\; S$

This is the ancient Latin motto which refers to the crucifixion of Christ. The remaining letters in HENRIKUS are R-U-N-E. Henricus always kept the basic IHS-K intact and distributed the remaining four letters in randomly selected positions so as to form pairs with the first four. This procedure was applied in each of the four cryptopuzzles by Henricus which were analyzed in Chapter 9.

The cryptographic effectiveness of this unique trademark is evident. By its use he managed to call attention to his religious profession (IHS-K), his hobby (RUNEMUNK), and his name. His cryptographic competence is evident throughout.

In the Spirit Pond carvings the principal purpose was to record that HENRIKUS SIKLA, that is, Henricus sailed. He repeats this five times in puzzle form but the Norse word, SIKLA, is present in his visible text, in its normal unscrambled form, only once. This is in line 10 of SP 3 which reads SIKLA SKIBI, that is, "sailed the ship."

This normal form of SIKLA is a clue. It tells the potential solver that the several *scrambled* forms of the word, which appear in the three inscriptions, signal the presence of a nearby, significant group of runes. This group delivers the principal secret message which reads, in whole or in part, "Henrikus sailed 34 days October 6, 1123 A.D."

After he had chosen SIKLA as the theme of his cryptopuzzle, Henrikus was virtually compelled to use a cover text that featured some form of travel. Hence, *the cover text contains no particular truth.* The visible text was concocted merely to serve as concealment for the secret messages.

The Kensington inscription presents an identical situation. The text contains seven numbers, 8, 2, 2, 2, 10, 14, and 10 as well as the year number 1362. These are all calendrical indicators which confirm in the perpetual calendar the date Sunday, April 24, 1362. There were no doubt Goths and Norwegians in the party but not necessarily 8 and 22 as is stated in the text. The whole story may be true in a general way but one thing only is certain. The numbers had to be those that are used in order to confirm the date—and he saw to it that they were.

In his four earliest puzzles, the numerical values of the runes that spell Henrikus confirmed their dates. .In the Spirit Pond puzzles, the 23 in the year 1123 had to be expressed in some other way. His name could not give the right numerical values. This is the reason that he chose SIKLA. It serves very well. The S in SIKLA provides the 11 and the combination of I (=9) and L (=14) gives the sum 23. Together, they indicate 1123 A.D. When his name is included, this appears as an associated transposition cipher.

The word SIKLA, and the date October 6, also had other advantages. The numerical values of K and A in SIKLA are 6 and 10 respectively. This represents the 6th day of the 10th month, which is October 6. In addition, the calendar shows DDL=6 and DGN=10 for October 6. *The date is therefore self-verifying!* This shows that there can be no doubt that October 6 was selected because it could be easily and neatly cryptogrammed. If October 6 was also an important day in the life of Henricus, such as the date on which he set sail or returned, or if it had some important connection with the history of Vinland, so much the better. But, if so, this can not now be proved.

Scrambled spellings of SIKLA are found once on the back of SP 1, once in SP 2, and three times in SP 3. The SP 3 "text" is written in three sections. They end with the pentathic numbers 1010, 1011, and 1011. While these numbers are a necessary part of the cryptography, they also are two of the years which historians believe that Thorfinn Karlsefni and his party spent in Vinland. That the year number 1011 is also associated with the map of Karlsefni's camp Hóp in SP 1, is certainly no coincidence. It is another instance in which Henricus, in common with other puzzlemasters, managed it so that his cryptographic details served more than one purpose.

The pentathic system alone can not express numbers as large as these. However, the decimal system is used in virtually all of the many dozens of dated puzzles which Mongé has solved. In the three parts of SP 3 the year numbers are expressed as follows:

FIGURE 89

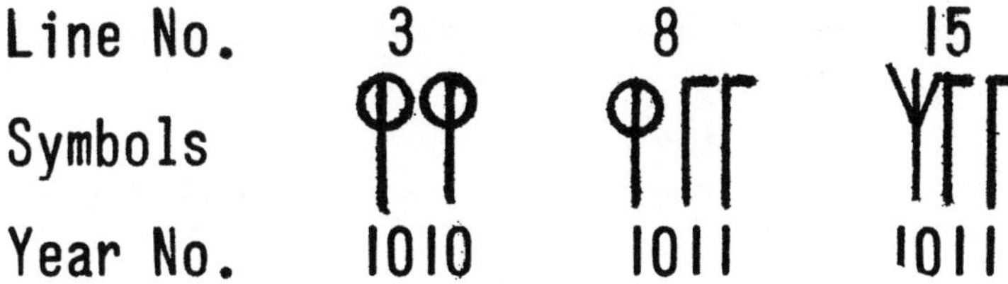

Line No.	3	8	15
Symbols	ΦΦ	ΦΓΓ	ΨΓΓ
Year No.	1010	1011	1011

The use in Line 15 of the rune M, whose numerical value is 15, was a deft cryptographic touch which requires an explanation. It actually represents the Roman numeral M whose numerical value is 1000. The three symbols, therefore, do represent 1011 A.D.

It so happens that, in this case, the pentathic symbol for 10, which was used in Lines 3 and 5, could not be used. The reason is cryptographic and will be explained later.

A.   Spirit Pond Number 1

In several respects SP 1 offers the most important information of the three stones. Even though it does not contain the name Henricus, it has several very significant features. The most intriguing is, of course, the outline map and that it is marked HOOB (HÓP). Below the four runes is the word VINLAND

FIGURE 90

Front   Back
A six-inch ruler indicates the dimensions.

and the year number 1011 A.D. It is as if Henricus wished to make certain that it was understood that this had been a part of early eleventh-century Vinland. The three Spirit Pond cryptopuzzles also suggest that this may have been an important port of call for Henricus himself, if it was not actually his headquarters.

On the same side of SP 1 is this inscription:

FIGURE 91

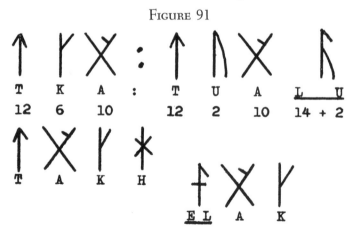

The eight runes in Line 1 appear to have no meaning in medieval Norse. However, they are cryptographically significant in two ways and take part in a third use. The last two runes are combined. This reduced the line into two groups which are separated by double points as three symbols followed by four symbols. This indicates the number 34. Since the four runes in Line 2, TAKH, means "days," the translation up to this point is "34 days."

Of course, the number 34 could have been indicated by any group of three and four symbols whatever. However, the special significance of these particular eight runes is not far to seek. Their numerical values add up to 68 which is twice 34. The association of 68 with 34 in this manner is found several times in the Spirit Pond inscriptions. It is natural to assume that it means 34 days and 68 days.[1]

The significance appears to be this. The arrow points south when the map is properly oriented. It presumably is intended to indicate that Henricus, during the summer of 1123 A.D., had sailed south along the coast for 34 days. There was no opportunity to say how much he had stopped along the way. A ship, such as the one he was probably using, could cover eighty miles during daylight hours with favorable winds. He could have reached the southern tip of Florida in 34 days at an average distance of less than 50 miles per day. This is not to suggest that he did so.

It is the three symbols in Line 3 which carry the bulk of the cryptography. This is our first encounter with a puzzle pattern which is found five or six times in the Spirit Pond carvings. The solution will therefore be analyzed rather carefully.

Line 3 has four of the five runes that spell the word SEKLA. The word means "sailed." Henricus seems to have preferred the spelling SIKLA, but, as here, when he wished to combine the I with an L, he had to change the I into an E by adding the crossbar. Had he not done so, all of the rune would have disappeared into the L. The change did not affect the cryptography because the word still had the same meaning and the numerical values of the runes E and I are the same.

We note that the S to spell SEKLA is still missing. Because there is good reason to believe that Henricus needed the S here, we try to find where he has it hidden. This turns out to be another case which resembles the John (under) wood (and over) Mass puzzle which was solved at the beginning of Chapter 9. The numerical value of the missing rune S is 11. There are a total of 11 *symbols* in Lines 1 and 2 so that the S is indicated by stating its numerical value! Let us therefore add the S to the four runes ELAK in Line 3 and see what happens:

FIGURE 92

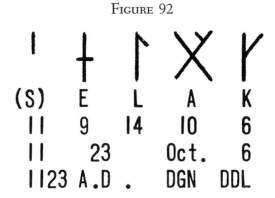

The S gives us the numerical value 11. The numerical values of the E and L have the sum 23 (9 + 14 = 23). The numbers 11 and 23 then combine to form the year number 1123 A.D. by a procedure which is found dozens of times in Norse dated puzzles.

The last two runes, A (=10) and K (=6), indicate the day. This could mean the 10th day of the 6th month (June 10), or the 6th day of the 10th month (October 6). The question is quickly resolved when it is observed in the calendar that, for October 6, DGN=10, and DDL=6. In other words, the day is self-confirming in the calendar! This makes it also certain that the date was chosen because of this very desirable property from the point of view of cryptography. If the date also happened to represent an important day in the life of Henricus, this was a bonus. But this we can not now know.

Henceforth, when we see the five scrambled runes that spell the word SIKLA, or SEKLA, we will know that Henricus is once again affirming the message, "sailed, October 6, 1123 A.D." Usually, the name Henrikus will be found nearby, or entwined with SEKLA, but invariably scrambled by the use of a transposition pattern such as the four such patterns that were analyzed in Chapter 9.

L here has the value 14 instead of 15 because Henricus used an alphabet in which L preceded M just as it did in the Roman alphabet. This change was made in the runic alphabet about the year 1100 A.D. It could probably be taken for granted that Henricus was abreast of the times in such matters.

On the reverse side of SP 1 is a group of eight runes which transpose to MILTIAKI. This is, also, not a Norse word or name. It will be shown that the secret meaning is "observed by me" or "beheld by me."

What Henricus had observed he shows by sketches which surround the runes. They include a flower, bush, fish, bird, deer, snake, Indian, an Indian paddling a canoe, a bow and arrow, and a skin. This is a representative selection from the fauna and flora of New England.

It has been suggested that these are Indian petroglyphs. This is not so for several reasons. They surround the runes MIL-TIAKI and there is more Norse cryptography below the figures. It is apparent that the cryptography was fitted to the figures, both above and below, and vice versa. The figures are also carved with lines of identical width, depth, and cross section. There is nothing to show that more than one carver was involved. It is also very doubtful that the Indians of the area ever carved such fine lines on hard stone.

Below the figures Henricus placed clues to the solution of MILTIAKI (see Figure 93 on next page):

FIGURE 93

The symbolic message of these figures is about as follows: "In MILTIAKI above, four incomplete and currently meaningless pairs of runes (as indicated by the half-length rungs on the ladder) are to be converted into four complete and meaningful pairs of runes (the four complete rungs). This is to be accomplished by the application of the Saint Andrew's Cross on the left. The excess stroke from one to the other upper limb of the cross is significant."

The excess stroke points out that something special is present at this location—something that is *not* present at the lower end of the cross.

Why did Henricus now change over to the Saint Andrew's Cross? The reason seems to be that he repeatedly used the Latin cross to cryptogram HENRIKUS. MILTIAKI does not contain his name. Note: If the above symbols are rejected as a clue to the solution, they have no purpose. This would make no sense. The solution is unaffected in any case.

The four pairs of runes, as they are carved on the back of SP 1, are:

FIGURE 94

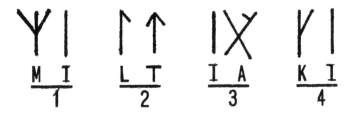

These pairs of runes were arranged by Henricus at the extremities of the Saint Andrew's Cross just as he repeatedly arranged the eight letters of his own name on the Latin Cross.

FIGURE 95

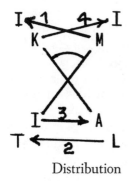

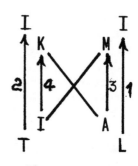

| Distribution | Transposition |

Note again that the distribution of the pairs is symmetrical. The special feature *which was signaled at the top of the Saint Andrew's Cross* is now apparent. In carrying out the distribution the indicating arrows are crossed above but not below.

The conversion to the original plaintext, which became the secret message, is shown by the numbered arrows in the figure at the right. Note that the conversion is also completely symmetric. This is a basic requirement in a transposition cipher. Without such symmetry there is no cipher. When symmetry exists, the probability that this happened by accident is very small in any given case. When the symmetry is found in one transposition after the other, this probability becomes zero.

The eight letters that come out of the transposition spell out the three Norse words LITI A MIK. The meaning is "Seen by

FIGURE 96

$$\underset{1}{\underline{L\ I}}\quad\underset{2}{\underline{T\ I}}\quad\underset{3}{\underline{A\ M}}\quad\underset{4}{\underline{I\ K}}$$

me" or "Beheld by me." What was it that Henricus had observed? It was obviously the items which he had illustrated on the same side of the stone—the fauna and flora of Vinland.²

The basic reason that Henricus confined his message to eight runes was that the Saint Andrew's Cross has four arms. Therefore, in order to avoid complications he could use only multiples of four runes. The transpositions on the Jesus Christ Cross in the Gol ciphers in Chapter 6 shows that Henricus had other options. The reason that he used only eight runes may also have been to mislead the solver into a futile search for the eight letters in his own name. His name appears in numerous other places.

Note: In symmetrical transposition patterns such as squares, rectangles, stars, crosses, etc., it can happen that two or even more systematically followed transposition routes will produce exactly the same *obviously correct message from the same cipher text.* In most such cases it is rarely possible to determine which route was originally used unless additional information is available. Usually this situation is not of great concern. The analyst can console himself with the knowledge that he has the correct end result.

This is the case with the four pairs of runes in MILTIAKI and the resultant plaintext LITI Á MIK. However, for several reasons the route that is used in the transcription above seems to be the most logical. It seems reasonable that Henricus, who never missed a chance to use a cross in one way or another— the more the merrier—joined the upper limbs of the Saint Andrew's Cross in order to indicate that something special and unique is present at this top position—something that is not present elsewhere among the pairs of runes that are inserted. This was the "crossed pairs."

B.   Spirit Pond Number 2

The stone is about five inches long. It has a dark blue color, is very fine grained and appears to be of igneous origin. The rounded form indicates that it was probably transported to this area during the last glacial period.

FIGURE 97

There are two lines of runes. The visible text, as usual, has no meaning:

FIGURE 98

In Line 2, we see again the five runes which, when rearranged, spell the word SEKLA. Again the runes E and L are combined. It was shown above that this combination of runes means "Sailed, October 6, 1123 A.D."

The second symbol in Line 1 is also a combined rune:

FIGURE 99

$$\text{R} = \text{H} \text{ and } \text{R}$$

In each of the closely related puzzles on SP 1 and 3, Henricus furnished at least one more or less obvious clue to the solution of his secret messages. In SP 2, however, the clue is not very conspicuous, or as easy to perceive, as was, for example, the "cross and ladder" on the back of SP 1.

In this inscription the principal clue to the secret message is the combined rune in Line 1. Here a rune O, of numerical value 4, was attached to the rune R in order to point out that the R is actually the 4th letter in a secret message. The message must have the same length as the unreadable text in which it occurs, that is, 8 runes. (Originally, as with all solutions, this was only an assumption. It became fact when the solution later confirmed it.)

The question is, *what* 8-letter group? In view of the known fondness of Henricus for recording his own name, what guess could be more logical than that it is the eight runes of his own name? The fourth letter in HENRIKUS is, indeed, an R!

When the indicator, the rune O, has been eliminated, Line 1, transliterated into Latin letters, becomes: N R K S L O L K.

We shall find that the name HENRIKUS is present but, as the inscription now stands, only four letters of the name are present. They are the first four runes NRKS. The other four runes are invisible or, more correctly, they are transposed.

FIGURE 100

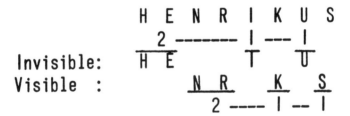

Before we proceed with the solution, it must be pointed out that Henricus had other fish to fry. It is seen that the eight runes were separated into visible and invisible groups so they form a double series of 2, 1, and 1. This suggests May 27 by ND=211. The matter will be discussed at the end of the chapter, but it is worth noting here that this is the only double left-to-right sequence 2-1-1 that can be arranged with eight letters.

In order to indicate the four additional runes that spell his name, Henrikus started with the four visible runes, NRKS. He used them to make counts in the 16-rune alphabet. It could be expected of Henricus that he would again use IHS-K to develop the numbers for this count. But he did not use the numerical values of the runes in IHS-K. Instead *he used the positional values of IHS-K in his own name.* The figure below shows that I is in the 5th place in his name, H in the 1st, K the 6th, and S the 8th.

FIGURE 101

H	E	N	R	I	K	U	S
1	2	3	4	5	6	7	8

Having in this way assigned numerical values to the four letters HIK-S, they were next distributed on the four arms of the Latin cross (See A below) in exactly the same order as they were distributed in earlier cryptopuzzles (Chapter 9).

FIGURE 102

A. Distribution   B. Transposition

It remains now to transpose the letters. This was done in the same order as a priest would move his hand when he said the benediction—from top to bottom and from right to left (See

B above). This generates the number series 6-1-8-5. This series will operate on the four visible letters from his name NRKS.

For the sake of convenience, the runic alphabet, in Latin letters is repeated here:

FIGURE 103

F	U	Th	O	R	K	H	N	I	A	S	T	B	L	M	Y
1	2	3	4	5	6	7	8	9	10	11	12	13	14	15	16

The count proceeds as follows in the order right, left, right, left from the letters NRKS in the alphabet.

Rune	Series Count	Direction	Indicated Rune
N	6	right	L
R	1	left	O
K	8	right	L
S	5	left	K

Now Henricus had the eight runes NRKS and LOLK which he carved in Line 1 of SP 1. The last four were derived from the four visible letters of his name by the use of his favorite device—a transposition cipher which he based on the Latin cross which he always associated with his own name. In this way the four invisible runes from his name, NRSK, were transformed into LOLK.

The second line in the inscription is again the five runes SELAK. They indicate, as before, "Sailed October 6, 1123 A.D." Note that here too, as elsewhere, 11 and 23 are adjacent to each other so as to invite the interpretation 1123 A.D.

Henricus could have arbitrarily chosen any four letters other than NRKS from his name. He apparently chose NRKS so as to produce the double sequence 2-1-1 for ND=211. If so, the date is May 27 but what would be its significance?

Any attempt at an answer must be speculative. It is perhaps most probable that May 27 in 1123 A.D. was the date that he set sail for the last time for Vinland from Greenland. His VM cryptopuzzle, which is dated August 23, 1122 A.D., must have been constructed in Greenland. This was probably too late in the year to undertake a sailing to Vinland. But by October of 1123 A.D. he was constructing and carving his SP 1, 2, and 3 runic puzzles in Vinland. He may have set sail for Vinland on May 27, 1123 A.D.

It is an interesting question why the Greenlanders were seeking a new bishop in Norway in 1123 A.D. when Henricus had apparently sailed to Vinland in the same year. Vinland was a part of the bishopric which he was trying to organize. Bishop Arnald was apparently sought in Norway in 1123 A.D., was consecrated by Ozur, Archbishop of Lund, which was then a part of Denmark, in 1124, and was installed in Greenland in 1125 A.D.[3]

Did the Greenlanders feel that Henricus was neglecting them with his three sailings to Greenland and long stays there? He was obviously trying to organize the church in Vinland. Did he, in fact, envision Vinland as his own special project, perhaps with a bishopric as an eventual goal? His actions seem to be consistent with such a plan. The action of the Greenlanders in seeking a new bishop, before they could possibly know of his death, suggests that the church authorities were acting according to some plan that would displace Henricus.

To pursue the matter one step farther, Legend 67 in VM seems to suggest something of the same nature. Henricus is lavish in his praise of the fine qualities of Vinland. He appears to have been happy to return there. VM does not mention his first visit to Vinland. But what prompted him to say, in Lines 7 to 9 of Legend 67 that he returned to Greenland *and then* "proceeded in most humble obedience to his superiors." We now know that he did, in fact, return to Vinland. His statement seems to say that he was ordered to return to Vinland by his "superiors." But there is nothing in the statement that implies that this was against his will.

Did his superiors, whoever they may have been, assign him to permanent duty in Vinland? The fact that a replacement was sought for him at the same time, in Greenland, can be so construed.[4]

These actions also seem to throw into doubt the belief that Henricus died soon after October of 1123 A.D. There is no longer a sound basis for such an assumption. It is possible that Henricus lived out his days in Vinland.

Who were the unnamed superiors whom Henricus said that he obeyed? They may have been the leaders of the Greenland colonies. It was they who sent emissaries to Norway to seek a new bishop. In those days the temporal power selected a candidate for bishop, and the Church, if it agreed in the choice, consecrated him. Henricus had been appointed in 1112 A.D. by the same Norwegian King Sigurd who appointed Arnald, his successor, in 1123 or 1124 A.D. In the temporal sense, the leaders of the Greenland colonies were both his superiors and his protectors.

There is, however, another possible interpretation. Henricus had reached Vinland as early as 1114 A.D. and had apparently found Norsemen scattered along a 300-mile-long coastline. His visit to Vinland, which is recorded in VM, was at least his second. There had been ample time for a report, which Henricus had undoubtedly written, to reach both the Archbishop at Lund and the Vatican. A reply could easily have reached Greenland by 1122 A.D. A suggestion from such a high source that Henricus should return to Vinland would have had the force of a command. This may well be the real answer to the problem.

The present chapter and that which follows deliver many cryptographic indications that Henricus made sailings of 34 and 68 days. For reasons which are stated, they have been interpreted by the author to refer to a voyage southward from the Spirit Pond site along the shores of what is now the United States. Mr. Mongé has recently uncovered two corroborating but independent cryptographic evidences which seem to prove that a different interpretation is correct. At the end of Legend No. 67 of the Vinland Map Henricus stated that he returned to Greenland *and then* "proceeded in most humble obedience to the will of his superiors." Mongé believes that this statement means that he complied with an order from the Vatican to report the status of the bishopric of Greenland-Vinland at the First Lateran Church Council which convened on March 18 of 1123 A.D. This would have required that he travel to Rome during the year 1122.

Since Henricus dated his Legend No. 67 August 23, 1122 A.D., it seems likely that he had already arrived in Rome before the legends and the outlines of Greenland and Vinland were written and drawn. (It would also have been possible for him to have returned to Vinland in time to complete and carve the inscriptions and map on SP 1, 2, and 3 by October 6, 1123 A.D.)

It would be strange if Henricus did not deliver a full written report to the Council. Such a report, together with the outline map of Greenland and Vinland and Legends No. 66 and 67, would certainly have been deposited at the Vatican library. There they may have been discovered and copied by the scribe who assembled the Vinland Map at the Church Council at Basle, Switzerland, in 1440 A.D. This leaves as a distinct possibility that the originals may still be found in the Vatican archives.

What then of the cryptographic indications? In Chapter 8 it was shown that Henricus indicated the year 1122 A.D. in Line 9 of Legend No. 67. In so doing the two letters U and I were spotlighted and their order reversed to IU as a part of the dating procedure. During medieval times the letters IU were used as an abbreviation for IPSE URBS, that is, "this city" and was exclusively used to indicate Rome. (In item 16 on page 130 of *The Vinland Map and the Tartar Relation* the word URBS is also interpreted to mean Rome. Furthermore, there were suggestions by the authors of VMTR that the author of Legend No. 67 meant to indicate that he had been ordered to sail to Europe but no corroborating evidence was cited.)

To this cryptographic indication Henricus apparently added

a second. The first letters of the eight words in Legend 66, taken in normal succession, spell out the two words VIA BRELS which seems to have no possible interpretation other than "by way of Brels." The only known town with this name is spelled Breles. However, as was noted in Chapter 8, Henricus could use only eight words in his Legend No. 66. The second letter e in Breles could be dropped without causing a misunderstanding. The hamlet of Breles is located on the inner end of a small bay on the extreme northwestern end of Brittany in France. Passage from Greenland to Rome by way of Breles would have provided the possibly shortest route since it would have avoided sailing around England on the east side.

These two indications, each constructed according to the best traditions of the Norse puzzlemasters, lend powerful force to the belief that Henricus had orders to travel to Rome and that this was the journey of which he hinted in the text of Legend No. 67 and which he confirmed by cryptographic means. It should be kept in mind that it was the cryptography which was the main reason for the existence of the legends and very probably also the outlines of Greenland and Vinland in VM.

CHAPTER 12

The Swan Song of a Bishop in Vinland

Very little of the visible text of SP 3 can be translated. Only a very few groups of two or three words have any meaning. The reason is that the text is only a vehicle for extensive cryptography. This is the sole reason for the existence of the inscription.

The first secret message of SP 3 begins with the first two groups of runes which are separated by double points in Line 1. The two groups contain eleven and five runes for a total of sixteen.

FIGURE 104

The last group of five symbols are by now familiar. They are the five runes that spell SIKLA and their numerical values indicate and confirm the date October 6, 1123 A.D. Again the I and L of numerical values 9 and 14 are adjacent to each other so they can express the number 23 in 1123 A.D. and the S, with numerical value 11, follows them.

In the first eleven runes a different system is in use. The key to the solution is the three overlined runes I, T, and Th. They serve both as counters of numerical values 9, 12, and 3 respectively, and as indicators of cryptographic procedures.

The three runes were inserted. They are not a part of the secret text. The text consists of the eight runes after the three overlined runes are removed. In the secret message, the eight will be supplemented by three runes from Line 2 and three

201

FIGURE 105

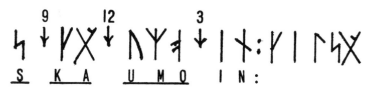

runs from Line 3. It is the function of the three overlined runes to point out which runes are to be selected from Lines 2 and 3.

In the figure above, the overlined runes *isolate* one, two, and three runes of the eight runes that supply the text in Line 1. This indicates that parts of the message are to be found in Lines 1, 2, and 3. But where? This the three overlined runes will point out.

Significant parts of Lines 1, 2, and 3 are reproduced in the figure below. Keeping in mind that the three overlined runes have values 9, 12, and 3, note this: from Line 1 there are 8 runes; the 9th position is occupied by a double point; the rune which is immediately below the double point becomes the 9th rune in the message; in Line 2 the 12th space is occupied by another double point; the rune which is immediately below it in Line 3 is the 12th rune in the message.

FIGURE 106

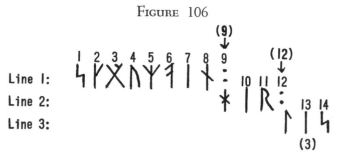

The first two of the three overlined runes have now served their purposes. Only the third, whose numerical value is 3, remains. Its function is to indicate that the number of runes that are to be taken from Line 3 is three.

We now have, as is shown in the figure below, a secret message of fourteen runes. It will be shown presently that the first eleven runes contain the name HENRIKUS. The sum of the numerical values of the last three runes is 34.

FIGURE 107

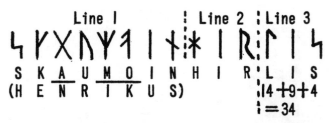

When to this is added the five runes KILSA in Line 1, the total message becomes: "Henrikus sailed, October 6, 1123, 34 [days]."

It will be noticed that three of the first eleven runes do not belong in the name HENRIKUS. These superfluous three are underlined in the figure. They spell the Latin word AMO which means "I love." This is, of course, no accident. It verifies that these three runes belong together, but are otherwise independent of the secret message.

Observe that three of the eight letters in the name HENRIKUS came from Line 2 so that only five were *needed* from Line 1. However, HENRIKUS needed *more than five runes* in Line 1 in order to separate them, as he did, in three groups of 1, 2, and 3 runes. This would require a minimum of six runes (1+2+3). He, therefore, chose to raise the number of runes from five to eight so that the extra three could convey some sort of meaning. They could be any runes whatever except one of the eight runes in HENRIKUS. It is characteristic of this dedicated bishop that he chose three letters which spelled out the key word in the Christian doctrine: AMO, I love.

No one will envy Mr. Mongé the task that he faced in solving this rather intricate puzzle. However, once the solution is known, almost anyone, given a little patience, can follow it and realize that it was carefully and intelligently arranged. It remains now to show how Henricus arranged his transposition cipher so as to scramble his name into the four pairs of letters SK-UI-NH-ER. They were transposed as follows:

FIGURE 108

Distribution   Transposition

The way in which Henricus transposed his name in this instance is shown in the two figures. The four runes, IHS–K, were first distributed on the Latin cross in the counterclockwise direction in the same positions as in the four transpositions which were analyzed in Chapter 9. The remaining runes, RUNE, were then paired with them as indicated by the arrows in the figure at the left. This completed the distribution. In the figure at the right, the four arrows show the order in which the eight runes in HENRIKUS were transposed into the four pairs which appear in Lines 1 and 2 of the SP 3 text, namely, SK–UI–NH–ER. As usual, both the distribution and transposition are symmetric as they must be for a transposition cipher to exist.

The second of the two principal hidden messages in SP 3 makes use of the entire fifteen lines, front and back. It is only a slight modification of the same two concealment ciphers in Legends 66 and 67 of VM. The analysis is quite detailed but is otherwise straightforward.

Figure 109

TRANSCRIPTION OF SPIRIT POND NUMBER 3

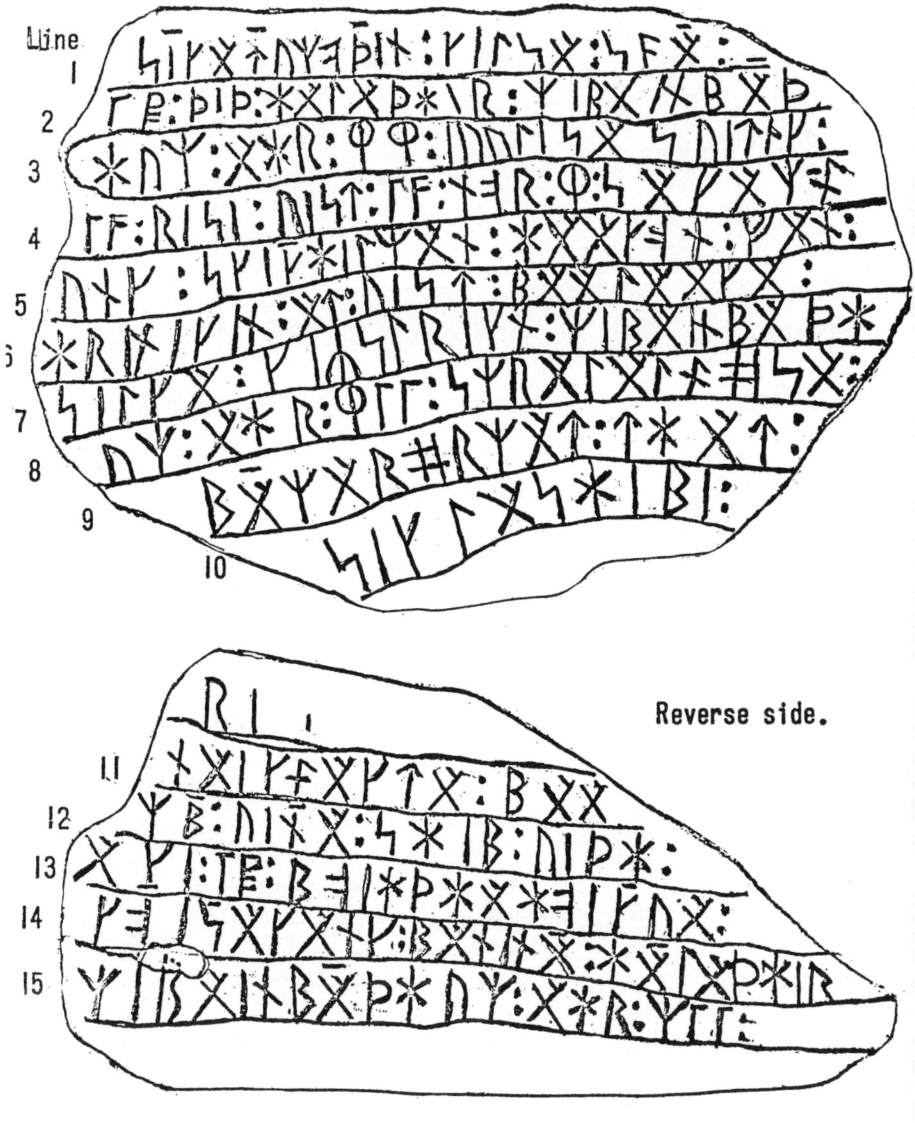

Reverse side.

Figure 110

Norse Acrostic (Part A) and Substitution Cipher (Part B) in Spirit Pond 3

Part A —

Line	② Number of Words	③ Runes	④ Latin Letters	⑤ Runic Numbers	⑥ Count of runes from the left end of the lines.
1	3	ᚴ	K		
5	4	ᛋ	S		
6	,4	ᛁ	I		
7	3	ᛚ	L		
9	2	ᛅ	A		
10	1	ᛋ		11	
11	2	ᛅ		10	
12	4	ᛁ		9	
14	3	ᛁ		9	

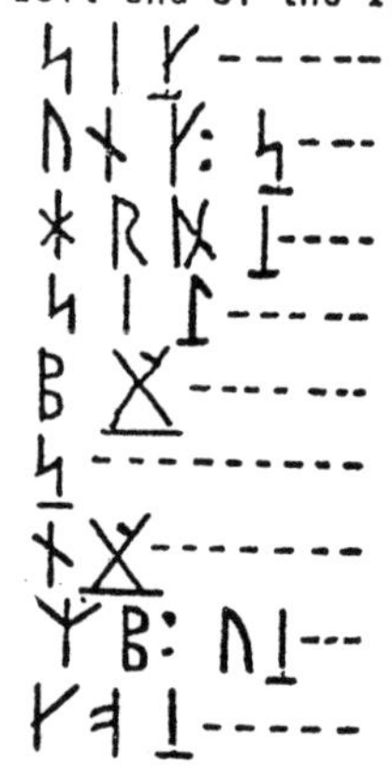

Part B —

Line	② Letters in Group	③ Runes	④ Latin Letters	⑤ Runic Numbers	⑥ Groups that have overlined runic symbols.
12	1	ᛦ		1	
12	3	ᚦ		3	
13	12	ᛏ		12	
14	8	ᛏ		8	
14	5	ᚱ		5	
14	6	ᛦ	K		
15	11	ᛋ	S		
1	8	ᛏ	N		
1	2	ᚿ	U		
2	7	ᚼ	H		
4	5	ᚱ	R		
5	9	ᛁ	I		
9	9	ᛁ	E		

Total—68

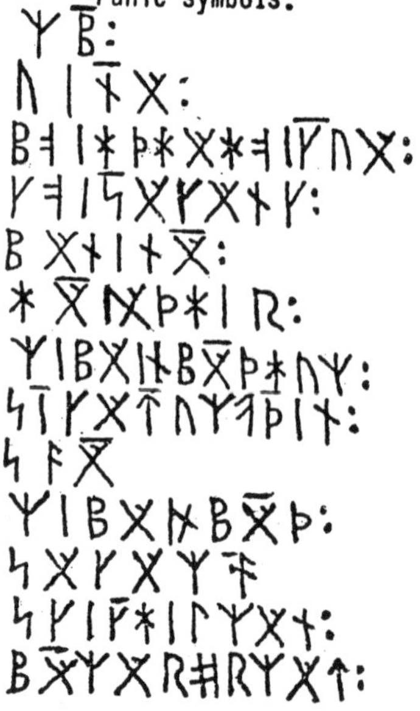

The message begins as a Norse-type acrostic *in those of the fifteen lines which contain no pentathic numbers*. They are Lines 1, 5, 6, 7, 9, 10, 11, 12, and 14 which are listed in order in Column 1 of Part A of the Table. Column 2 lists the number of *groups of runes* which are separated by points in each of these lines. In Column 3, the rune which is located *this number of spaces from the left end of the line* is recorded. (The first runes in each line are reproduced in Column 6 and the rune in Column 3 underlined.)

The runes in Column 3, Part A, play two separate roles. In Column 4 the first five runes are changed into their equivalent Latin letters. The last four are converted into their numerical values in Column 5.

Part B of the Table analyzes a Norse-type substitution cipher. Because this cipher is integrated with the acrostic in Part A, both must be recorded in the same table and analyzed as a unit. Part B begins with Line 12 and includes only those groups of runes *which contain one or more overlined runes*. There are thirteen such groups of runes.

In counting the numbers of runes in each group, *the overlined runes themselves are not counted, and combined runes are counted as only one rune*. The resulting counts are listed in Column 2 of Part B. In Column 3 the counts in Column 2 are changed into the runes which have the same numerical values in the 16-rune alphabet.

The *last eight runes* are changed into Latin letter equivalents in Column 4. In Column 5, the *first five runes* are changed back into their numerical values. (Again Column 6 shows the groups of runes in question and shows which runes are overlined and which are combined.)

We are now ready to interpret the message which has emerged in Column 4 and 5. In Column 4 the first five letters, when they are rearranged, spell SIKLA. As before this means "Sailed, October 6, 1123 A.D."

The last eight letters in Line 4 of the table represent overlined runes which appear in succession in the text of SP 3.

Taken in pairs in the order in which they appear, KS–NU–
HR–IE, they are the result of a cipher which distributed and
transposed the runes in the name HENRIKUS.

FIGURE 111

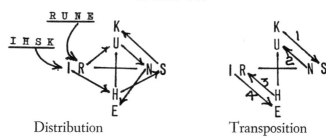

Distribution   Transposition

The figure at the left shows that Henricus first separated
the runes which spelled his name into his unique two-part
pattern, IHS–K and RUNE, which indicate his vocation and
avocation respectively. He then distributed these two groups of
four runes separately, beginning in each case at the left of the
distribution pattern, IHS–K is going to the counterclockwise and RUNE in the clockwise direction. In order to
attain the desired transposition KS-NU-HR-IE, which is shown
in the transposition figure at the right, it was necessary to inter-
change the letters H and E at the lower end of the distribution
pattern. This caused the pattern to be "crossed" in the same
manner and for the same reason as when LITI A MIK was
transposed to MI-LT-IA-KI on the reverse side of SP 1.

The sum of the numerical values in Column 5 is 68 (days).
This is assumed to have been the elapsed time for the entire
journey. The number 68 is also repeated two more times in the
inscription of SP 3. When the numerical values of the *overlined
runes* are added separately on the front and back of the inscription, the sum, in each case, is 68: Front: 9-12-3-10-10-8-6-10.
The sum is 68. Back: 13-8-6-11-10-10-10. The sum is 68.

This makes a total of three indications of the number 68.
It is clear that, whatever its· significance, Henricus wished to

impress this number on the mind of any potential solver of his cryptography. The sums were obviously so arranged because many of the overlined runes serve no other purpose than this. They were selected so their sum was 68.

The entire secret message in SP 3 is therefore, "Henrikus sailed 68 days, October 6, 1123 A.D." Taken together with the number 34 this seems to mean that Henricus sailed to the south for 34 days and returned in another 34 days. (*Note that, if the number of days out and back were not equal, this would have been very difficult to make clear in this type of puzzle. It may have been necessary to make them equal.*)

It would be surprising if Henricus had not made use of his pentathic numbers for cryptographic purposes. He did so, and here we find another element of similarity between the cryptography in SP 3 and the Kensington inscription. Both use the pentathic numbers in place of the Arabic digits in decimal numbers. Both experienced the same difficulty in so doing because there was no pentathic symbol for zero. Both overcame this difficulty in the same way. Both used exactly the same form of the pentathic numbers. In the table which follows, the pentathic numbers in Lines 2, 4, and 13 were treated differently from those in Lines 3, 8, and 15 out of necessity and so are listed separately. They are all decimal numbers but the first three do not involve a problem which is encountered with the larger numbers below them.

The numbers in Lines 3, 8, and 15 in the table have four digits and, in each case, the thousands and hundreds digits are 1 and 0 respectively. Since there was no pentathic symbol for zero, these two digits could only be expressed by the use of the single pentathic symbol for 10 to represent both.

Henricus shows that he was well aware of the situation and he made good use of it. He arranged his numbers so that the sum of the *numbers* in Lines 2, 4, and 13 was 68. In addition, the *symbols* in Lines 3, 8, and 15 have the sum 34.

In Line 15 Henricus faced a special problem. If he had allowed the thousands and hundreds digits to be expressed

FIGURE 112

Line	Symbols	Numer. values	The sums
2	Γ ℞	17	17
4	Γ F-Γ F-Φ	12 -12 -10	34
13	Γ ℞	17	17
3	A H R Φ Φ	10 -10	20
8	A H R Φ Γ Γ	10 -1 -1	12
15	A H R Ψ Γ Γ	1 -1	2
	↑	Totals 34	68

by pentathic number 10 as he did in Lines 3 and 8, the sum
would have been 44 instead of 34. His remedy was simple and
effective. In place of pentathic number 10 he substituted Roman
numeral M whose numerical value is 1000. By so doing, his
number still had the value 1011. However, the M is not pentathic, nor is it a part of a decimal number. Therefore it could
not be counted as a digit. This reduced the sum of the digits
in the three lines to 34.

Finally, there is the spelling AHR for "year." We have
previously seen this spelling in Gol V C (1329 A.D.) and the
Kensington inscription (1362 A.D.). Some scholars have con-
tended that this spelling was not yet in use by the mid-fourteenth century. Now we find it in SP 3 (1123 A.D.) almost two
and a half centuries earlier.

In both Gol V C and the Kensington inscription the puzzlemaster would have had to spell the word as AHR for cryptographic reasons even if he had believed that the correct spelling
was AR. On the other hand, there was nothing to force Henricus to use the spelling AHR in SP 3. Yet he did so on three
separate occasions.[1]

This spelling has not previously been found in Scandinavian
sources from the eleventh through the mid-fourteenth centur-

ies. But this does not prove that it was not used. The absence of a certain spelling among scanty surviving documents can not establish that the spelling did not exist.

The same can be said for a number of other usages which had also been unknown in Scandinavia from the eleventh to the thirteenth centuries. Among them are the decimal system, pentathic symbols, the Old Norse runes and, most important of all, Norse dated puzzles and ciphers.

It is quite possible that these things were known mainly among the Norse clergy and, particularly, that segment of it which was devoted to the art of Norse-type cryptography. This may be the key to the question of the source of these long forgotten features. Henricus was one of the foremost of the puzzlemasters. Harrek, the author of the dated puzzle and ciphers in the Kensington inscription nearly two and a half centuries later, also used the spelling AHR. In the next chapter it will become quite clear that he was a pupil and disciple of Henricus.

CHAPTER 13

From Spirit Pond to Kensington

There is a close relationship between the inscription which is carved on Spirit Pond Number 3 and on the Kensington Stone. At first glance this seems surprising because they were carved 239 years apart and are separated by about 1,300 miles. These figures are deceptive, however. They leave out of consideration a substantial body of pertinent fact, some of which is inherent in the inscriptions themselves. To this is added independent indications which are rooted in the history which surrounds them both.

Because the connection between these inscriptions are of great historical importance, their major similarities will be summarized and discussed in this chapter.

1. Both use the decimal system. It had been invented by the Arabs many centuries earlier and had been introduced into the Benedictine monastery schools of Northern Europe more than a century before the time of Henricus. The evidence is beyond dispute that the decimal system was known, and used, by Norse priests in their runic puzzles from shortly after 1000 A.D. and into the mid-fourteenth century.

2. In both SP 3 and Kensington medieval pentathic symbols were substituted for the Arabic digits in decimal numbers. There is no essential connection between the Arabic digits and decimal numbers. Historically, it has been the custom to use the Arabic digits but any number of different sets of symbols can be arranged to use in their stead. Pentathic numbers are only one of such sets.

a. In both inscriptions the same difficulty was encountered in trying to write decimal numbers with pentathic symbols. This was that there was no pentathic symbol for zero just as there was no rune which had zero numerical value.

212

b. Henricus in SP 3, and Harrek, the runemaster of the Kensington inscription, overcame this difficulty in the same way. Both expressed the two-digit decimal number 10 by using the single pentathic symbol whose numerical value was 10.

c. The forms of the pentathic symbols which are used in the two inscriptions are identical.

d. Decimal numbers, with pentathic symbols as digits, are scattered liberally throughout both inscriptions. These numbers play a vital role in the extensive and varied cryptography which each contains.

3. The word for year is spelled AHR instead of AR in both inscriptions. Some experts in the medieval Norse language have said that the word should have been spelled AR even as late as the mid-fourteenth century.

4. Both are carved with the Normal runes of the 16-rune alphabet. The only difference is that, in the Kensington inscription, points were added to some runes in order to change their inflections. When Henricus carved his inscriptions, points were not yet used for this purpose.

5. In both inscriptions an anomalous form of the rune A is used throughout. Runologists have apparently not found this form of the rune in normal runic inscriptions during the twelfth to the fourteenth centuries. A theory which will be advanced later in this chapter can apparently explain the origin of this strange form for the rune A.

* * * * *

Both inscriptions use decimal numbers but it is not this feature which makes them unique. Decimal numbers were used by Norse puzzlemasters from the early eleventh century. The thing which distinguishes these two inscriptions from others is that both Henricus and Harrek substituted pentathic symbols for the Arabic digits in their decimal numbers. As was noted above, this forced both to express the two-digit number 10 with the single pentathic symbol which also had numerical value 10. They deserve no credit, or blame, for using the same method because, once they had decided to use the pentathic symbols, there was no alternative. The figure shows the actual numbers which appear in the two inscriptions.

FIGURE 113

Spirit Pond

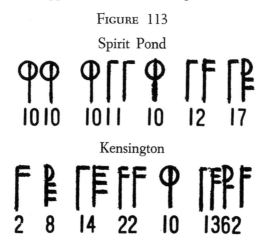

Kensington

The figure shows that both runemasters used the pentathic figure with numerical value 10 whenever the decimal number presented a digit 1 followed by a digit 0 (zero). A large majority of dated puzzles, whose number runs into the dozens, used runes in the same way. For example, the 1012 A.D. year number in the Heavener No. 1 inscription (Chapter 7) was indicated by the runes A and I whose numerical values were 10 and 12 respectively. This is the same procedure as when two blocks, whose faces are numbered 10 and 12, are placed adjacent to each other.

This is indeed the decimal system but a basic principle is violated. This is that a four-digit decimal number must have a separate symbol for each digit. After Henricus wrote the number 1010 with only two pentathic symbols, the number could not be used in addition, subtraction, multiplication, or division. Of this fact Henricus was certainly aware but he only wished to write a readable number, and did. Harrek was more fortunate with his year number, 1362. It required only digits which the pentathic number system could supply.

Pentathic numbers are based on the number 5 instead of 10 as in the decimal system. In medieval times pentathic numbers were written by the use of a large number of different sets of symbols of which only a relatively few have survived. The figure compares the way in which the transition was made from the base number 5 to two times 5 in the tenth-century calendar of Athelstan, in the Spirit Pond and Kensington inscriptions, and in sets of Golden Numbers which are illustrated in Worm's *Fasti Danici*.

FIGURE 114

Athelstan. 900 A.D.	Spirit Pond and Kensington. 1123 A.D. 1362 A.D.	Fasti Danici. (Ole Worm)
↑ ⳾	Ρ Φ	Ρ ⴲ
5 10	5 10	5 10

It is clear that the transition from 5 to 10 which was used by Henricus and Harrek, and which Henricus very probably invented, is more logical than the other two. If 5 is represented by a half circle, nothing could be more logical than to let 10 be written as a full circle.

This discussion should help to dispel the veil of mystery and misunderstanding which many commentators have thrown over the pentathic symbols which Harrek used in the Kensington inscription. There is no mystery about them and they are not in any sense in error. The question which is here raised is why Henricus substituted pentathic symbols for the Arabic digits with which he was certainly familiar and why Harrek decided to follow suit. The answer is very probably that pentathic symbols, mixed among runes where they were seldom used, would be sure to attract much more attention than ordinary decimal numbers. This was very important because the main burden of the cryptography in both inscriptions was hidden in these numbers. (Pentathic symbols were normally used only for the Golden Numbers in the perpetual calendar. However, Golden Numbers which were written with symbols of runic type were sometimes used in dated puzzles. Henricus used the Golden Number 18 in his Popham Beach inscription nine years before he carved Spirit Pond Number 3.)

The implication that Harrek knew about the cryptographic work of Henricus and decided to use this and other features is clear. Another indication that this must have happened is that the Kensington inscription used the same special form for the rune A which is found in SP 3. The symbols are identical in the two inscriptions except that Henricus did not use points to change inflections of certain runes.

FIGURE 115

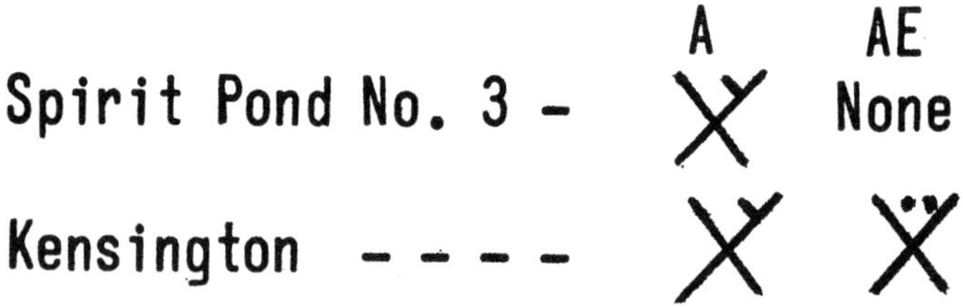

Spirit Pond No. 3 -   ⟨A ✗⟩   ⟨AE None⟩

Kensington - - - -   ✗   ✗

If Henricus copied this form for the rune A, the source is not known. It is also unlikely that he did so, not only because an earlier use has not been observed from Greenland but because it appears to have been one of Henricus's cryptographic inventions. If this was, in fact, its origin, it permitted him to display still another symbol for the Christian cross in the text of SP 3. The reader will recall that a Saint Andrew's Cross was carved on the reverse side of SP 1. It was an auxiliary part of a cipher which Mongé interpreted to suggest that the eight runes, MILTIAKI, had been transposed on a Saint Andrew's Cross. It was proved that the message which had been so transposed was LITI A MIK which translated as "observed by me." Outline drawings of objects which had been observed were carved around the eight runes.

In fashioning this special symbol for A, Henricus apparently began with the rune from the 16-rune Normal alphabet. The simple conversion into the Saint Andrew's Cross is indicated in the figure.

FIGURE 116

A is for Andrew

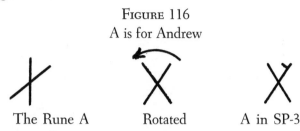

The Rune A   Rotated   A in SP-3

What Henricus appears to have done is to rotate the Normal rune for A slightly in a counterclockwise direction until its staff and slanting crossarm assume the same angle with respect to the vertical. He then added a short spur to the upper right arm to indicate the direction of rotation.

Normally, the slanted crossarm of the rune A was carved shorter than its staff but instances are not lacking in which they are equal in length. Its length lies within the rather broad range of permitted runic variations. When, as here, the intention was cryptographic, more drastic distortions were routine. This conversion of the rune permitted Henricus to *display another form of the Christian cross no less than fifty-two additional times* in the text of SP 3. There are five instances in which two runes for A are carved in succession. Since these occurrences have no connection with the cryptography or with any textual meaning, their only purpose seems to be to increase the number of these symbols and to call attention to them.

In the Kensington inscription there are 22 such special symbols for the rune A. Four have the spur replaced by double points in order to change the inflection from A to AE. It is possible that puzzlemaster Harrek was not aware that Henricus had designed the symbol so as to represent the Saint Andrew's Cross. Nevertheless, he also used the symbol for cryptographic purposes. There are exactly 22 such symbols for A in the Kensington inscription. This supplements the double indication of YDL=2 for the year and DDL=2 for April 24 which Harrek delivered in his text with the words "...22 Norwegians..." and the single indication, "...2 skerries...." It raises the total number of such indications to five.

This might be mistaken for a coincidence except for the fact that Harrek did not stop there. He also changed the runes K and U into strange forms, and he arranged it so that there were 14 changes of K (and G) and 10 of U runes in his text. These numbers correspond to YGN=14 for the year 1362 and ND=10 for April 24. These are additional confirmations which supplement the indications of the pentathic numbers in the text. It was done in recognition of the principle that, in the longer texts, calendrical indications must be repeated in order to overcome the tendency for the cryptography to become overlooked.

The cryptographic origin, and the calendrical functions, of these strange symbols were unknown to the runologists and linguists. It was, therefore, not strange that they questioned them. The solutions of the Kensington cryptography, and that in many other inscriptions, show that their objections were based on faulty assumptions.

*   *   *   *   *

We now turn our attention to what is perhaps the most intriguing similarity between the two inscriptions. The table near the end of Chapter 12 shows that, in Lines 3, 8, and 15 of Spirit Pond Number 3, Henricus spelled the Norse word for year as AHR. This is very interesting because, as noted above, some experts in the medieval Norse language have claimed that the spelling should have been AR even as late as the mid-fourteenth century. As a result, objections have been raised to the spelling AHR in the Kensington inscription.

Three inscriptions are known which use the spelling AHR:

	Name	Location	Year
1.	Spirit Pond Number 3	Maine	1123 A.D.
2.	Gol Number 5 C	Norway	1329 A.D.
3.	Kensington	Minnesota	1362 A.D.

The three inscriptions are widely separated both in distance and in years but a strong probability exists that the two fourteenth-century puzzles are direct descendants of the cryptographic work of Henricus in Vinland. Both appear to be a part of a strong resurgence of interest, and activity, in Norse cryptography which seems to have been centered in western Norway in the early fourteenth century.

Henricus used the spelling AHR in three different places in SP 3. There is nothing in the cryptography which could have forced him to use this spelling. Therefore, the most logical assumption seems to be that this was the accepted spelling in Greenland in the early twelfth century at least with Henricus and, perhaps, among his church-oriented and puzzleminded colleagues.

No documentary evidence has survived from Greenland which can settle this question one way or the other. This remains no less true if the approximately one hundred brief and, often hopelessly confused, runic inscriptions from Greenland are included. The Greenlanders became progressively more isolated from Scandinavia and Iceland. As a result runologists such as Magnus Olsen have been impressed with the independence with which both runic symbols and the Norse language developed in the Greenland colonies. (It can be taken for granted that Norsemen who settled in Vinland and beyond felt the isolation even more keenly.)

Added to the tendency of the Greenlanders to go their own way, is the fact that the spelling of words in runic inscriptions even in Scandinavia varied widely. For example, the word AEPTIR, whose meaning was "after," was spelled in at least twenty-eight different ways. They ranged all the way from AT and HAFT to ITIR and YFIR. Under such conditions it is doubtful if the term misspelling can be appropriately applied to any spelling whatever.

Compared with such aberrations from the norm, the insertion of a silent letter H in AR to make it AHR is insignificant. It was also in line with a natural development of the Norse language which made AHR the correct spelling in later centuries. Bishop Henricus, who was very likely educated in England or Germany, may have been ahead of his time in this respect. There seem to have been only two ways by which Harrek, the puzzlemaster of Kensington, could have had the opportunity to learn, and to adopt, so many of the cryptographic procedures of Henricus. Either, or both, may have been in operation. It is inconceivable that Henricus, or any other major producer of dated puzzles and ciphers, could have developed his cryptographic skill, and could have nurtured and executed his considerable volume of complex cryptography, except under one condition. This is that he kept a file of his own procedures and completed puzzles as well as those of other puzzlemasters. Such a file by Henricus must inevitably have found its way to the establishment of the bishop at Gardar.[1] Those Norse puzzles which have been solved from Greenland prove that Henricus was by no means the only puzzlemaster who left his mark there and who presumably made Greenland his base of operations.

These facts may have a direct connection with Harrek and his Kensington inscription. Norse priests, who were assigned to accompany expeditions to the North American continent, were either appointed directly from Gardar or they were sent from Norway or Iceland. When they arrived in Greenland, they were presumably under the protection of Gardar and probably also under its jurisdiction. It was necessary to stay over the winter in Greenland because, when the expedition arrived, it would be too late in the year to mount another major voyage to the western continent. It can be assumed that members of the clergy were invited to stay at Gardar. Such of them as were interested in Norse cryptography would therefore have had ample opportunity to study the work of Henricus and other puzzlemasters.

Harrek, who constructed the hidden date and two brief ciphered messages in the Kensington inscription, included in it devout religious references such as the well-known Catholic abbreviation AVM (Ave Virgo Maria, that is, Hail to the Virgin

Mary) and the last petition of the Lord's prayer: Save us from evil. This leaves little doubt that he was a Norse priest. His cryptogram makes it equally obvious that he was an avid and talented student of Norse cryptography. During his long enforced stay in Greenland on his way to America he probably had ample opportunity to study Norse puzzles such as Spirit Pond Number 3 and the Kingigtorssuaq inscription.[2]

There is a second way by which Harrek may have learned of the cryptographic procedures of Henricus. As more information comes to hand, it is steadily becoming more plausible that Harrek may have visited the Spirit Pond site in Maine. If he did so, he may have had the opportunity to study the Spirit Pond puzzles at first hand. "8 Goths and 22 Norwegians on a journey of exploration from Vinland westward." That is the startling opening statement of the Kensington carving. The implication is strong that the Kensington party proceeded westward from Vinland. Persuasive, but not yet conclusive evidence that such a route was followed will be presented in Chapter 15. What seems to be established is that Norsemen had crossed the Appalachian Mountains or more probably had flanked them to the north, and had reached the upper Ohio River basin and points as far west as the Missouri River in the Dakotas.

This raises the question how Harrek and his party could have known that they had rediscovered the Vinland in New England which had been discovered, and at least to some extent explored and settled by Norsemen during the eleventh century, and which Bishop Henricus had favored with so much attention nearly two and a half centuries earlier. Only a positive identification of Norse sites in Vinland seems to justify the positive and unambiguous statement in the Kensington text. Landings, followed by careful searches, would have been necessary to identify such sites if they were abandoned and overgrown. (The most conservative view is taken here that the Norse settlements in Vinland had disappeared by the mid-fourteenth century but this is by no means certain.)

The Kensington inscription states that their ship had been

left "by the sea" 14 days journey from the site of the stone. Some have argued that this excluded a direct passage from Vinland to the west because it could not be accomplished in 14 days. While this is true, this does not either prove or disprove the theory. In the Kensington carving all pentathic numbers, of which the number 14 is one, had as their primary function to indicate and to confirm the date. For the year 1362 YGN was 14. This is all that is needed to justify the presence of the number 14.

It seems probable that the expedition traveled along routes where other Norsemen had preceded them. The most likely appears to have been by way of the St. Lawrence River, across Lake Ontario and southward across the low continental divide east of Lake Erie into the upper Ohio River basin. There appear to be a number of runic inscriptions in this large area, all of which are apparently undated. Some are quite well carved while others are no better than the most carelessly cut Greenland inscriptions. This problem will be pursued further in Chapter 15.

CHAPTER 14

The Narssaq Inscription from Greenland

In late 1967 the Danish runologist Dr. phil. Erik Moltke mailed to the author a reprint of an article which he had written in 1961 about a runic inscription. It had appeared in the Danish periodical *Grønland* under the title, "A Greenland Runic Inscription from the Time of Erik The Red." In the article Dr. Moltke expressed, in strong terms, his conviction that the inscription had been carved in heathen times in Greenland and certainly not later than 1025 A.D.[1]

The article discussed one of about one hundred runic inscriptions which are now known from Greenland. It was pulled out of the ground in 1953 while earth was being removed for fill. Since professional excavation had to wait until the following year, and the site had been occupied over a long period of time, reliable dating based on archeology was not possible.

The site lies near the mouth of Eiriksfjord in the Eastern Settlement. It was at the inner end of this fjord that Eirik the Red established his estate, Brattahlid, in 986 A.D. Because this site now bears the Eskimo name, Narssaq, the runic inscription is referred to as *Narssaqpinden*, that is, the Narssaq stick. It will henceforth be referred to here as NS.

The piece of pine on which the inscription is carved is roughly square in cross section. Its length is about seventeen inches and the four sides taper in width from about an inch at one end to a half inch at the other. Each side carries some part of the inscription. Two sides are covered with symbols from end to end.

A large part of the inscription consists of conspicuously non-runic features. Dr. Moltke ascribed them to attempts at magic and sorcery. Nevertheless, he requested, in his cover letter, that they be examined to determine if they contained Norse-type ciphers or a hidden date.

223

At that time Mr. Mongé was very busy with a number of quite important solutions. Probably largely for this reason, he did not discover any cryptography. However, in June of 1972, his interest was rekindled by the expressed concern of Professor Cyrus Gordon of Brandeis University that the texts of the three Spirit Pond inscriptions from Maine apparently contain almost no literal meaning. In this respect the Spirit Pond carvings and NS appear to be very similar.

To his only mild surprise, but considerable delight, Mongé soon discovered that, not only does NS contain a dated puzzle, and the name of the puzzlemaster, but the structure of the cryptography was relatively simple and the solution was both complete and convincing.

It turned out that, far from being an early eleventh-century inscription which was heathen in tone and which Eirik the Red himself might well have carved, NS was dated from the early fourteenth century. What is more, it bears a religious date, Advent Sunday, November 28, 1316 A.D. NS is, therefore, another of the large number of dated runic inscriptions which Norse priests constructed well into the fourteenth century. Because it was carved in Greenland, the Norse gateway to the North American continent, it obviously is a part of an interesting backdrop for the two American dated fourteenth-century

FIGURE 117

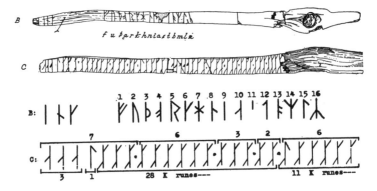

inscriptions, the drinking horn from the vicinity of Winnetka, Illinois, and the Kensington inscription.

With this introduction we shall proceed with the solution of NS. Above are reproduced the two sides, B and C, in which the cryptography is to be found. They are followed by transcriptions according to which the analysis will be carried out.

The year number is revealed in much the same way that the year was disclosed in the Kingigtorssuaq inscription from northern Greenland which was carved seventy-two years earlier. The difference is only that, in NS, counts are made in a special alphabet which is carved in the inscription instead of the Dionysian cycle of the Golden Numbers in the perpetual calendar. This difference is unimportant except for its implications.

Note that, at the extreme left end of Side C, are *three* runes for A and *one* rune for L. In the alphabet which is used, the numerical value of the rune A is 10, and for the rune L, 15. The three runes for A indicate that 3 is to be added to the 10. The single rune for L means that one (1) is to be added to 15. The sums are 13 and 16 and the indicated year number is 1316 A.D.

As usual, this is so far only an assumption. That this is the intended year, is confirmed by the groupings of the first three groups of symbols in Side C which are *separated by single points*. The groups number 7, 6, and 3 symbols. For the year 1316 A.D., Rati = 7, YGN = 6, and YDL = 3. This confirmation is complete and convincing.

The day is indicated in this manner. After the first four symbols in Side C, which have already been used, come fourteen identical symbols of novel shape. Each symbol is actually a double rune for K. The second K is an inverted and mirrored image of the regular rune. Therefore, there are 28 runes in the fourteen symbols. (Note that while similar symbols follow the fourteen, the fifteenth symbol is different from the fourteen which preceded it. For this reason, the count had to be terminated with the fourteen.)

The next six symbols also have two runes for K in each symbol, except for the first which has only one. Therefore the total number of K runes in this group is 11. We now have the indication of the 28th day in the 11th month which is November 28. Again this is an assumption up to this point. But let us now count the number of symbols in the next two groups of symbols *between single points* (groups four and five). They have 2 and 6 symbols respectively. The two numbers are the digits in the decimal number 26. ND for November 28 is 26.

The dating is now complete. It will be noticed that, as is usual, the elements which perform the dating and provide the confirmations are gathered into a compact group. The year, the day, and the day of the month are separately represented by distinctive, but consecutive groups of special symbols. By using the same symbols, the confirmations are all accomplished by separating them into groups with single points.

NS also contains the name of the puzzlemaster. It is stated by the three runes, ING, at the left end of Side B, and the two runes, AL, at the left end of Side C. His name was INGAL. This is a good medieval Norse name. It is listed, for example, along with Inggard, Ingulf, Ingvald, and Inge in Ivar Aasen's *Norsk Ordbok*, 1873 edition, on page 325. The arrangement is as follows:

FIGURE 118

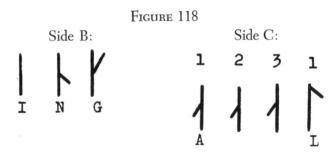

Ingal presented his name in approximately the same way which his predecessor, Henricus, had used in four puzzles in New England two centuries earlier. The main difference is that, by Ingal's arrangement, he needed only two letters of his name *to state the year number.* The three runes for A at the left end of Side C does not make the spelling of his name INGAAAL. In stating the year, only the first A was used as a rune. Three runes for A were used to indicate that 3 was to be added to the numerical value of the A, which was 10, to make 13.

Actually Ingal also served another purpose with the three runes for A. He prevented anyone from reading his name directly as ING plus AL. No puzzlemaster wished to make his solution obvious or easy. The other side of the coin was that, if he made it too difficult, no one might discover it to say nothing of solving it.

It was necessary for Ingal to use the early eleventh-century Sw.-N. alphabet which he carved on Side B. Only so could he indicate, with only seven runes, his own name and the year 1316 A.D. For example, the fourth rune on Side C must be an L so as to supply the last letter in his name. At the same time, this rune for L must have the numerical value 15. Then 15 + 1 gave the 16 which was needed to state the year. The alphabet which Ingal used has the L after the M so it is in the 15th position and has numerical value 15. His own fourteenth-century alphabet had the L before the M so its value was 14. This would not do.

Having chosen this three-centuries-old alphabet, Ingal had no choice but to alert anyone who might try to solve his puzzle of what he had done. It was this necessity which caused him to carve the alphabet in his inscription.

This is the crux for understanding the cryptography in NS. Since Dr. Moltke did not know that this substitution of alphabets had been made, he pointed to the L after M situation in the alphabet as proof that NS itself was from the eleventh century. This conclusion was based on false premises.

The eleventh-century Sw.-N. alphabet necessarily brought with it all of the other features which Dr. Moltke also mistook for evidence that NS was from the eleventh century. They included the forms of several runes which are distinctive to the

Sw.-N. alphabet. Another feature was the absence of points which, in later centuries, were used to change the inflections of certain runes in the alphabet.

Ingal's Advent Sunday date, and his obvious familiarity with the perpetual church calendar, makes it almost certain that he was a priest as well as a puzzlemaster. This raises the question from what source he had acquired the ancient Sw.-N. alphabet. There seem to be two major possibilities. As a practicing puzzlemaster, he may simply have dipped into his own files of cryptographic materials. If so, his files would also, in all likelihood, have contained Norse puzzles which were based on this alphabet.

It would seem far more likely that his source was cryptographic materials which were preserved from past centuries at the episcopal see at Gardar. Whatever the source, here was an alphabet which had already gone out of use for normal runic writing when Henricus made dated and autographed puzzles in New England two centuries earlier. The alphabet, in fact, belonged to the very years when an early eleventh-century puzzlemaster carved dated inscriptions in New England and Oklahoma. It could, as Dr. Moltke said, have been used by Eirik the Red himself.

This reenforces the belief that cryptographic materials had been accumulating in Greenland from the earliest times. NS shows that, three centuries after this alphabet had been in normal use, Greenlanders were still studying cryptographic materials and procedures. Ingal had been able to reach back three centuries for some of his source material.

The existence of the Narssaq puzzle is historically very significant. Greenland was the inevitable way station on the course to the North American continent. But, by the time an expedition had reached the Greenland colonies, it would not be possible to continue until the following summer. As previously noted, Harrek, the puzzlemaster at Kensington in 1362 A.D., was certainly also a member of the Norse clergy. And it is almost certain that he was invited to spend the winter at the bishop's establishment at Gardar.

At that time NS, which Harrek did not necessarily see, was less than fifty years old but it harks back three centuries before that time. Such materials Harrek would presumably have had the opportunity to study. Among them may well have been the cryptographic output of Henricus. Chapter 13 demonstrated that Harrek had borrowed many features and procedures from Henricus.

The Narssaq puzzle is actually one in a group of eleven Norse cryptograms whose solutions have been analyzed in this volume. All bear dates which fall in a comparatively narrow span of years from 1297 to 1362 A.D. The number could easily have been doubled. This shows that there was a strong surge of interest and activity, particularly in Western Norway during the two generations before the Kensington inscription was carved. (The Black Death, which fell with an especially heavy hand on the Norse clergy, may have contributed to the demise of Norse cryptography. It reached Norway in 1349 A.D. Other factors were also at work. Gunpowder, which had just come into use, made the Norse longship obsolete. It is notable that the only known cryptogram which is dated after 1329 [Tatai's Gol inscriptions] is the Kensington carving. But it was produced in America under quite special circumstances.)

Below is a list of late thirteenth and fourteenth-century inscriptions:

Year	Name and Location	Number
1297	Gol Stave Church, Norway.	4
1297	Buslabaen, Norway.	1
1297	Urnes Church Number 20.	1
1316	Narssaq, Greenland.	1
1317	Horn, Winnetka, Illinois.	1
1329	Gol Stave Church, Norway.	2
1362	Kensington, Minnesota.	1

This represents less than one half of the Norse cryptography which has already been solved from these years. It is probably only a small fraction of what will eventually be solved. A great deal has certainly been lost.

It would appear that cryptographic activity was centered in Western Norway during the first half of the fourteenth century. This is the area from which the bulk of the Norwegian contingent of the expedition which resulted in the Kensington inscription in 1362 must have come. It is probable that among them was the priest, and superb puzzlemaster, Harrek. It is, perhaps, not likely that he was the last of the breed, but he is the last about whom anything is known.

There are also other non-runic features in NS. This is reminiscent of a well-worn riddle: What is it that has *six legs,* wags its tail, scratches fleas, and barks? The answer is a dog. The two extra legs were thrown in to make the riddle more difficult! Ingal added the last half of side C for the same purpose of confusion.

CHAPTER 15

The Westward Trek

Attention is directed here to rock carvings some of which were briefly mentioned in Chapter 1. While some were observed from early colonial times, the majority have come to light during this century and particularly in the last four decades. These carvings, which number several dozen, are distributed in the same general areas in which the dated puzzles are found in the United States but are also spread into neighboring regions which in some cases extend several hundred miles.

Many factors combine to indicate that these are runic inscriptions. One such indication is that they contain a large proportion of acceptably formed runic symbols of the same types as those which are found in the American dated puzzles. They appear, in fact, to be the direct descendants of the early eleventh-century American cryptograms. They are similar in that, with almost no exceptions, their texts can not be translated. Unlike them they do not, so far as one has yet been able to determine, contain hidden dates and ciphers. That difficult art was, naturally enough, easily and quickly forgotten. As runic inscriptions they show to a varying degree signs of degeneration. In this respect they bring to mind the assessment by Moltke of a large proportion of the runic inscriptions carved by the Norse colonists in Greenland that they were a confused mixture of runes with no meaning.

In Vinland, and in the areas which lay beyond it, the isolation from the ancient runic traditions of Scandinavia was certainly even more complete than it was in Greenland. The early American puzzlemasters were also of little help. For cryptographic reasons their visible texts had no meaning and their runic symbols represented only numbers from the perpetual calendar. Their successors and imitators could copy their symbols but there were no words or sentences to remind them of the sound values of the runes. These may have been unknown from the beginning or they were soon forgotten so that their representations of runes became nothing but symbolism. Meanwhile Norsemen in America, like Norsemen everywhere, persisted in honoring the culture of their forefathers by carving the runic symbols which were the only visible reminders of it. This background for carving runic symbols during many generations after the dating puzzlemasters goes far towards explaining why it developed in the direction which it did as judged by their inscriptions.

The most important examples of non-dated runic writing by Norsemen in America have been discovered in quite recent years not by new excavations but by research into archeological exhibits and reports. Among them are the discoveries of prestigious institutions such as the Peabody Museum at Harvard University and the Smithsonian Institution in Washington, D. C. Other sources have been illustrations and descriptions of the results of archeological discoveries in books and encyclopedias of archeology. All are reputable sources whose discoveries cannot be beclouded or besmirched as to their origins. They have the substantial additional advantage that in no case did those who discovered them and reported them have the vaguest notion that the carved symbols were runes or that the Norsemen might once have reached the area. In two cases it is admitted in the report that these are deliberately carved symbols, such as the Indians never produced, but the question of who had carved them was left unanswered.

It would be strange indeed if more conventional runic inscriptions were not associated with dated puzzles. There was no separation in Scandinavia. There, runic writing had developed over many centuries before puzzlemasters arrived on the scene. Both types exist side by side. The same is also true in New England and Oklahoma except, on account of the totally different historical background, it was the makers of runic puzzles who led the way a very few years after Vinland had been discovered.

When other Norsemen later copied the symbols, they knew nothing about dating from the perpetual calendar—or they were not interested in it. Nor is there any but very slight evidence that they were aware of the use of the sound values of the runes to spell words. At any rate, they failed to make use of them just as had their puzzlemaking predecessors. (It may some day be shown that some of these inscriptions do have textual interpretations. There are many Scandinavian inscriptions also which yield translations only by the exercise of great ingenuity and imagination on the part of the runologist. On the other hand, many inscriptions in both Scandinavia and Greenland have not been translated despite persistent effort.)

What this absence of textual content and other unusual features means in terms of the passage of years may prove very difficult to determine. But it probably did not take long to forget the sound values of runes. A difficult art such as writing must be cultivated and passed on to each new generation or it is lost. This would be an especially hazardous situation in an untamed wilderness. Meanwhile the symbolism could survive, and in fact develop, because it conforms to no fixed rules other than those of the moment and it changes so as to satisfy the needs of those who, for one reason or another, are concerned with it.

There are other similarities which suggest, and indeed approach the status of complete proof, that the early American dated puzzles were the source of the runic forms which appear in later non-dated inscriptions. One very significant likeness is that they contain an equally high percentage of the Old Norse runes which the runologists have said were not used after 1000 A.D. There seems to be no other possible explanation for their appearance in later carvings.

It is true that an occasional Old Norse rune is to be found in Norwegian inscriptions during the Middle Ages but they are treated as whimsies by the runologists and this is probably the best explanation for their existence. This leaves only two runic inscriptions in Scandinavia which use Old Norse runes after

1000 A.D. They are the two Swedish inscriptions, with year numbers 1008 and 1015 A.D., which were solved in Chapter 7. While they do prove that Old Norse runes were still in use for cryptographic purposes at that late date, no connection has yet been established between them and their contemporary American dated puzzles.

Many of the non-dated American inscriptions repeat the same rune, or a pair of runes, several times. This is also a feature of many Norwegian and Greenland inscriptions. It is not possible to prove that the motives for the repetitions were in all cases the same but the example was there for others to follow. No matter where it is encountered, it is a principle of symbolism that if one statement of a theme is good it is still better to repeat it. (The words magic and sorcery are avoided here because there is no evidence of such intent.)

*   *   *   *   *

Some Norsemen must have reached an area which lies west of the Kensington site in Minnesota, to the banks of the Mis-

FIGURE 119

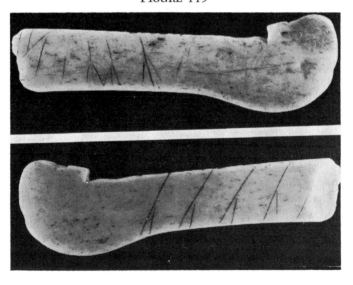

souri River in the Dakotas. The two sides of the bone which are photographed (Fig. 119) are only a part of this evidence. It was excavated in 1905 from one of the oldest Mandan Indian sites along the Missouri north of Bismarck in North Dakota. The discovery was made by an archeological expedition from the Peabody Museum at Harvard University. It was illustrated and described as a part of a report which was published the following year.[1]

These are clearly carved symbols. It was to be expected that the Peabody report expressed no opinion as to the origin of the carving. However, a comparison with corresponding symbols in the Kingigtorssuaq inscription from northern Greenland (1244 A.D.) shows that they are Norse runes.

The illustration below reproduces four runes from the Kingigtorssuaq carving which are flanked by the two kinds of symbols on the Mandan bone. At the left is the rune Y. (When this rune is inverted it is the rune M. Since the orientation of the symbols on the bone can not be determined they may represent either a Y or an M.) Even more significant is a comparison of the symbols at the right of the figure with the rune U from the Kingigtorssuaq carving. This is a special form of the rune which was developed in Greenland. Its appearance in an American inscription therefore takes on added significance.

FIGURE 120

The Peabody bone is broken at both ends so that only a central part of the inscription remains. Its repeated symbols obviously have no meaning as a runic text. A number of Norwegian inscriptions which have repeated runes have been solved in this volume but the best inscription for comparison in this case is perhaps the Greenland dated puzzle which is known as the Narssaq Stick and which was solved in Chapter 14. Its side C contains a continuous series of repeated symbols nearly all of which are combinations of more than one runic symbol.

Repeated symbols are very common in non-dated runic inscriptions in the United States. This seems to be especially true in the areas which are farthest removed from the occurrences of the dated puzzles and which were therefore, presumably, among the latest that were carved. Especially is this true of carvings in the Dakotas and those which are found among Indian rock carvings along the major rivers of southwestern Texas which drain into the Gulf of Mexico.[2] In such carvings it is clear that all pretense of a textual meaning is gone and that the inscription is purely symbolic.

By way of contrast the Kensington inscription was carved with Normal runes except when Harrek deliberately altered them for cryptographic reasons. It would seem that its only possible connection with runic carvings from the Mandan sites is that it was carved by a member of an expedition which was in search of "lost" Norsemen in this area. If so, it is a fair question how they could possibly have proceeded to the very heart of the continent unless there were other Norsemen to direct them on their way. That the Kensington inscription was evidence of such an expedition was the thesis which Holand upheld with such energy, and so effectively.

The Mandan bones appear to prove that Norsemen did, in fact, penetrate to the heart of the continent. They thereby indirectly, but persuasively, support Holand's contention that the Kensington party was in search of Norsemen who had reportedly defected from the faith and migrated to the mainland from the western colony in Greenland. Such an expedition was ordered in 1355 A.D. by Magnus, king of Norway and Sweden. The circumstances suggest that the expedition may have been successful in its search in this area. However, the evidence supports the assumption that these particular Norsemen had worked their way from Vinland over a long period of years. It is unlikely that they were late migrants.

The bone from the Peabody Museum is only one of seven which apparently are carved with runic symbols and which have been excavated from Mandan and Ariskara sites since the turn of the century. (The Ariskara were friends of the Mandans and had similar life styles. They were united in their resistance to the nomadic Sioux and Cheyenne. Nevertheless, both were of Sioux stock and had once migrated from the Ohio River valley with the other Siouan tribes.) The bones have been excavated from points along the Missouri River near Mobridge, South Dakota, and Bismarck, North Dakota. It was a few miles north of the location of Bismarck that La Vérendrye became acquainted with the Mandans and discovered that they had many of the characteristics of white people. It was also nearby that he found the inscribed stone, mounted in a cairn, which was very probably a runic inscription but which was lost somewhere in France.

Five of the eight bones were discovered by archeological expeditions from prestigious museums. One, which was described

FIGURE 121

Runes Carved on Bones from Mandan and Ariskara Sites

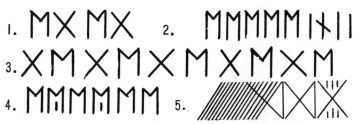

1. From Moorehead's *Archaeological Encyclopedia.* (1910)
2. Excavated by R. S. Thompson from a Mandan, N. Dak., site.
3. In Smithsonian exhibit. From Ariskara site, Mobridge, S. Dak.
4. From Fort Lincoln Memorial Museum at Mandan, North Dakota.
5. Straight-line pattern on bone. Similar to Greenland pattern. On exhibit at Fort Lincoln Memorial Museum.

above, is in the keeping of the Peabody Museum, another is a part of the exhibit of the Plains Indians at the Smithsonian Institution at Washington, D. C.,[3] three are on display at the Fort Lincoln Memorial Museum at Mandan, North Dakota, and a sixth is reported in the *Archaeological Encyclopedia* by Warren Moorehead.[4] The present whereabouts of this bone is not known. The seventh and eighth bones were uncovered recently by an amateur archeologist, Ralph S. Thompson, during an attempt to salvage as much as could be saved from Mandan sites before they were covered by the waters from a new dam. Finally, a straight-line pattern is carved on one bone which has a very close counterpart among the carvings from the Norse colonies in Greenland.[5]

These are transcriptions because, except for the bone at the Peabody Museum, the most significant examples are on exhibit under glass and not readily available for photography. However, the lines are cleanly cut with a sharp edge and, with a few exceptions, can be easily read.

Greatest interest centers on the Old Norse symbols because they must inevitably have been taken from the eleventh-century dated puzzles of the puzzlemasters. These bones contain only the ancient runes E and G even though several other forms are found in inscriptions from the Ohio River basin. But the O.N. symbols in the Mandan carvings are repeated 34 times so that they are a large majority of all runes.

It is interesting to note that there are many Mandan and Ariskara sites along the Missouri River and that some cover a considerable number of acres. Only a relatively small part has been completely excavated. This leaves the prospect that eventually more bones which are carved with runic symbols may be recovered.

*   *   *   *   *

If the theory of a trek by the Kensington party to the west from Vinland is correct, it poses some interesting questions. Did the expedition encounter Norsemen who were settled west of the Appalachian Mountains, perhaps in the upper reaches of the Ohio River valley? If so, did they receive further information of other Norsemen far to the west and north? Did they, in fact, come upon Norsemen in the territory which lies west of the Mississippi and north of the Missouri Rivers? In that event, were these Norsemen to become a part of the Mandan Indians in whom, in 1738 A.D., the French trader, Sieur de la Vérendrye, believed that he observed many physical and cultural traits of white men? Hopelessly outnumbered as they would have been, eventual amalgamation of the races would seem to have been inevitable. But the process may have been in its early stages in 1362 A.D., nearly four centuries before 1738. During these centuries of isolation, how long could the demonstrated fondness of the Norsemen for their runes have survived? The answer may well be: much longer than one might at first expect if one is to judge by the actions of Scandinavians elsewhere, and even of Anglo-Saxons.

Space can be allotted here for only two evidences of the presence of Norsemen in the large area between the Appalachian Mountains and the Mississippi River. In 1952, Ronald E. Mason, now of Gulfport, Mississippi, saw what turned out to be an elegantly ornamented drinking horn which had been carved from the horn of an ox. The site was along his milk route in a new subdivision near Winnetka, Illinois, about twenty miles north of Chicago. It was found at an approximate fourteen-inch depth embedded in the yellow clay of a freshly graded bank of a street. On the open prairie of eastern Illinois such clay usually is windblown soil of considerable age.

It is quite unlikely that the horn had been lost by a Scandinavian pioneer during the nineteenth century. However, it is the internal evidence of the character of its decorations, including its dated and ciphered runic inscription, which makes this possibility quite remote. Figures from Norse mythology adorn one side of the horn. This is balanced on the other side by a figure which appears to represent a pagan priest who was a worshiper of Odin and Thor. Mr. Mason did not know, until he was so informed in 1971, that the very small and expertly cut symbols were Norse runes. They consist of two columns of words most of which have no meaning and the whole covers an area no larger than a large postage stamp.

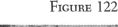

FIGURE 122

The runic inscription is carved on the inside curve of the horn. To the left is depicted a battle between the dreaded Fenris Wolf with one of the Norse gods at the final settlement at Ragnarök, the end of the world. The fierce wolf, as was predicted, is worsted.

The inscription is, in fact, a double telestic cipher. Its date is December 15, 1317, and the ciphers deliver the message: "Audin carved the runes." In a letter which is dated July 10, 1971, Mongé made known the solution with these words of explanation:

"The inscription on the Norse horn is now completely solved. It apparently is directly related to the acrostic-telestic cipher which Henricus built into Legend 67 of the Vinland Map. It is also a close relative of the acrostic and telestic in the Kensington inscription. . . . I am quite certain that this double telestic could not have been faked by modern man. It is just as authentic as the Vinland Map and the Kensington inscription."

The last statement also leaves out of consideration the fact that no one in modern times has known of the existence of dates from the perpetual calendar in runic inscriptions. The authenticity can not be successfully questioned. Because its date precedes the Kensington year number by only 45 years, it is entirely possible that Audin had made a gift of the horn to Harrek. What more appropriate gift for a puzzlemaking colleague?

The so-called Piqua tablets had been discovered some time before 1910 when they were illustrated, and discussed, by the well-known anthropologist Warren G. Moorehead in his *Archaeological Encyclopedia*. At that time they were owned by a Mr. J. H. Rayner. It was he who supplied the illustration of the tablets and a full description. He reported that they had been excavated from an Indian mound near Piqua, a county seat in western Ohio. The tablets themselves have apparently since been lost.

Dr. Moorehead recognized that these were symbols and that they had not been carved by Indians. However, as with nearly

FIGURE 123
Tracing of the Piqua Tablets

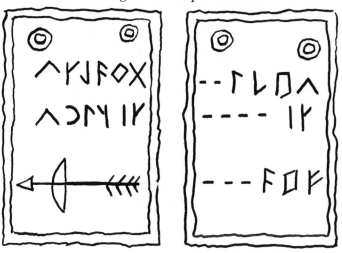

all American anthropologists until recent years, he knew nothing about runes. Nor did he, or they, suspect that Norsemen had ever reached the upper Ohio River basin. Therefore, he declined to express an opinion about who might have carved the inscription. Under the circumstances it is clear that neither he, nor Mr. Rayner, could have done anything to favor the interpretation that the symbols are Norse runes.[6]

It is undeniable that most of the twenty-one symbols in the Piqua inscription are entirely acceptable likenesses of runes. (See the transcription and transliteration below.) Of the remainder, three are irregular but occasionally used forms of the rune U. Four others are either reversed or inverted, but otherwise acceptable, forms of the runes K, L, and T. Such variations are also found in Scandinavian inscriptions such as the inverted and mirrored runes in the Narssaq Stick.

Five of the twenty-one symbols are good likenesses of Old Norse runes. They are drawn with heavy lines in the transcription. Another nine symbols also appear to be runes which occur in both the ancient and the medieval alphabets.

FIGURE 124

Transcription of the Piqua Carving

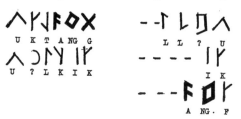

The presence of Old Norse runes in non-dated American inscriptions is of considerable importance. It has been suggested previously that the only reasonable explanation for their use is that they were copied from dated runic puzzles which had been carved earlier by Norse puzzlemasters. On this assumption the Piqua tablets from western Ohio, the Mandan inscriptions from the Dakotas, and many others, testify to the progress of the Norsemen from their original foothold along the coast which they called Vinland. Because these inscriptions are not dated, it will no doubt prove to be very difficult to establish even an approximate timetable.

For the present, the most important consideration is, however, that these runic carvings, together with the Kensington inscription, prove that Norsemen did reach areas that lie far to the west of the Appalachians. This gives additional meaning to the words of the Kensington inscription, "...on a journey of exploration westward from Vinland." They also support the conclusion, which seems to flow naturally from the great interest which Henricus had in the Vinland of his day. This is that the Norse occupation of the New England coastline was a long-term affair which may well have continued into the mid-fourteenth century and beyond.

It has been possible in this chapter to give only a brief glimpse into the nature and occurrence of non-dated runic inscriptions on the North American continent. To do justice to the subject, even as it has developed to the present, would require a fair-sized volume. It is quite certain that future progress in the study of runic inscriptions will be centered largely in this field. Its aim, as now, will be to define as clearly as possible the time scale and the scope of the activities of the Norsemen on this continent.

Notes and References

CHAPTER 1

1. Some historians believe that the contents of the Vinland Sagas were copied from earlier written sources which have been lost. If so, the period over which the saga accounts were transmitted orally would be materially reduced but must, as a minimum, be considerably more than a century.

2. *Explorations in America Before Columbus,* by Hjalmar R. Holand, Twayne Publishers, Inc., New York, 1956. On page 352 Mr. Holand lists twenty-six sites for Vinland which have been favored "by the more prominent writers." Of these, seventeen selected a site on, or near, Cape Cod. It is along these same shores that seven dated and secretly autographed runic puzzles have been discovered and solved.

3. The latest attempt to correlate locations along the northeastern shores of North America with places that are described in the sagas was made by the historian Frederick J. Pohl. In his *The Viking Settlements of North America* he claims to have established no less than eighty-five correspondences. (Crown Publishers Inc., New York, 1972.)

4. *Antiquitates Americanae,* by Christian Rafn, 1837.

5. His last book on the subject was *A Pre-Columbian Crusade to America,* Twayne Publishers Inc., New York, 1962.

6. *Ancient Norse Messages on American Stones,* by O. G. Landsverk, Norseman Press, Rushford, Minnesota, 1969. Chapter 5.

7. Chapters 5, 6, and 7 contain many examples which illustrate the difficulties which confronted the runologists when the inscriptions were Norse puzzles instead of normal runic inscriptions. In many cases no translation exists and none was intended, in others, a correct translation was made difficult, and in some cases virtually impossible, until the distortions that were introduced to fulfill the needs of the cryptography are first removed.

8. Goodwin's best known book is *The Ruins of Great Ireland in New England,* Meador, Boston, 1946.

9. Vinland was called an island about 1070 A.D. by Adam of Bremen, rector of the cathedral school of that city. He reported that a very good authority, Svein Estridson, King of the Danes, had informed him that Vinland was an island. In 1122 A.D. Bishop Henricus, an educated man who was personally well acquainted with Vinland, called the territory *Vinilanda Insula* in Legend 66 of the Vinland Map. It

may be, however, that Henricus knew better but that he needed the nine letters in *Vinilanda* as the first number in his substitution cipher. An added suggestion that this is so is the fact that he misspelled Vinland by inserting an extra letter I. See the solution in Chapter 8.

CHAPTER 2

1. Leif Erikson's discovery is generally believed to have taken place in 1003-1004. Most historians believe that Torfinn Karlsefni's colonizing expedition began in 1009 and ended three years later. Some have suggested that the date was as late as about 1020 A.D.

2. *De Gamle Nordbobygder ved Verdens Ende,* by Poul Nørlund, Nationalmuseet, Copenhagen, 1967. Chapter 2 gives a good description of church life in the Norse Greenland colonies. English edition: *Viking Settlers and Their Descendants During Five Centuries,* Cambridge University Press, London, 1936.

3. *Ibid.,* p. 38.

4. *Conquest by Man,* by Paul Herrmann, Harper, New York, 1954, parts seven and eight. Herrmann states that excavations have shown that at Brattahlid, the estate of Eirik the Red, the barns could house well over a hundred cattle and sheep. Poul Nørlund confirms this and estimates that the establishment of the bishop at Gardar could house an equal number.

5. A Dutch explorer, James Cnoyen, wrote a report of unknown date which has since been lost in which he stated that an expedition had been made "to the lands near the North Pole." This was the mistaken notion which cartographers had long held about the position of Iceland, Greenland, and neighboring territories. Cnoyen dated this expedition at about 1360 and attributed his information to a report which a "priest who had an astrolabe" had rendered to the king of Norway in 1364. (The astrolabe was an early form of sextant.) The priest could only have been Ivar Baardsson who returned to Norway from Greenland in 1364. No other ship from Greenland is known over a period of several years before and after 1364. The account of Cnoyen stated that the astrolabe had been given to the priest by an Englishman, Nicholas of Lynn, Oxford Franciscan and mathematician who was a member of the expedition. Excerpts from Cnoyen's report were written by the cartographer Gerard Mercator on one of his maps which is preserved at the British Museum. That Nicholas of Lynn actually took part in this expedition is confirmed by the fact that he reported to the English king what must have been the same voyage. This report is also lost.

6. *Explorations in America Before Columbus,* by Hjalmar R. Holand, Twayne Publishers Inc., New York, 1956, p. 126.

7. *De Gamle Nordbobygder ved Verdens Ende,* by Poul Nørlund, Nationalmuseet, Copenhagen, fourth edition, 1967, p. 27.

8. See the *Sagas of Olaf Trygvason and Saint Olaf.* Their sagas are translated into English in rearranged form in *From the Sagas of the Norwegian Kings,* Dreyer, Oslo, 1967.

9. *Explorations in America Before Columbus,* by Hjalmar R. Holand, Twayne Publishers Inc., New York, 1956, p. 90.

10. *Runerne i den Oldislandske Literatur,* by Björn Magnússon Ólsen, Gyldendal, Copenhagen, 1883.

11. *A History of the Norwegian Church,* by Bishop A. Chr. Bang, Gyldendalske Boghandel, Nordisk Forlag, 1912.

12. *Breve til og fra Ole Worm,* Vol. I, II, III, 1607-1636, translated by H. D. Schepelern, Munksgaard, Copenhagen, 1965.

13. *Ibid.,* I, 225.

14. *Ibid.,* I, 323.

15. *Runerne i den Oldislandske Literatur,* by Björn Magnússon Ólsen, Gyldendal, 1883.

CHAPTER 3

1. *The Runes of Sweden,* by Sven B. F. Jansson, The Bedminster Press, Totowa, N. J., 1962, p. 7.

2. *Fasti Danici,* by Ole Worm, 1643.

3. *New Catholic Encyclopedia,* Volume 13, pp. 858-60.

4. *Ancient Norse Messages on American Stones,* Norseman Press, Rushford, Minnesota, 1969, Chapter 4.

5. See reference 1 above, pages 11 to 17.

6. *Stuttruner,* by Ingrid Sanness Johnsen, Universitetsforlaget, Oslo. The Rök inscription, pp. 140-41; Sparlösa, pp. 153-61.

7. *The Norseman,* published by Nordmanns-Forbundet, Oslo, No. 4, 1971. "Nine Centuries of Organized Church in Oslo," by Fridtjof Birkeli.

8. *Danske Mindesmerker,* 1806. R. Nyrup stated that "The carving of runes was, presumably, the task of the priests and it gave them a good income."

9. *Norges Innskrifter med de Yngre Runer,* Volumes 1 to 5, 1941 to 1960, Norsk Historisk Kildeskrift Institutt, Oslo.

10. *Ibid.,* Vol. 5, pp. 175-88.

11. NIYR Vol. 4, p. 157: "Men rimeligere er det vel å tenke sig at runegåten i Borgund stavkirke Nr. V har fåt stå uløst i påvente, enten

av en bestemt person som man viste snart ville intreffe ved Borgund kirke, eller av en senere ukjendt besøkende."
NIYR Vol. 4, p. 117: "I senere tids runekunstlerier kan så å si enhver rune bli brukt som bestanddel i den avdeling av lønskrift vi her har å gjøre med."
12. *Runer frå Bryggen,* by Aslak Liestøl, 1963.

CHAPTER 4

1. The first permanent missionary to Norway appears to have been a Benedictine monk, Rudolph. He carried on his work at the inner end of Viken which is now known as the Oslo Fjord area. Near the site of the present city of Oslo is an area which is called "munkeholmen," that is, the monk's island. This was the site of the first known monastery in Norway.
2. Dionysius Exeguus was an eminent sixth-century Christian theologian who was regarded as an authority on the ordinances of the Church. It is he who is given the credit for introducing the now existing method for calculating the Christian era.
3. *Fasti Danici,* by Ole Worm, 1643.
4. This is only a part of the total evidence that the Kensington inscription is a dated cryptogram. In addition, it contains two very difficult ciphers in the form of an acrostic and a telestic. They reveal that the name of the puzzlemaster was HARREK, and of the runecutter, TOLLIK. The entire solution is analyzed in Chapter 5 of *Ancient Norse Messages on American Stones,* by O. G. Landsverk, Norseman Press, Rushford, Minnesota, 1969.
5. About a century after the time of Athelstan, a Benedictine calendar repeats the 20 letters of the Latin alphabet throughout the year. The DLs are also expressed with Latin letters but Roman numerals are used for the GNs. In addition, this calendar has three extra columns which were taken from the pagan Julian calendar including the ides, the nones, and the calends for the months. It is clear that the perpetual ecclesiastical calendar developed under a variety of different traditions.
6. *Fra Runesten til Almanak,* by Mogens Lebech, Thejl, Copenhagen, 1969, pages 5 to 43. The first calendar which was printed by Gutenberg with movable type was also "indexed" by the addition of a repeated alphabet throughout the year.

CHAPTER 5

1. *Norges Innskrifter med de Yngre Runer,* Volumes 1 to 5, 1941-60.
2. *Ancient Norse Messages on American Stones,* Norseman Press, Rushford, Minnesota, 1969.

3. *Runestenen fra Kingigtorssuaq,* by Finnur Jónsson, 1914, Grønlandske Selskab, Aarskrift, Copenhagen.

"Kingigtorssuaq—stenen og sproget i de Grønlandske runeinnskrifter," Magnus Olsen, *Norsk Tidsskrift for Sprogvidenskab,* Volume 5, Oslo.

4. See Chapter 4 of reference 2 above.

5. LOSNE and A are correctly spelled Norse words but the spelling of the word which referred to an expanse of ice was ISAR instead of ISAN. This is, however, a minor variation which would not have been misunderstood. It may be a misspelling which was forced on the puzzlemaster by the requirements of the cipher.

It also seems likely that the I in OIRVAR was an intrusion for the same reason and that the desired spelling had been ORVAR. An alternate interpretation is also possible, namely: LOSNE A ISA NORVAR VALRSLEThN. ISA may still be a misspelling but both the first and second syllables of NÓRVAR are known in such names as NORVAL and INGVAR.

VALR was the correct spelling for the word for battleground. SLETTA was a flat plain. The name VALRSLEThN therefore apparently referred to a flat battlefield.

In an extensive and complex cipher such as this, it is very difficult to determine whether an apparent misspelling may have been unavoidable. On the other hand, *normal runic inscriptions* contain a great many misspellings or words which are spelled in various ways. Furthermore, many names which appear in runic inscriptions have strange spellings or are totally unknown.

6. *Runeinskrifter i Sverige,* by Sven B. F. Jansson, Almquist & Wiksell, Stockholm, 1963, p. 176.

7. *Runer frå Bryggen,* by Aslak Liestøl, 1963. No publisher given.

CHAPTER 6

1. *Gulatingslovi,* translated from Old Norse by Knut Robberstad, Det Norske Samlaget, Oslo, 1969.

2. *Norges Innskrifter med de Yngre Runer,* Volume 5, pp. 175-88.

3. *A Pre-Columbian Crusade to America,* by Hjalmar R. Holand, Twayne Publishers Inc., New York, 1962.

4. *The Book of Saints,* Ramsgate, London, 1934.

CHAPTER 7

1. *Stuttruner,* by Ingrid Sanness Johnsen, Universitetsforlaget, Oslo, 1968, p. 51.

2. *Runinskrifter i Sverige,* by Sven B. F. Jansson, Almquist & Wicksell, Stockholm, 1963, pp. 16 to 20.

3. This happens to be a feature whose probability that it could have happened by pure chance, and so had not been arranged by a runemaster, can be calculated. Let us first take note that, at least in all written European languages, the A is used more often than the average for all of the symbols in the alphabet. This is true also with writing in which the 24-rune alphabet was used. A check reveals that, on the average, runic A is used approximately once for each twelve runes. This becomes a basic figure in the calculation.

As a consequence of this, the probability that the rune will appear in any specific position in a *normal runic inscription* is one in twelve. Mathematically this is stated by the fraction $1/12$. If, therefore, we examine every fourth rune in any inscription that uses O.N. runes, what is the probability that all will be the rune A, without a miss, six times in succession?

Unless the runes were deliberately rigged, which we are here assuming that they were not, the answer is $1/12$ multiplied by itself six times. It is the same problem as with tossing a penny. The probability of heads is one out of two tries, that is, $1/2$. The probability of tossing heads two times in succession is therefore $1/2$ multiplied by $1/2 = 1/4$.

In this case the answer is $1/3,185,984$. That is, there is less than one chance in three million that the six runes A appeared in succession in this way *by pure chance.* That is, *they have been rigged.*

4. *The Vikings Were Here,* by Gloria Farley, Poteau Independent, Poteau, Oklahoma, December, 1970.

5. *Norse Medieval Cryptography in Runic Carvings,* by Alf Mongé and O. G. Landsverk, Norseman Press, Rushford, Minnesota, 1967.

6. *Ancient Norse Messages On American Stones,* by O. G. Landsverk, Norseman Press, Rushford, Minnesota, 1969.

CHAPTER 8

1. *The Vinland Map and the Tartar Relation,* by R. A. Skelton, Thomas E. Marston, George D. Painter, Yale University Press, 1965.

2. *Explorations in America Before Columbus,* by Hjalmar R. Holand, Twayne Publishers Inc., New York, 1956, pp. 90-91.

3. *History of the Crusades,* by J. F. Michaud, A. C. Armstrong and Son, New York, p. 289.

4. *The Vinland Map and the Tartar Relation,* by R. A. Skelton, Thomas E. Marston, George D. Painter, Yale University Press, 1965. Ierlanda is discussed beginning p. 128; Isolanda Ibernica, beginning p. 138.

5. *Plutarch's Lives* is found in many translations. The best known in English was written during Elizabethan times by Sir Thomas North. The latest translation is by A. H. Clough, New York, five volumes, 1909.

6. An "opportunity date" is one for which the perpetual calendar provided one of two situations:

a. The date is expressed by an unusual combination of numbers such as 6,6,6,6,6 for the date June 6, 1297. (This is the sixth day of the sixth month of a year, 1297, whose Rati = 6, Golden Number = 6, and Dominical Letter = 6.) Such a dating is spectacular.

or

b. The date is "self-confirming." For example, sometimes the number of the day in the month and the number of the month itself also happened to be the same numbers as the Golden Number and the Dominical Letter for the same date. This permitted the dated puzzle to be exceptionally compact, which was an important feature and objective.

7. This is the same situation which exists with the Kensington text. The eight numbers in the inscription are the calendrical indicators which state and confirm the date, Sunday, April 24, 1362 A.D. The expedition undoubtedly consisted of Goths (western Swedes) and Norwegians as the text states, and there were probably men killed etc., etc. But it is very unlikely that there were exactly eight Goths and exactly twenty-two Norwegians or that any of the other numbers, except the year 1362 which is repeatedly confirmed, are exact. The function of the numbers was to state and confirm the date. The function of the entire text was to serve as a vehicle for embedding the dated puzzles with added ciphers. A secondary function of the text was to conceal the cryptography without hiding it so well that it would never be discovered. This was a requirement in all Norse cryptopuzzles.

CHAPTER 9

1. Dr. Edward J. Kealey, professor of history at the College of the Holy Cross at Worcester, Massachusetts, offers a different explanation for the origin of the symbol IHS—K. In Greek the name Jesus was spelled IHSUS. According to this explanation, the symbol was composed of the first three letters, IHS, followed by a letter to signify the cross which, in Norse, was K.

2. See the symbol for Golden Number 19 in Columns 1 and 2 of the table from Worm's *Fasti Danici* which is illustrated in Chapter 3.

CHAPTER 10

1. *Vinland the Good,* by Anne Holtsmark, translated by Joan Tindale Blindheim, Johan Grundt Tanum, Oslo, 1966.

2. The runes in the Kingigtorssuaq inscription together with an assortment of auxiliary (cryptographic) cuts, were apparently cleanly cut and easily read just as are the symbols in the three Spirit Pond inscriptions. However, credit for an exact copy must also be given to the one who reproduced it in 1843 A.D. The Kingigtorssuaq inscription contains a very intricate and skillfully made dated puzzle with a difficult added cipher which completes the message of the text. A part of it had long been thought to have been omitted but no one, before Mongé, had managed to find it. The inscription contains several dozen runic symbols and special markings which are cryptographically significant. If even one of these runes or markings had been omitted, or had been changed in relative position, a major part of the solution may have become impossible. The fact that the solution is complete and logical throughout justifies the assumption that the copy was carefully made and is accurate. Exactly the same situation prevails with the two Latin legends of the Vinland Map in which the fifteenth-century scribe in Switzerland seems to have copied the legends exactly as Henricus wrote them in 1122 A.D. This included a considerable number of "errors" which he had introduced into his text as was required by the cryptography.

CHAPTER 11

1. It is interesting to note that the fifth rune in Line 1 is the standard form from the Normal alphabet. But, in the last symbol of the same line, the curved part of the rune U was moved down the staff so as to leave room for the slanted cut of the combined rune L at the top of the staff.

2. For LITI see, for example, *Gamal Norsk Ordbok,* by Leiv Heggstad, Det Norske Samlaget, Oslo, 1963 under the entry LITA.

3. *The Norse Atlantic Saga,* by Gwyn Jones, Oxford, 1964, pp. 191-93.

4. A theory which Mr. Mongé favors is discussed later. This is that Henricus intended to say in the last part of Legend 67 of VM that he had been ordered to return to Iceland, to Scandinavia, or even to Rome. That he intended to sail to Iceland in 1123 A.D., and perhaps farther to the east and south, but was driven back to Vinland by bad weather, seeems to be too much of a coincidence to be credible.

CHAPTER 12

1. Variant spellings or misspellings are quite common in what are assumed to be normal runic writings. The aberrations are also often

more serious than those which are found in the texts or the hidden messages of Norse cryptograms. There is no mystery about this. The puzzlemasters were knowledgeable about runic symbols and the spelling of words. When they misspelled words, either in their texts or in the hidden messages, these were deliberate acts for the purpose of fitting the cryptography into the inscription. In all cases the result must be understandable wherever the presence of a meaning was intended.

To object to these minor misspellings, while at the same time accepting drastic aberrations even to the extent of changing the roots of difficult words, is illogical.

CHAPTER 13

1. On Gardar, see *Viking Greenland*, by Knud J. Krogh, The National Museum, Copenhagen, p. 92.

Based on excavations by Poul Nørlund and Aage Roussell in 1926, Krogh states that the foundations of the cathedral measured 90 by 53 feet. The house, which formed the west side of the group of buildings, was no less impressive. Its façade was 165 feet long and the largest of its rooms, the great hall, measured 56 by 26 feet. Along the south side was an extremely long byre, 213 feet in length. The bishop had room for about 100 cows on his farm. Round about were "innumerable" buildings, both large and small: barns, storehouses, byres, and stables, and there was a dam for irrigating the main field by a system of canals.

2. Valrslethn, the puzzlemaster of the Kingigtorssuaq dated puzzle and cipher, was, in all probability, a priest. This is so not only because it is certain that nearly all Norse dated cryptography was the work of the Norse clergy. The Kingigtorssuaq inscription also suggests the religious associations of the puzzlemaster in other ways. He tied the date, May 7, 1244 A.D., by multiple confirmations to the two major holy days of the church year, Easter Sunday and Ascension Day. The last six special symbols at the end of the inscription also employ the same method for stating the day and year as is found on the Swedish baptismal font which is called Norumfonten, and which was carved in 1103 A.D., 141 years earlier. This again indicates a connection of the Kingigtorssuaq carving with the church. It is significant, also, that these are the only known Norse puzzles which use this particular system for dating. This is another illustration that time and distance was no barrier to the far-ranging Norse priests.

CHAPTER 14

1. "En Grønlandsk Runeindskrift fra Erik den Rødes Tid," by Dr. phil. Erik Moltke, *Grønland,* November 1961.

CHAPTER 15

1. *Peabody Museum Papers, Volume III*, report by G. F. Will and H. J. Spinden, August, 1906.

2. Whether all of the Texas inscriptions still exist is not known. They were carefully copied in the 1930's by experienced artists who were commissioned by Texas universities in order to record as many as possible of Indian rock carvings in Texas before they were destroyed by vandals. The result was between one and two thousand photographic plates in several large volumes. Among them are about a dozen plates many of whose symbols show strong runic similarities. Some of these contain nothing but clearly cut runes, almost all from the ancient alphabet. Under the conditions there is no possibility that the artists were influenced to draw the symbols like runes since they knew nothing about runes and no one had the least thought that Norsemen had reached the area.

3. This bone is a part of the anthropological exhibit on the Plains Indians among whom the Mandans and Ariskara are counted even though they lived in permanent houses. It is about three quarters inch wide and eight inches long and only about one eighth inch thick. It was excavated from an Ariskara site near Mobridge in South Dakota. The Ariskara were allies of the Mandans against the Sioux and the Cheyenne. Before they were devastated by smallpox in the last half of the seventeenth century they were dominant in the area. This was reported to be so by La Vérendrye when he visited them in 1738 A.D.

4. *Archaeological Encyclopedia*, ed. Warren Moorehead, Volume II (1910) p. 152.

5. *Meddelelser om Grønland, Sandness and the Neighboring Farms,* by Aage Roussell, C. A. Reitzel, Ltd., Copenhagen, 1936. Appendix by Erik Moltke, pp. 223-32. The bone is on exhibit at Fort Lincoln Memorial Museum.

6. *Archaeological Encyclopedia*, ed. Warren Moorehead, Volume I (1910) p. 350.

Index

Hellespont, 140
Henricus (Bishop to Greenland and legate of Pope Paschal II), 3, 4, 5, 6, 12, 13, 14, 16, 20, 22, 23, 25, 29, 30, 32, 34, 37, 61, 63, 78, 89, 100, 118, 126, (Chapters 8 through 13, pages 127 to 224, are entirely devoted to Henricus. They contain sixty references to him.), 226, 227, 229, 240, 243.
Henrik, 129
Herjulfsson, Bjarni, 133, 145
Herrmann, Paul, 24
Hettusvein (*see* cryptograms)
historians, Catholic, 131
history, American, 11
Hjalti, 28, 29
Holand, Hjalmar Rued, 14, 27, 30, 31, 89, 128, 236
Holar, monastery, 33
Hóp, Hoob, 170, 173, 178, 182, 185
Hudson Bay, 128, 130, 181
Hy Connall, Irish monastery, 106

Iceland, 6, 7, 22, 23, 24, 26, 27, 28, 29, 30, 31, 32, 35, 51, 130, 136, 137, 219, 220
Icelanders, 6, 22, 25, 29, 30, 32, 34
Icelandic literature, 60
Icelandic Parliament, 23
Illinois, Winnetka, 239
Indian Rock, 122
Indian rock carvings, 236
Indians:
Arikara, 237
Cheyenne, 237
Choctaw, 122, 187, 232
Mandan, 235, 236, 237, 238, 242
Sioux, 237
Ingal, 226, 227, 228, 230
Inscriptions, runic (*see also* cryptograms), 6, 11, 14, 15, 31, 45, 46, 47, 48, 49, 51, 62; pornographic, 80, 83; Scandinavian, 106, 129, 150, 151, 175, 211, 212, 213, 215, 233; American, Greenland, Swedish, 234, 235
Ireland, 130, 136, 137
Isleif, bishop of Skålholt, 23, 30

Isle of Man, 45
Ita, 88 (continuous, pages 93 through 106), 133
Italy, 35

Jansson, Sven B. F., 39, 45, 47, 76, 111
Jerusalem, 31, 128
Jesuit, 175
Jesus Christ cross (symbol), 61
jigsaw puzzle, 80
Johnsen, Ingrid Sanness, 45, 110
Johnson, Arngrim, 33
Jónsson, Finnur, 71
Jorsalfarer, King Sigurd, 30, 128, 198
Julius Caesar, 51

Kahn, David, 142
Karlsefni, Thorfinn, 12, 21, 22, 25, 170, 172, 173, 185
Kennebec River estuary, 166, 178, 182
Kensington inscription (*see* cryptograms)
Kensington, Minn., 2, 3, 5, 6, 14, 25, 42, 43
keys, cryptographic:
key word, 134, 144
numerical key, 138, 139, 140, 141
operating key, 143, 144
transposition key, 141
Kingigtorssuaq inscription (*see* cryptograms)
Kings:
Aethelstan, 60, 215
Baldwin, 31
Haakon, 26
Magnus the Good, 89
Olaf Haraldson, 29, 46
Olaf Trygvasson, 28
Sigurd Jorsalfarer, 30, 128, 198
Knutson, Paul, 89, 90
Kylver (ancient runic alphabet), 39

Laborador, 12, 181
Landsverk Foundation, 3, 4, 30, 168, 174
Landsverk, O. G., 4, 142